# THE ETHICAL EDGE
# OF
# CHRISTIAN THEOLOGY

Forty Years of Communitarian Personalism

# THE ETHICAL EDGE
# OF
# CHRISTIAN THEOLOGY

### Forty Years of Communitarian Personalism

## WALTER G. MUELDER

Toronto Studies in Theology

Volume 13

The Edwin Mellen Press
New York and Toronto

Library of Congress Cataloging in Publication Data

Muelder, Walter George, 1907-
    The ethical edge of Christian theology.

    (Toronto studies in theology ; v. 13)
    Includes bibliographical references and index
    1. Theology--Addresses, essays, lectures.
2. Social ethics--Addresses, essays, lectures. 3. Ethics
--Addresses, essays, lectures.  I. Title.  II. Series.
BR85.M73  1983       230'.044       83-21935
ISBN 0-88946-754-4


Toronto Studies in Theology  ISBN 0-88946-975-X

        The Edwin Mellen Press
        P.O. Box 450
        Lewiston, New York    14092

Printed in the United States of  America

To

*Martha Grotewohl Muelder*

who has honed the ethical edge of theology with me.

# Contents

## ACKNOWLEDGMENTS AND PERMISSIONS

These essays written over a period of forty years are indebted to many scholars and to the generous permissions of many publishers. Essays not previously published enhance these debts. The author acknowledges the permissions newly granted and renewed as follows: to Robert Bierstedt for permission to quote from Robert M. MacIver, *The More Perfect Union*; to Doubleday and Co., for excerpts from John Dillenberger, *Protestant Thought and Natural Science*; to Harper and Row Publishers for passages from H. Richard Niebuhr, *Christ and Culture*, Baker Brownell, *The Small Community*, Paul Lehmann, *Ethics in a Christian Context*, Gunnar Myrdal, *An American Dilemma*, Amos N. Wilder, ed., *Liberal Learning and Religion*, Ruth Nanda Anshen, *The Family: Its Function and Destiny*, Paul Tillich, *Dynamics of Faith*; to Macmillan Publishing Co. for material from Abraham Edel, *Ethical Judgment: the Use of Science in Ethics*; to McGraw-Hill Book Co. for sentences from Clyde Kluckhohn, *Mirror for Man*; to Oxford University Press for sentences from Rudolf Otto, *The Idea of the Holy*; to Charles Scribner's Sons for passages from Reinhold Niebuhr, *The Nature and Destiny of Man*, Fritz Kunkel, *How Character Develops*, and J. A. Hutchison, ed., *Christian Faith and Social Action*; to Florence R. Taylor for excerpts from Clyde Kluckhohn and H. A. Murray, *Personality in Nature, Science and Culture*; to Wadsworth Publishing Co. for material from John C. Bennett, ed., *Christian Ethics in a Changing World* and O. Hobart Mowrer, *The Crisis in Psychiatry and Religion*; and to Westminster Press for quotations from David L. Mueller, *An Introduction to the Theology of Albrecht Ritschl*. Precise references to these and other works are found in the endnotes of the respective essays.

# SOURCES

SOURCES

SOURCES

## An Autobiographical Introduction
## Forty Years of Communitarian Personalism

The chronological span of my self-awareness embraces two world wars, the Korean War, the Indo-China War, and an endless ideological war between super-powers; it encompasses unregulated prosperity and economic speculation, the Great Depression, an era of American domination of world economy, and a global stagflation; it began in the midst of triumphant European colonialism and imperialism and reflects on massive areas of Marxist domination and Third World demands for a new international economic order; it participates in Protestant missionary denominationalism and subsequently in the great Christian ecumenical movement and the release of the Roman Catholic Church from the bondage of Trent and the First Vatican Council; its adolescence notes the victory of suffrage for American women and its senior citizenship finds equal rights for women a dubious outcome; it covers parts of eight decades of racism and the civil rights struggle.

Reared in a German Methodist parsonage where Boston Personalism and Rauschenbusch's social gospel were the liberating agents from individualistic evangelical pietism, my formative years were lived in the turmoil of the nineteen twenties. To be sure, I was born in 1907 and experienced anti-German prejudice during World War I, but my intellectual self-awareness became acute in high school. High school (Burlington, Iowa), college (Knox, Galesburg, Illinois), and theological seminary (Boston University) were the extra-parental matrices for a pilgrimage of commitment to the causes of organized labor, pacifism, socialism, ecumenism, and personalistic idealism. In that decade from the

1

Palmer Raids to the Crash of 1929 mid-western churches were
not only torn by social questions, but they were also tor-
mented by the "warfare of science and theology," more particularly by the issue of the place of human life in nature.

The Scopes trial took place while I was in college. The
death of Debs closed a period in Socialist Party history;
Norman Thomas became the new standard bearer for socialism; reaction against World War I provided the impetus for
the Kellog-Briand Peace Pact; Bruce Barton wrote a biography
of Jesus with a bourgeois mentality. Today's Moral Majority
pietists and Prayer Breakfast Republicans would have read
that biography avidly and found its mood consistent with
Coolidge's dictum that "the business of America is business."  Those were the years that called forth the American
Civil Liberties Union and the American Legion, that resound-
ed with the cries of union busting, that witnessed the decline of the A. F. of L. and the hey day of company unions.
Employers organized mass production on a philosophy of
individualistic time-clock piece work.  Today's sociology of
labor refutes the old individualistic assumption that each
individual worker's happiness depends solely upon his own
achievement and wage level. Teamwork is important; productivity is enhanced by a "learning curve" of cooperation over
and above individual skills.  The politics of religion made
of Prohibition a "single cause" surrogate for the earlier
and broader "social gospel."  There was widespread revolt of
youth, lawlessness, bootlegging, and false optimism.

My generation was not the pioneer group that met the
intellectual and spiritual challenges of the doctrine of
evolution in biology or of social Darwinism.  Ours was
really the third generation which felt those shock waves.
For many college teachers and ministers Borden Parker Bowne
had shown how to handle those challenges and the philosophy

of Herbert Spencer. Then came the generation of E. S. Brightman and of clergymen like my father who faced the issues in classroom and local churches. Likewise in higher criticism of the Bible. There had already been heresy trials and expulsions from teaching posts in the era of Hinckley Mitchell. The point is that my generation had at its disposal a significant literature in German, French and English which dealt with these vital problems and we were free to move forward on several fronts.

Theologians of a philosophical bent and philosophers of religion did the constructive work as bridgebuilders between evangelical Christianity and the realms of science. Whereas some thinkers were comfortable in making a sharp differentiation or separation of the realms of theology and of science, idealistic metaphysicians like Knudson, Brightman, and Hocking and process philosophers like Whitehead persisted in the classical tradition of organic and synoptic reflection. The Hegelian dictum that the true is the whole and, hence, that all reductionism must be vigorously combatted, dominated these perspectives, even when Hegel was himself roundly criticized. On the other hand, theologians of a neo-Augustinian bent, responding with approbation to Barth's theology of the Word of God and emphasizing proclamation, made virtually no contributions to the dialogue between religion and science.

At the philosophical level the continental divide between a religious outlook on life and secularistic or naturalistic scientism peaked on the question: Is there more-than-human purpose in the world? Within the above idealistic metaphysical framework scientific evidence and method were viewed neither as dualistic nor as monistic alternatives to theism. Personalists insisted that the purposes of science logically should never be lost to view.

They insisted, furthermore, that what was directly experienced as conscious ought not, empirically speaking, be regarded as epiphenomenal.  Mind is "nature's" profoundest
resource, the most concrete key to the nature of reality.
Naturalism, a widely held position, contested these idealistic claims and held that purpose in the universe is
strictly local.  Naturalism and pragmatism, accompanied by a
corresponding humanism in ethics, were in their ascendancy
in the 1920s and continued so into the 'thirties.  For personalists the human presence *in* nature requires a radical
reassessment *of* nature.

The synoptic alternative to reductionist tendencies
appreciated the contributions which analytical, specialized,
and abstract methods make, but rejected materialism, behaviorism, neo-realism, operationalism, and pragmatism on wholistic experiential grounds.  Brightman sometimes referred
to his own view as the more-inclusive-naturalism.  The persistent militant criticism of religion by naturalists, whether physicalists or humanists, prompted me to write the essay
which is first in the subsequent chapters.  "Naturalism
Faces Prophetic Religion" appeared in 1938.  While rejecting
metaphysical naturalism I affirmed not only some of its
ethical claims but also insisted that religious leaders
continue a dialogue with it.

The widespread interest in these issues is reflected in
the three-way debate between Max Otto, Henry Nelson Wieman,
and Douglas C. Macintosh which ran for an extended period in
*The Christian Century*.  For many people the empirical and
scientific appeals in these articles were commonly assumed,
but what distinguished the options were pragmatic humanism,
theistic process philosophy of religion, and a theism based
on "theology as an empirical science."  The personalistic
option cuts across these options, as my essays generally

show, but the option requires an affirmative interpretation
of the scientific method within the disciplines of
philosophy, theology, and ethics.

The late nineteenth century liberalism in theology made
a sharp differentiation between the *Naturwissenschaften* and
the *Geisteswissenschaften*, the former conceding to natural
science a necessitarian view of causality, the latter
emphasizing the claims of freedom for the sciences of mind
or spirit. The resultant problem was how to resolve the
relation of the two in persons as subjects and in reality as
a whole. One way was to eschew metaphysics and to base
judgments of religion on value-decisions, thus making value
judgments the entering place for theological statements, for
example, about Christ and God. This path was blazed and
taken by Albrecht Ritschl, the subject of the second essay
included in this volume.

Although I wrote this essay in 1979 as a lecture for
the Boston University Institute of Theology and Philosophy
of Religion, my initial study of Ritschl goes back fifty
years earlier. At that time any advanced graduate student
in theology at Boston University took a seminar under Dean
Albert C. Knudson on Schleiermacher and Ritschl, the two
giants of liberal German theological reconstruction. The
dissent from Ritschl in Boston Personalism is emphasized in
this lecture. It is placed immediately after the essay on
Naturalism to provide a dialectical contrast. For the past
hundred years the tradition of idealistic personalism, while
recognizing the relative autonomy of Christian theology (one
of the major themes in neo-orthodoxy as well), has tended to
view theology and philosophy as supplementary disciplines.
Knudson is explicit about this in dealing with ethics.
Knudson was particularly critical of all philosophies which
treated religion as an illusion.

Of the personalists the most influential thinker in my
spiritual formation was Edgar S. Brightman.  Both in method
and substance he was very persuasive.  Like Martin Luther
King, Jr. thirty years later, I found that Brightman's method and metaphysics gave me satisfaction in thinking about
God as the personal ultimate real and the basis for moral
reflection on the dignity and worth of all human personality.  In my subsequent ethical reflection I moved beyond him
particularly at two points:  (1) toward an historical communitarian view of human personality and (2) toward a much
larger use of empirical social science.  Of the Brightmanian
affirmations my thinking was congenial especially to the
following:  (1) the nature of the self as conscious experience and of the person as a self capable of reason and
criticized values; (2) the synoptic method as superior to,
but including, the analytical; (3) the epistemological dualism of idea and object; (4) the correspondence definition of
truth; (5) the coherence criterion of truth when it includes
empirical as well as rational coherence; (6) the primacy of
the practical reason, including the concrete unity of theory
and practice; (7) the experient as the real moral agent; (8)
all value claims as *of*, *by*, and *for* persons; (9) the
objectivity of ideal norms; (10) the organic character of
reality qualified in its personal monism by the pluralism of
finite persons.   It is evident in this list that the
Hegelian accents in idealism are stronger than the Kantian
ones.  I appropriated Brightman's temporalist view of God
and his finitistic solution of the problem of good-and-evil.
These motifs are found in several of the essays below.

Personality is viewed by me not only as experience, but
experience is understood as social or communitarian.  The
self is not an individual experient who *has* a social
environment which influences the self; the self *is* its

social experiences (which comprise its identity) as well as
its uniquely private experience. The self is conscious and
a person is self-conscious; and both are temporal, hence
historical. The self is not, however, just an ensemble of
social relations, for the self is a real subject. The self
is a *socius* with a private center. To be truly known a self
must share its experiences and meanings with others. At the
level of self-transcending reflective self-consciousness a
person's experiences are both private and social, the socius
having a private owner and the private finding itself
interpenetrating with its social identity. When we ask any
person who he or she is, the *identity* response always is
largely socially oriented, though also biologically oriented
as to gender or sex. My ethical theory appeals to person-in-
community.

Social and philosophical concerns are not the only
elements that have informed my religious and ethical attitudes in life. The great mystics have drawn me to them and
their quest and have guided my spiritual development in
significant ways. By mysticism I mean an unusually persistent concentration of consciousness toward God. I mean a
direct awareness of divine presence. Mysticism is not only
an appreciation of those who have explored theories of direct acquaintance and appreciation of the "Other" who is
"within," but a cultivation of the interior life that seeks
to be directly open to the "Thou," a development of trust in
the One. For me the mystical experience has been mild rather than ecstatic, and it has been primarily fed by fellowship with Christian masters of prayer, meditation, and
contemplation. The essays in this volume do not directly
reflect this dimension of my religious and moral consciousness, but the context of the "Holy" always surrounds the
awesome aspects of the moral order. The crucifixion of

Jesus has a central place in understanding the meaning of
suffering and reconciliation in an ethic of nonviolence and
love which I seek to espouse; it expresses God's solidarity
with us all.

In a course on the Classics of Mysticism under Edgar S.
Brightman in 1928 I learned to ask four questions of a
mystic's writings: (a) what was the preparation for the
experience? (b) how was the experience described? (c) what
was the mystic's interpretation of the experience? and (d)
what were the practical fruits?  These four questions have
subsequently been very helpful throughout my life.  And
hence, this is the appropriate place to state why I count
myself a Christian now despite a life-long exposure and
wrestling with many philosophies and rival faiths and
ideologies.  First, I have never doubted my initial loyalty
to Jesus Christ, though I have considered many competing
interpretations of the person and work of Christ; secondly,
I believe that the personal theism presumed by the central
tradition of the Christian faith is philosophically as well
as theologically the most coherent and hence true; thirdly,
I accept the objectivity of the moral order of the universe
and hence the ultimate imperatives of justice and love; and
finally, I believe that these three statements are universally worthy of acceptation and historically relevant.  My
ecumenical involvements have only deepened these convictions.

The early 1930s were almost as formative in my development as the '20s.  In 1930 - 31 I spent a year at the University of Frankfurt as a fellow of the International Institute
of Education, primarily under Paul Tillich.  While there I
deepened my critical understanding of Hegel and Marx at the
Institute of Social Research headed by Max Horkheimer, whose
work *Die Anfänge der bürgerlichen Geschichtsphilosophie*

appeared in 1930. Tillich's dialectical method and his
efforts to bring Lutheranism and socialism unto a mutual
dialogue became dramatically significant as Hitler was
rising to power and Germany's ill-fated Weimar Republic
splintered into a score or more of political parties. For
example, Tillich offered a seminar on the philosophical
presuppositions of the major political parties. Subsequently, when his works on the religious situation and his
*Interpretation of History* appeared I read them avidly. The
meaning of history became an existential problem while in
Frankfurt and I decided to ask my major professor (Brightman
was on sabbatical leave in Berlin) for permission to do my
doctoral dissertation on Ernst Troeltsch's philosophy of
history. Research on Troeltsch gave me an opportunity to
struggle with issues relating history, personality theory,
theology, socialism, and constructive social ethics to each
other. In this way social ethics became my professional
destiny.

Is there a group mind? In interpreting "Objective
Spirit" was Hegel correct in conceiving it as a real subject? Is individual personality the most concrete category
in contrast to any supra-personal wholes? Here Troeltsch
was helpful. In my dissertation research, "Individual
Totalities in Ernst Troeltsch's Philosophy of History," I
explored the nature of historical wholes. I appreciated his
view of historical wholes, in contrast to Hegel, as unities
of meaning and value. They defy reductionism. However,
Troeltsch surrendered finally the category of personality as
a true universal, an unnecessary sacrifice. Instead of
Troeltsch's view I developed later a communitarian conception of personality which is expressed below in the essay,
"Personality and Christian Ethics." It reflects the
influences of Brightman, Marx, and Troeltsch. It rejects

group mind as a real subject.

Troeltsch reinforced my developing ethical method to keep theological, philosophical, and scientific factors in dialectical tension with each other. He was magnificent in his mastery of historical material and in showing at innumerable points the pluralistic roots of Western Civilization interwoven into new unities of meaning and value. He had an amazing capacity to dissect and disentangle the various strands found in such phenomena as democracy, capitalism and socialism.

Troeltsch was a socialist who served in the government of the Weimar Republic following World War I. But he was not a Marxist. When he felt that German democracy had to be socialist, it was not on theoretical or idealistic grounds, but because of economic need and the changed conditions of industrial labor. The economy needed to be organized in the interests of the whole. For him socialism was not simply the necessary consequence of the full development of political democracy. If this were the case, equality before the law politically would have to be transformed into economic equality, but Troeltsch did not equate socialism and equality. Indeed, the roots of democracy, he argued, do not lie in the French Revolution. They lie in the Anglo-Saxon twofold revolutions, the Puritans against the Stuarts and the American Revolution. Both of these arose out of religious considerations and older English legal traditions. Hence political democracy does not inevitably result in economic democracy. Socialism required a new emergent combination with democracy. Socialism, for example, can mean domination by the social whole and democracy, rooted in certain forms of religion, can cling to the inviolability of private property. Socialist democracy, Troeltsch argued after World War I, is the response to a new need where diverse roots are used to bring forth a new historical whole. Without accepting Troeltsch's whole analysis here, I should acknowledge that he has been a tutor in reinforcing a decision for democratic socialism of a Norman Thomas type. Practically, I stumped for him in 1928, 1932, and 1936.

The complexity of the above issues had not only anthropocentric and philosophical aspects but also theocentric and theological ones. The problem of evil is not only personal and social but also natural and cosmic in an ultimate sense. Knudson and Brightman pressed their students to reflect on the nature of reality, not least the doctrine of God. Here again Brightman's hypothesis of God's finitude as formulated in *The Problem of God* and *The Finding of God* was on the right track. This means that I was concerned radically not only with pacifism and socialism as questions of human and historical sin and evil, but with excess evil in nature, with surd evil, and with evil as a problem in the metaphysics of divine reality. Brightman's work raised a theological storm. It was a privilege to be close to the storm center as a graduate student. A group of his students resided in Berlin for a period of weeks while he was composing his responses to criticisms of *The Problem of God* by his equally courageous *The Finding of God*. No one can rightly accuse personalists of not taking evil and sin seriously at all levels of reflection on the realms of being. On such issues they persistently grappled with them more than Tillich, the process philosophers, or the humanistic naturalists. No neo-orthodox theologian can put the cross-of-Christ deeper in the nature of God than this form of personal idealism. Since naturalism seemed to be the most serious challenge to the personalistic position, I elected to spend a summer session at the University of Wisconsin in order to experience the direct impact of naturalistic and

pragmatic humanism in the teaching power of the exciting
teacher, Max Otto, a co-signer of "The Humanist Manifesto."
The other side of my concerns I nurtured the following summer (1936) at the Harvard Tercentennary by studying under
Werner Jaeger, author of *Paedeia*, and C. H. McIlwain, the
famous historian of political philosophy in the West.

If personality is the irreducible and wholistic key to
reality, Reinhold Niebuhr's theology was bound to be a challenge. *Moral Man and Immoral Society* shook the American
scene with its Marxist sympathies and its even more post-
Marxist neo-Augustinian view of the relation of individual
human nature to collective human behavior. *The Nature and
Destiny of Man* offended my philosophical training and my
empirical sensitivities partly because of the assault on
reason and partly because it lacked a coherent account of
person-in-community as a constructive redemptive doctrine.
My criticism first appeared in *The Personalist*. I include
here also a hitherto unpublished paper delivered at Garrett
Biblical Institute in the late '40s.

The first of these essays, "Reinhold Niebuhr's Conception of Man," has special interest for the reason that later
Martin Luther King, Jr. directly appealed to it in his criticism of Niebuhr. King endorsed my assertion that Niebuhr
was weak in not recognizing the relative perfection that is
a fact in Christian living. He did not adequately deal with
the redemptive forces that can be released into history by
committed human beings and by the immanence of *Agape* in
human nature and history. King's acceptance of this correction of Niebuhr's view of *Agape* was crucial to the formation
of King's philosophy of non-violent resistance. While other
Personalists were deeply involved in this pilgrimage, a
passage from this essay was quoted by King in a paper written for DeWolf's course and the idea in it is alluded to in

*Stride Toward Freedom*:

> There is a Christian perfectionism which may be
> called a prophetic meliorism, which, while it
> does not presume to guarantee future willing,
> does not bog down in pessimistic imperfection-
> ism.  Niebuhr's treatment of much historical
> perfectionism is well founded criticism from an
> abstract ethical viewpoint, but it hardly does
> justice to the constructive contributions of the
> perfectionist sects within the Christian fellow-
> ship and even within the secular order.  There
> is a kind of Christian assurance which releases
> creative energy into the world and which in
> actual fellowship rises above the conflicts of
> individual and collective egoism.

We shall look more directly at King in a subsequent
context.

Most of my writing up to this point was either philosophical as in the book with Laurence Sears, *The Development
of American Philosophy* (1940), or in philosophical theology.
Initially, I had followed Niebuhr's activities as a fellow
pacifist and socialist with enthusiasm, but the late '30s
brought about a major evaluation of his perspective which
was to endure.  But first, more must be said about the decade of the Great Depression.

With the completion of the Ph. D. (1933), the quest for
a teaching position in philosophy and religion began.  Jobs
were scarce, the marketplace being beset not only by
economic recession but by the influx of many distinguished
exiles from German universities after the Hitler revolution,
not least among them two of my professors from Frankfurt,
Paul Tillich and Max Horkheimer.  Therefore, instead of
teaching, 1933-34 was spent in a Methodist parish on a
two-point circuit in a "cut-over" county of northern
Wisconsin.  Here abject poverty, bank failures, the spo-
liation of forests, bootleggers of the Prohibition Era, CCC
Camps, and sectarian religious rivalries provided the agenda

for a young pastor who was challenged to make the Gospel
relevant through the church in such a community under such
circumstances.

Even more was learned about social neglect of human
beings and the consequences of massive poverty the next six
years as a teacher of philosophy and Bible in Berea College,
Kentucky.   About this area of Southern Appalachia Harry
Caudill was to write a classic forty years later, *Night
Comes to the Cumberlands*.  The '30s were deep twilight.

God bless Berea College!  To this day the "cause of
Christ" as envisioned by President William J. Hutchins has
been an inspiration.  The college motto, "God has made of
one blood all nations" and the dedication of Hutchins'
forebears "to lift the mountains from the bottom" were for
me practical responses to one-sided neo-orthodoxy.  After
almost fifty years they have a deep lodgement in my religious and moral loyalties.   President Hutchins wanted a
Christian personalist theist to head the Department of
Philosophy and Bible and in appointing me gave me the
assignment "to build a golden bridge from an impossible
mountain theology to the modern world."  Ninety percent of
the students, too poor to go anywhere else, were the cream
of the two hundred mountain counties which Berea regarded as
its territory.   Since these students came from the same
social and cultural milieu, teaching Bible and philosophy
meant leading them through many religious and personal
crises which were sometimes acute.   Inasmuch as many of
these were common to the whole group, the educational task
was also a therapeutic one to which the College was sensitive.  The religious reconstruction had a socially constructive as well as reformative function in their total reassessment of mountain and non-mountain culture.  In this work
"moral man" and "immoral society" are partially useful

analytical tools, but one must not miss the power of a redemptive community as a synoptic reality.

With Gordon Ross, Willis Fisher, and Walter Sikes I taught there at various times Old Testament, New Testament, psychology of religion, and a whole settee of philosophy courses, including the history of political philosophy. As a tool I brought out a revision of E. S. Brightman's *Historical Outline of the Bible* (1936) and in 1940 with Laurence Sears the book of readings with critical introductions on American Philosophy noted above. A second edition appeared in 1960 with the assistance of Anne V. Schlabach.

To a reader principally oriented to the intellectual sources of new movements in theology and church life, the world crises and conflicts of the mid and late '30s may seem far removed from "Bloody Harlan" and Federal relief to alleviate Appalachian poverty, but spiritual life at Berea had a lively interest in the wider world of ecumenical striving and conflicts like the Spanish Civil War. The rise of Fascism, the Third Reich, the New Deal, the Japanese rape of China, and the ecumenical conferences at Oxford and Edinburgh may have been centered a continent or two away from hook worms, county agents, and coal operators and miners of Eastern Kentucky, but the Berea faculty were gathered from centers like Sian, Yale-in-China, Chicago, New York, Boston, and Oberlin, not to speak of Durham, Lexington, and New Orleans. A constant stream of graduates not only returned with experimental ideas to the valleys and hollows of mountain counties to do their part in lifting the mountains from the bottom, but entered the best of the nation's medical schools, social work centers, agricultural colleges, law schools, teachers' colleges, and theological schools. They made the "golden bridge" a two-way road.

Interest groups abounded at Berea in the absence of

many intervarsity athletic sports, except for basketball.
Societies flourished on such themes as voluntary poverty,
the Fellowship of Reconciliation, the Socialist Party of
whose local I was secretary, drama groups, debating, dance
and musical clubs, and much else. Interest in peace and
socialism were sufficient for me to be, for example, a
delegate in 1937 to a specially called convention of the
Socialist Party in Chicago. The religious focus of the
faculty was self-consciously ecumenical in both well-
conceived required chapel programs and in the vitality of
Union Church, the historical ancestor of the college. I
shall say more about my ecumenical development further on.

Barth, Brunner, and Bonhoeffer may not have been as
well known to the Berea faculty as Robert Hutchins, John
Dewey, or Arthur E. Morgan (of T. V. A. fame), but the
issues debated at Oxford and Edinburgh were by no means
ignored in prayer meetings and discussion groups in the
Union Church. Franco, Hitler, Stalin and Mussolini, like
the latest Soviet Five-Year-Plan, the co-operative movement
in Antigonish, and selling scrap iron to Japan were as
common faculty table talk as the new Highlander Folk School,
the Southern Tenant Farmer's Union, and the Wagner Act.
There was openness and pluralism in the mix of conservative,
liberal, and radical segments of faculty and staff both in
matters of theology, educational theory and practice, college discipline management, and social ideology. Perhaps
because Berea was the legatee of the "gospel of impartial
love," the college community tended to regard itself as
vocationally responsible to be open to national and world
movements while being a light in the night which rapacious
owners and victimized illiterates sought to survive in the
Cumberlands and beyond. Part of that light was the revival
of dignity through indigenous handicrafts of which Berea was

stimulus and leader.

Of Reinhold Niebuhr's rising star more must now be said against the background of the creative and redemptive Berea years (1934-40). It was not Niebuhr's "realism" or neo-orthodoxy that was the "golden bridge" for students who came from homes in many cases where parents were illiterate but nevertheless believed in the Bible from 'kiver to kiver'. Despite Niebuhr's concerns for social and historical problems, there seemed to be a split in his view of human nature that he never resolved, that between classical individualism of the anxious finite self and egoistic collectivism. Somewhere constructive community was lost in the glaring power struggles of corporations, trades unions, and sovereign national states. But industrial research was showing even in the '30s that individual incentives did not work as well as team work and group appeals. Teamwork produces attitudes and skills and even productivity over and beyond individualistic efforts and incentives. As noted above, however, already as a seminary student I had addressed the new "theology of crisis" and admired Niebuhr's *Leaves from the Notebook of a Tamed Cynic*. Yet the attacks on liberalism by both Niebuhr brothers left me feeling that they had not grasped the radical realism of Boston Personalism. H. Richard Niebuhr argued that liberalism had lost its dialectical element, the tension with transcendence. In the *Kingdom of God in America* he charged: "A God without wrath brought man without sin into a kingdom without judgment through the ministrations of a Christ without a cross." This meant, somewhat elaborated, that the ideas of evolution, growth, development, the culture of the religious life, the nurture of the kindly sentiments, the extension of humanitarian ideals and the progress of civilization had taken the place of the Christian revelation. Whoever the

representatives of this gestalt of liberalism were, I knew
that it was not what Boston University School of Theology
had taught.  Like Reinhold Niebuhr, I had no sympathy for a
faith that was only "the consciousness of the highest social
values" or for sentimental parlor pinks who had no sense for
the dialectical unity of theory and practice in politics or
economics.  Of course, anxiety, temptation, sensuality and
pride afflict all human beings.  But these can be terribly
formal categories and abstract individualistic issues in the
face of abject poverty and powerlessness.  Much alienation
can be overcome by some enabling personal and group power.

Like the Niebuhrs I was suspicious of those who read
Marx through the eyes of sectarian socialist fundamentalism;
or of church persons who went to the Soviet Union and returned with only a Kingdom-of-God glow on their faces.  Yet,
they had at least gone to Russia, while their compatriots
wallowed in anti-communist hysteria.  The Marxism I had
studied at Frankfurt was historically self-critical in
method.  Real dialectics had its own "Protestant Principle"
as Tillich was later to call it. Personalists like myself
were aware that Stalinist Communists had no real belief in
civil liberties. Christians had a basic conflict with the
Marxist doctrine of human nature so far as transcendent
reference goes, both within the self and in relation to God.
Human problems can not finally be resolved by social reconstruction external to the self.  Moreover, I appreciated R.
Niebuhr's continuing role in the Socialist Party, was
excited about reports of his participation in the Oxford
Conference (1937), and was equally disappointed when he
advocated intervention in World War II.  Niebuhr the social
prophet did not persuade me about Niebuhr the theological
pessimist ("realist").

Methodologically there is a deeper problem in neo-orthodoxy—its theological positivism, an attribute which it strangely shared with the anti-philosophical bias of Albrecht Ritschl. It held that the validity of Christianity depended entirely on an act of faith in the Bible as God's Word. It resorted to a "leap of faith" rather than to experience taken as a whole and including the venture of faith. Hence its ethic was exclusively heteronomous and deontological. Hermeneutics dominated exegesis of Scripture. The "liberals'" historical and exegetical conscience seemed to be discounted. These traits made for an irritating Olympian posture and even arrogance in theology. Later in my career I was less offended by those who perceived Christianity with only the "eyes of faith" because I understood better the corrective character of every ideology and particularly the cultural crisis which precipitated the "theology of crisis" in Germany. Kerygmatic proclamation was a style in theology that had a prophetic social function. It corrected a whole range of social accommodation to certain evil social movements. Barth's "No" was a necessary response to culture religion and specifically National Socialism. The cry at Oxford, "Let the Church be the Church", had an heroic ring in the confrontation of church and state, of religious liberty in the face of totalitarianism. But today the real intellectual challenge to Christian existence is the creeping penetration of science-based secularism and individualistic humanism. Neo-orthodoxy cannot really engage the new naturalism because kerygmatic proclamation is not dialogue.

Culture is, to be sure, always in need of radical criticism from an ultimate perspective. And this applies particularly to the basic values ascribed to persons-in-community and the social order whose hierarchy of values they are likely to adopt. Thus, for example, the equality of human dignity with its implicit democratic claims is

often reduced to the slogan of equal opportunity, which is
only relatively defensible since it may be limited in practice to the equal opportunity to compete for entrance into
the main stream of an ambiguous status quo. Such competition may be devoted more and more to energies by women and
men, minorities and majorities in a society dominated by
mass culture, bureaucracy, technology, privatized values,
war, materialism, and lived out in a bored, well-fed, thrill-
seeking, pleasure and consumption-oriented selfish state of
affairs. The radical "No" of a new Barth may be propheti-
cally welcome in such circumstances, but the constructive
ethical foundations of an alternative realm of values must
be wholistically laid. For this task deontology needs the
corrective of a teleological and relational personalism.
Equality of opportunity as a deontological principle is
necessary but not sufficient. Society needs more than
marketplace philosophy extended to business, entertainment,
the arts, and the professions which are in a state of moral
decadence.

Radical criticism requires the trustworthiness of
reason; else it is arbitrary. Yet the dominant theology of
the '30s and '40s waged an unrelenting attack against the
"pride of reason." This attack seemed both abstract and
unfair, tending on the one hand to identify all reasoning
with the intellection of the Enlightenment and to overlook
the relational character of reason and its critical humility
in the face of objective reality. John Dewey stressed the
idea that the quest for "certainty" was empirically in vain
and that open-ended certitude was the most the mind could
intellectually hope for. Analysis is brilliant, but it is
subordinate to constructive synopsis. All sciences are only
relatively autonomous and point beyond themselves. This
principle holds for ethics also. Brightman's Fifteenth

Moral Law is, accordingly, a metaphysical law: "All persons ought to seek to know the source and significance of the harmony and universality of the moral laws, i. e., of the coherence of the moral order." Human moral laws point beyond themselves. Moral choice has a context in the whole person, the person-in-community, the community in history, history in cosmic action—in God. A moral decision is not a mere intellectual syllogistic conclusion; it is a venture and in the moment of action it is a practical absolute; but the practical absolute of present decision-making has a context of theoretical relativism, an openness to new data and further reflection. A decision is more than a conclusion. Theoretically speaking, persons have certitude, not certainty.

Such reflections as the above show that my problems tended to be couched in terms of philosophical theology more than in those of systematic theology, though at the center of my religious life was a deeply felt loyalty to Jesus Christ. Indeed, his choice to accept death on the cross still keeps me in the pacifist fold and committed to non-violence, even when utilitarian considerations and the rough-and-tumble compromises of political life urge deviations from that Christian way of life. That this is still a minority position in the church has been evident since the great Oxford Conference (1937). At that very time the Spanish Civil War required an existential decision which World War II was not to change.

Division in the body of Christ on matters of violence/non-violence is but one aspect of the ecumenical problem. Ecumenism is hard patient work; and nowhere is it harder than in Europe whose churches dominated the ecumenical movement for many decades. Christian unity demands hard choices and honest searching dialogue. The unity we

have in Christ is deeper than the scandalous disunity that
denominationalism perpetuates.    Yet eucharistic visible
organic unity can come only through the churches.

I represented my seminary in 1928 at a biennial meeting
of the Federal Council of Churches and reported back to the
School of Theology my enthusiasm for what I had experienced.
Presently I became aware that the Social Creed of the
Methodist Episcopal Church, formulated and adopted in
1907/8, was substantially that of the newly organized
Federal Council. The leaders and the heroes of the Council
became mine and many of them were also Methodists. Already
at Knox College my weekly diet in preparation for sermons as
a student pastor fed on *The Christian Century*. Conferences
on Preaching at Boston University enlisted the whole spec-
trum of Protestant leadership. Boston as a city provided an
envigorating ecumenical climate among Protestants and Jews,
not least on its social ethical side, with outstanding
national figures to be heard at The Community Church and The
Ford Hall Forum. No topic was too controversial to be aired
or debated.

My ecumenical perspective was further broadened during
my graduate year in Frankfurt under Tillich's concern for
religious socialism and through frequent visits to churches
and synagogues. But my self-consciousness of the Church as
the *una sancta* was not well developed at that time. Cooperative Christianity and openness to the truth in all
great world religious and their classics characterized that
stage of growth.

As I worked on my doctoral dissertation on Ernst
Troeltsch's philosophy of history and his theses in *The
Social Teachings of the Christian Churches* in the years 1930
to 1933, my grasp of history and of the inner development of
the churches deepened. In 1932 I was excited to note new

formulations of the Social Creed in the Federal Council of
Churches and in my denomination, a movement from single
reform resolutions to criticisms of the capitalist system as
a whole. That was an election year when I campaigned somewhat for Norman Thomas. Also, as a student-pastor in North
Hampton, (N.H.) Congregational Church I broadened my experience of parish polity beyond that of the Methodism into
which I was ordained in 1931.

During the church year of 1933-34 at Crandon-Argonne,
Wisconsin, the depth of the Great Depression taught me how
to live on a total of $600.00. All around the Methodist
Church were the crying needs of public relief, C. C. C.
Camps, bootlegging in the cut-over forests, small communities in need of organizing their human resources, and the
negative impact of conservative ethnic Lutheran and Roman
Catholic parishes. The pastoral ecumenical imperative was a
word that fell on a stoney ground of closed minds and hard-
ened hearts in the midst of human need crying out for Christian co-operation and service.

Then came six years at Berea College (1934-40), happy
ones ecumenically because of the close ties between the
college and Union Church. While there in the      hills of
the Cumberlands with the strange variations of "mountain
religion" I followed from afar with interest, zeal, and
excitement the preparatory studies for the Oxford and
Edinburgh Conferences. The marvelous convergence of the
Life and Work Movement and the Conference on Faith and Order
into the Provisional World Council of Churches provided
vision and insight into the meaning of the Church and its
witness to the world in social ethics. "Let the Church be
the Church!" was a clarion cry for rededication to the cause
of Christian unity. Suddenly the problem of philosophical
theology and ethics had a new dimension for service among

rival faiths in an age of universal history. The ecumenical
in relation to the merely international was akin to the City
of God in relation to the City of Earth, akin but not quite
identical.

    If I was primarily a Bible teacher and philosopher at
Berea College, at the University of Southern California
(1940-45) I had more explicit duties in Christian Theology
and Christian Ethics.  Ecumenically I served as Chairman of
the Commission on Race Relations of the Los Angeles Church
Federation and concurrently as a citizen on the Council on
Civic Unity which was formed to keep ethnic tensions in the
area within civil bounds in wartime.  Ill-conceived pru-
dence, war hysteria, anti-Japanese racism, economic competition, and plain unadulterated land greed conspired to force
100,000 American citizens of Japanese origin and Japanese
aliens into concentration camps.  The policy was a major
violation of civil liberties and a dark racist stain on the
history of California and the U. S. A.  As an ecumenical
churchman I was afforded the duty to witness and feebly
serve the suffering relocation of persons of Japanese ances-
try and subsequently visit in some of the camps.  When all
Japanese were ordered in 1942 to be relocated, The Methodist
Church opposed the action as un-American and unchristian.
Once they were in the camps, Methodists co-operated with the
federated churches that were set up in the Relocation Camps,
there being thirty-one ministers in these camps.  The converse side of the emptying of "Little Tokyo" was the large
influx of Negroes into Los Angeles and the rise of
"Bronzeville."

    In the U. S. A. there were four lynchings of blacks in
1941.  Discrimination was widespread in industry, labor
unions, housing, and in almost every phase of national
defense.  Since Hitler was a racist, it was obvious that in

effect racists in America were the allies of the enemy despite patriotic pretensions. Hispanics and Native Americans
also fared poorly. President Roosevelt eventually issued
Executive Order 8802 and appointed the first Committee on
Fair Employment Practices.

Concurrently, the drafting of men and the volunteering
of women in the armed services, the practice of defensive
"blackouts," the burgeoning of defense industries, efforts
to place qualified Japanese-Americans (Nisei) of college age
in midwestern colleges, voluntary labor dispute arbitration,
counseling conscientious objectors and visiting Civilian
Public Service Camps—kept changing the agenda for
theological and ethical reflection and action. Not least in
time consumption were the meetings on post-war
reconstruction to make relevant and to implement the "Four
Freedoms." It was during World War II that I wrote the
enclosed essay on Niebuhr and the one on "Personality in
Christian Ethics." When I left Los Angeles in 1945 to take
over the deanship of Boston University School of Theology, I
wrote a compact study for the *Annals* of the American Academy
of Political and Social Science called "National Unity and
National Ethics." The whole volume, edited by Gordon A.
Allport, was called *Controlling Group Prejudice.* It is not
included here, but some may find it a helpful summary of
wartime thinking and aspiration.

What was the resultant and emerging conception of the
nature of Christian social ethics from the foregoing succession of experiences? Christian social ethics is not yet a
coherent discipline. It is eclectic. It is a dialectical
unity of theological input, history and social science, and
philosophical principles. Through this dialectic ethics
seeks emergent coherence. As a young normative science it
is the natural legatee of the social gospel movement. In

this tradition Christian social ethics has a concern for the
place of values in social science and the relation of theology to the social sciences.  This concern carries forward
some of the issues of the '20s on the relation of religion
and science, for social science prior to World War II was
often trying to emulate natural science with a value-free
objective, a rather sterile venture.

"Norms and Valuations in Social Science," written for
*Liberal Learning and Religion* (1952), edited by Amos Wilder,
reflects these issues and the impact of the War.  I recall
how many university people were carried away by value relativism about 1940 and tended to view all social behavior as
just social conditioning.  But Hitler's "war against the
West" made it evident that the dignity of human personality
in science and in the scientist was at stake.  Today, a
whole literature on value and science carries the debate
forward.

In 1966 the Department of Church and Society of the
World Council of Churches convened a study conference in
Geneva, a follow-up of the 1937 Oxford Conference, for which
I wrote a preparatory essay, "Theology and the Social
Sciences."  The volume was edited by John C. Bennett.  This
paper was subsequently published also in German.  Taken
together this and the above essay illustrate how seriously I
take social science and also the preliminary state of the
art of Christian social ethics.  Readers of *Moral Laws in
Christian Social Ethics* (1966) may find these papers of
supplementary interest.  Likewise, two papers which appeared
in *Christendom* during World War II, not included in this
collection, bear on this theme:  "From Sect to Church" and
"The Ecumenical Significance of the International Labor
Organization."

In teaching and research the study of the sciences is

much more than developing a metaphysical or theological
posture about the scientific standpoint. As E. S.
Brightman learned early in his career, a metaphysics which
sees science as dealing with the merely phenomenal order
tends toward emphasizing the relative unimportance of science. Theologians who maximize ultimate loyalties tend to
develop superiority complexes and habits of mind toward
"lower" realms of knowledge. Learning from such deficiencies and the positive postures of naturalism and pragmatism
toward science, I have found the dialectic of theology-sci-
ence-philosophy indispensable in social ethics. But not
only must Christian ethicists have a friendly attitude, they
must study the sciences seriously. And too few do.

Two books that permanently influenced my work appeared
in the '40s: Gunnar Myrdal's *An American Dilemma* and Robert
M. MacIver's *The Web of Government*. Myrdal was persuasive
on the principles of multiple causation and cumulative causation, and hence of the possibilities of a benign spiral and
a vicious circle in social development. His treatment of
valuation in social science was also determinative. MacIver
clarified the relation of community and state, the ubiquity
of government, and the role of myth in community. He
stressed the error of the appeal to force in understanding
power in government. Thus my communitarian personalism was
reinforced and enriched by serious attention to thinkers
like Myrdal, MacIver, Troeltsch and many others.

Commitment to an inclusive church in an inclusive society became evident in the ethos of Boston University School
of Theology in the '50s. From 1952 to 1962 and beyond, half
of all the doctorates in religion earned by black students
in the U. S. A. were awarded there. One of these was to
Martin Luther King, Jr. (1955) who was the leader of the
Montgomery Bus Boycott and in due course was awarded the

Nobel  Peace  Prize.   King  made  the  final  stage  of  his
pilgrimage  to  nonviolence  at  Boston  University,  as  his  book
*Stride  Toward  Freedom*  testifies.   He  notes  that  during  his
doctoral  studies  he  had  the  opportunity  to  talk  to  many
exponents  of  nonviolence.   Here  he  found  a  passion  for  social  justice  that  stemmed,  not  from  a  superficial  optimism,
but  from  a  deep  faith  in  the  possibilities  of  human  beings
when  they  allow  themselves  to  be  co-workers  with  God.   In
the  process  he  realized  that  Niebuhr,  as  noted  above,  had
overemphasized  the  corruption  of  human  nature  and  that
Niebuhr's  pessimism  concerning  human  nature  was  not  balanced
by  an  optimism  concerning  divine  nature.   "He  was  so  involved  in  diagnosing  man's  sickness  of  sin  that  he  overlooked  the  cure  of  grace."  What  sustained  King  in  the  great
civil  rights  struggles  that  lay  beyond  Montgomery  until  his
assassination  in  Memphis  (1968)  was  a  Christian  faith  philosophically  grounded  in  the  idea  of  a  personal  God  and  a
metaphysical  basis  for  the  dignity  and  worth  of  all  human
personality.   This  personalism  he  learned  directly  under  E.
S.  Brightman  and  L.  Harold  DeWolf,  with  S.  Paul  Schilling
serving  on  his  dissertation  committee.   Racial  inclusiveness,  nonviolence,  and  personalism  dominated  the  ethos  of
the  whole  School  and  helped  translate  New  Testament  love
(*agape*)  into  activist  nonviolence.   Half  of  all  the  Boston
black  doctorates  in  religion  in  that  period  were  in  social
ethics.   King's  doctorate  was  in  Systematic  Theology  and
Philosophy  of  Religion.

     Ecumenical  activity  became  ever  more  intense  after  the
First  Assembly  of  the  World  Council  of  Churches  (1948).
Symbols  played  their  part.   As  dean  of  Boston  University
School  of  Theology,  beginning  in  1945,  three  possibilities
opened  up  as  a  new  building  was  being  erected:  (1)  placing  a
permanent  ecumenical  symbol  over  the  main  entrance  of  the

building; (2) a dedication ceremony with honorary degrees awarded to Orthodox, Roman Catholic, and Protestant scholars; (3) making more ecumenical faculty appointments. These were promptly accomplished. The next move was the ecumenical development of program and curriculum. In 1950 the Summer Term inaugurated a special ecumenical leadership curriculum in cooperation with the newly constituted National Council of Churches, a program which continued throughout the decade. Depth and leadership were augmented by the appointment of Nils Ehrenstrom as the first full-time professor of ecumenics in any theological seminary. He had headed research and studies from Amsterdam (1948) to Evanston (1954) for the W. C. C., having earlier been lent by the Church of Sweden to prepare for the Oxford Conference already alluded to above.

By 1951 preparations for the Second Assembly were in full swing. A special commission of twenty-five theologians was constituted to write a report on the main theme: Christ—the Hope of the World. As a member of that Advisory Committee I worked for three successive years. This ten-day per year face-to-face encounter with theologians from across the world caused me thereafter to be more explicit in articulating my Christian theology, to appreciate Christian faith in its many guises, and to grasp the Barthian and neo-orthodox corrective of conventional liberalism in a new way. This meant being less content with implicit loyalty to Jesus Christ, though, as Hendrik Kraemer was wont to note, I still did not wear all my theology on my sleeve as European theologians often do. The nature of ecumenical dialogue became clearer; there are no short cuts to unity. In 1952 I began duties on the Faith and Order Commission, continuing until Nairobi (1975). In 1953-54, while on sabbatical leave, I taught a semester at the Graduate School of the Ecumenical

Institute (Chateau de Bossey).   In 1954 I was a consultant
at  the  Evanston  Assembly  and  became  co-chairperson  of  the
Commission  on  the  Co-operation  of  Men  and  Women  in  Church
and  Society,  continuing  until  New  Delhi  (1961).   That  commission  was  a  sort  of  gadfly  to  the  whole  ecumenical  establishment  respecting  the  life,  status,  role  and  service  of
women—including ordination—in the Church.   The essay   "The
Togetherness  of  Men  and  Women"   reflects  my  thinking  in  the
context  of  the  Commission  of  which  Madeleine  Barot  was  the
executive  leader.    In  1955  the  Faith  and  Order  Commission
took  the  unprecedented  step  of  enquiring  into  the  so-called
Non-theological  Factors  that  affect  unity  and  disunity  in
the  churches.   First,  came  a  request  to  make  a  proposal  on
how  a  manageable  unit  of  research  might  be  conducted.   Next,
came  a  request  to  write  an  illustrative  essay  on  Institutional  Factors  affecting  Unity  and  Disunity.   Thirdly,  came
the  appointment  to  be  chairman  (with  Nils  Ehrenstrom  as
secretary)  of  a  special  commission  on  Institutionalism  and
Church  Unity.   A  report  and  a  volume  edited  by  Ehrenstrom
and  myself  appeared  in  preparation  for  the  Montreal  Conference  of  Faith  and  Order  in  1963.

       This  long  recital  outlines  the  almost  non-stop  ecu-
menical  study,  research,  teaching,  commission  meetings,
Assemblies  of  the  '50s  as  concurrent  activities  with  the
deanship  and  the  professorship  in  social  ethics.   Ecumenical
dialogue  required  constant  fresh  reflection  on  Christ  and
the  Church,  his  relation  to  social  and  ecclesiological
change,  and  attention  to  theory  and  practice.   In  this  context  I  read  a  paper  in  1953  to  the  American  Theological
Society  on  "Distinctive  Characteristics  of  Christianity,"
which  has  not  hitherto  been  published.   I  include  also  one
on  "Religion  and  Human  Destiny"  (1951)  read  at  the  University  of  the  Pacific,  one  on  "Christ  Transforming  Culture"

(1957) presented to the Council of Methodist General Board
Secretaries, an essay on "Social Problems and the Christian
Hope" (1956), and one on "The Necessity of the Church"
(1956). If the essays of the '40s have a focus on the human
person seen against the background of theistic Personalism,
those from the '50s show a concentration on the insepara-
bility of Christ as person and Christ as lord of the Church,
but always with a relevance to social change. There is no
less concern with metaphysical reality, but there is also a
communitarian hope which is more characteristically American
than I found among the European colleagues in that decade.

"Religion and Human Destiny" (Pacific Philosophy Institute) was one of a symposium dealing broadly with American
politics, education, and religion: William D. Nietman on
human nature, T. V. Smith on democracy, Gustav E. Mueller
on freedom, and myself on religion. All were semi-popular
statements. I showed the merits of Boston Personalism and
the findings of Troeltsch on the permanent contributions of
the Christian ethic. My view rejects Troeltsch's loss of
nerve in not adhering to the principle of personality in his
latter years as stated in his *Christian Thought*.

"Distinctive Characteristics of Christianity" focuses
on the concreteness and historical reality of Jesus Christ.
Through the years various Christian movements have selected
aspects of his teachings or doctrines about him, as in Paul.
Historical developments of the Church and its theology have
featured Christianity as a "religion" which can be compared
with analogous features or functions of other great religions. Such comparisons are not my specialty. This essay
focuses on the personality of Jesus Christ. Christianity
is not fully itself when it neglects the concrete person in
the interest of some doctrinal comparison. The revelatory
personality of Jesus transcends all interpretations in all

historical circumstances. Jesus' words are influential but
as a person he exerts power in history, in the happy formulation by H. Richard Niebuhr of "Christ Transforming Culture."    All teachings about Christ are born from reflections on worship, i. e. on supreme values. The essay,
"Christ Transforming Culture," shows how religion and the
church function in culture and the function of the church to
set goals and to be in mission to change culture. These
efforts require that the church be self-critical about its
cultural accommodations.    There is urgency for self-criticism and self-reform. The essay is more programmatic than
definitive—and proved to be controversial.

An eschatological aspect of the theme of Evanston,
"Christ the Hope of the World," is its social activism.
Since my social ethics development in the '50s revolved
around the "idea of the responsible society," which was the
great middle-axiom of the social ethic of the Amsterdam
Assembly, it was important to relate the Christian hope to
responsible social action. "Social Problems and the Christian Hope" expresses this. It is dangerous to separate
eschatology and Christian ethics. Moreover, it is a mis-
fortune if a middle-axiom like "the responsible society"
degenerates into a mere slogan; the lordship of Christ
refers not only to "faith and order" but also to "life and
work."

In Faith and Order the persistent impact of "leading"
theologians tended to be Christocratic. Indeed, one often
had the impression in the early '50s that the doctrine of
God was in danger of becoming Christomonistic; i.e., instead
of a well-balanced doctrine of the trinity, Christian theology was ecumenically Christocentric, with natural theology
and creation a neglected theme and the idea of the Holy
Spirit a dependent, if not unimportant aspect of church

life. One heard much about Christ and His Church. It was
not until the Uppsala Assembly (1968) that the doctrine of
the Holy Spirit received much emphasis, but by then the
charismatics and the pentecostals were inciting minor rebel-
lions in mainline denominations. The neglect of nature for
history left the churches unprepared, as a whole, to deal
with ecology systematically.

Personally, I was working on three fronts: Christian
theology both Biblical and natural, Christian sociology
(church and society), and Christian social ethics. My social ethical writing still reflected the language of philosophical theology or natural theology. This was both delib-
erate and inevitable, since I did not wish to expand the
voluminous literature of systematic theology, already in
excess supply, while social ethics and the "idea of the
responsible society" were underdeveloped. One disvalue of
this, however, was that critics sometimes charged me with
having no theology. Having distinguished colleagues in
Biblical, historical, and systematic theology and assuming
that devotion to evangelical Christianity and the mission of
the Church were the natural context of the deanship of a
theological seminary, I assumed that my theological critics
were better informed about my participation in helping write
"Jesus Christ, the Hope of the World" (1954) than was in
fact the case.

My endeavors have generally been to build on what has
already been accomplished rather than to invent an original
idiom. Emergent empirical coherence is the goal. There was
much groundwork to do in the post-World War II situation,
given the United Nations, the Universal Bill of Rights and
Freedoms, the Marshall Plan, the independence of India, the
revolution in China, the Taft-Hartley Act, the Korean War,
and the McCarthy scene. Through it all throbbed the task of

relating  new  movements  to  the  idea  of  the  responsible
society.    "Rapid  social  change"  and  development  had  special
relevance  for  new  nations  in  Africa.    Suddenly  the  "Third
World"  appeared.    Between  Amsterdam  and  New  Delhi  East-West
confrontations  had  a  new  global  context  in  church  and  state.

Meanwhile,  a  personal  attack  in  *The  Readers  Digest*
(February,  1950),  called  "The  Pink  Fringe  of  Methodism,"
brought  home  the  challenge  of  anti-communism  and  of  rising
McCarthyism.    This  incident  coincided  with  an  invitation
from  Ralph  Lowell  to  give  Lowell  Institute  Lectures  for  1951
in  King's  Chapel  on  current  topics  in  religion.    The  series
was  published  as  *Religion  and  Economic  Responsibility*.    It
afforded  an  opportunity  to  state  explicitly  how  I  evaluated
communism  and  particularly  Stalinism.    In  1954  I  was  honored
by  Boston  University  to  give  its  annual  Boston  University
Lecture  and  chose  the  theme  which  linked  me  to  the  World
Council  of  Churches,  "The  Idea  of  the  Responsible  Society."
Later  it  served  as  the  substance  of  the  opening  chapter  of
the  book,  *Foundations  of  the  Responsible  Society*  (1959).

This  book  was  not  published,  however,  according  to  its
original  plan.    It  is  applied  ethics.    The  theoretical  foundation  had  to  appear  later  because  of  publisher's  fears
about  length.    *Moral  Laws  in  Christian  Social  Ethics*  appeared  in  1966.    By  that  time  the  field  was  buzzing  with
discussions  of  "situation  ethics"  and  "contextualism."
Accordingly  I  took  the  occasion  to  pay  my  respects  to  the
principal  contemporary  rivals  to  "moral  law"  and  added  a
chapter  which  explicitly  stated  my  understanding  of  how
Jesus  Christ  is  related  to  the  idea  of  the  responsible  society.    It  states  my  Christology.    Nevertheless,  coherence  is
still  the  criterion  of  truth  and  Christian  social  ethics
must  proceed  eclectically.

In  1969  the  Council  of  Bishops  of  the  United  Methodist

Church invited me to address them on the Christian Bases of
Morality and Ethics for Today. It was an effort to help the
bishops with principles for choosing responsibly in a revolutionary world. The moral situation in the '60s was bad and
two weaknesses in the churches contributed to their silence
in the face of the civil rights struggle and the Indo-China
War, racism and war being much more obscene than the language of protesting youth that offended their elders and the
Establishment. First, the churches were too confused to
speak out and secondly, their members were sufficiently
well-off within the status quo to manage without getting
involved in radical protest or revolution. In addition to
race and war issues, they also avoided commitment to rising
feminism, Hispanic liberation movements, and the morality of
abortion. The Kerner Report spoke for more than racial
unrest when it said that the people lacked social and political will. The phrase, "choosing responsibly in a revolutionary world," pointed to four elements in the moral situation: (a) responsibility rather than freedom was the majority's moral need; (b) action alone would convince those who
were impatient with hypocrisy and freedom deferred; (c)
revolution referred to the multiphasic social change that
was upsetting the patterns of power; and (d) world described
the scope of the theater and the drama that was being enacted despite the apathy and defensiveness of the Establishment. The ecumenical movement was alert to the situation
at the top and in its conferences, but the grass roots made
of its utterances a dialogue of the deaf.

The paper which is reproduced here may be regarded as a
summary of my general ethical position at that time or an
introduction to my book length treatises in Christian social
ethics. Coming only four years after the 1966 Geneva Study
Conference on Church and Society, its statements on theology

and social science are meant to reflect the views of the
essay, "Theology and Social Science" and to serve as a formulation of regulatory moral principles which lead to the
middle axioms already noted above.   Related essays interpreting the 1979 Conference on Faith, Science and the Future
are found in the *Andover-Newton Quarterly* (vol.   20:   March,
1980) and *NEXUS* (vol.   23,  1980) No.   59 under the titles
"The New Debate on Faith, Science and the Future" and "A
Just, Participatory and Sustainable World Society" respectively.   The moral laws embrace a wholistic standpoint,
running the regulatory gambit from formal logical consistency and autonomy to comprehensive communitarian demand and
pointing toward an ultimate ecological metaphysics.   In this
perspective the human person's domination over nature is
integrally united with stewardship which is responsible for
the earth's sustainability.   One might say that nature does
not belong to persons, but persons belong to nature; and
nature belongs to and is within God.

    Once again, the social ethics presented in the fore-
going acknowledges the eclectic stage of the art.   Too early
closure of theory in the interests of tight Christian or
Biblical consistency is likely to distort synoptic truth.
The gospel is nonreducible and theology spells out its meanings from that affirmation and perspective. Jesus Christ is
Lord and Savior. History and the social sciences describe
and partly interpret the data of social experience, social
problems, institutions and processes. Philosophy reflects on
experience as a whole and performs a bridge function in
pointing out the principles that connect the ethical edge of
the gospel to social science. Such principles constitute
regulatory moral law.

    Theology provides much more, of course, than grist for
the ethical mill. The gospel is Jesus Christ with the mes-

sage that he is the Saviour of the world. And the gospel
entails the Church. Jesus called forth a community to carry
forward his politics of the Kingdom of God and his mission
of inclusive redemption. The gospels were formulated for the
Church and hence the evangelization of the world is unthink-
able without the reality (being) and mission of the people
of God. The early church was legally illicit. Its refusal
to acknowledge Caesar as Lord is essential to its affirmation of Jesus Christ as Lord! The gospel thus conceived
created a revolutionary new community. Its universalism
burst the old wine skins of the Jewish synagogue and Torah.
In Christ a universal fellowship as an historically concrete
*ecclesia* became manifest. Indeed, a new age was born.
Hence Christian social ethics cannot be understood apart
from the faith of the Church, the new creation in the
Church, and the transforming mission of the Church in
society.

The remaining essays of this book may be read as various emphases in the meaning and role of the Church as part
of the ethical edge of theology. The specific nature of the
Church cannot be concretely expressed apart from the ecumenical movement, to which theme I now return.

Two exalted movement in the Lund Conference (1952) of
Faith and Order noted (a) that the closer persons and
churches draw to Christ the closer they draw to each other
and (b) the dictum that the churches ought to do all things
together except those which conscience prevents them from
doing. Unfortunately, these dicta are complicated and compromised by the historical circumstances and the disobedience of the churches, not least their institutional intro-
version. On the first point, it is often the case that when
the churches begin to draw together in matters of theological consensus they do not get close enough to Christ to be

transformed empirically and institutionally. Hence their
dialogues on doctrine make them aware that they want to be
fully united, but not just now. On the second point, the
scandal continues that churches do only those things together which they cannot do disunitedly. They institutionalize
their disunity by organized co-operation. In thirty years
since Lund, despite theologies of covenant and conciliarity,
the cause of unity goes forward with painful hesitation.
The essay on "The Necessity of the Church" reflects my concerns in 1956 because of the ambiguous situation. It recognizes my acceptance of a cosmic and historically oriented
Christology which entails a communitarian view of the Church
and the unity of ecumenism and renewal.

Of the modes of renewal which unity requires, two moral
imperatives in the transformation of denominations are noteworthy, one rooting in the "order of creation" and the other
in the "order of redemption." The first has to do with race.
The Church cannot be the Church when any church deliberately practices segregation. The inclusiveness of the
Church is a precondition of its authenticity. The second
has to do with gender or sexism. Here it is not a question
of the "mixed" character of the community, but of the vocation and offices of women and the relationship of men and
women to each other. We have noted this earlier. The
co-operation of men and women in the Church is one aspect of
the larger question of their mutuality and equality in society as a whole. The renewal is, therefore, one of both
church and society. Any study which seeks to isolate these
realms (e. g., equality in secular society but only male
ordination in the church) is theologically suspect and morally compromised. The *kairos* of this issue is now.

As we have seen, three key terms are vocation, ministry, and responsibility. Ecumenism affirms their interpene-

tration.  The World Council of Churches has been a prime
influence in emphasizing the ministry of the laity and in
interpreting the vocations of clergy and laity as aspects of
the continuity of Christ's ministry through the Church and
in the world.  The short article  "Theological Aspects of
Vocation" (1960)  combines my personalistic theology with a
community-oriented understanding of Christian vocation.   A
longer statement appeared in the study book  *In Every Place
a Voice*.   These ideas were carried forward in the present
essay, "Diakonia: The Christian in Society," published in
German in 1968 and appearing here in English for the first
time.  It also shows, when compared with statements developed in the '40s, a more explicit theological formulation.
One of the reasons for this accent is that in the earlier
period a Christian ethos and context could be presumed in
the audiences to whom my writings were addressed (except for
the naturalistic humanists), whereas by the '60s there was
less certitude and vital faith.   This shift in the ethos
even of many theological seminaries in the late '60s modified the division of labor for the Christian social ethicist.   One had to wear more theology on one's sleeve.

Important as the ecumenical movement is, not least the
leadership of the top, the findings of study commissions,
the  pronouncements  of  conferences  and  assemblies—the
Christian witness is made primarily in and through the local
congregation.   In 1951 I expressed this in an address at
Howard University, which is published here for the first
time.  It indicates certain criteria of prophetic integrity
which are persistently relevant along with elements of strategy to guide local churches.   The book  *In Every Place a
Voice* amplified the theme, already part of the message of
Amsterdam (1948), that in the local congregation Christians
should be a home for those who have no home and a voice for

those who have no voice.  Given ethnic minorities, world
hunger, unemployment, the handicapped, refugees, the tor-
tured  and  imprisoned,  battered  children,  and  homeless
elderly—no  more  relevant  vocation  still  beckons  the
churches in the 1980s.

     The ethical edge of theology is global.  Although key
terms  of  the  '60s  were  rights,  vocation,  ministry,  and
responsibility,  hardly  less  so  were  witness,  service,  and
mission.   The  Church  is  mission,  domestic  and  world-wide.
When "Life and Work" and "Faith and Order" united in a provisional plan for a World Council in 1937/38, they did so in
association with the World Missionary Council.  This body, a
council  of  councils  and  of  missionary  agencies,  became  formally  a  division  of  the  World  Council  of  Churches  in  1961
(New  Delhi).   Ecumenical  work  requires  a  renewal  in  and  of
and  by  the  churches,  but  also  of  world  mission.   Some  aspects of this renewal are reflected in the essay, "The Christian Faith and the Renewal of World Mission" (1963).   This
paper, not previously published, was circulated at a Regional Study Conference in Washington, D. C.

     The  final  essay  makes  plain  that  my  commitment  is  a
transformational view of Christ's relation to church, culture,  and  social  order  globally  understood.   "Christian
Responsibility  with  Respect  to  Revolution"  is  not  an
analysis of violence.  The term revolution is here used as a
more  radical  concept  than  either  violence  or  nonviolence.
From  the  perspective  of  Christian  pacifism  my  current
thinking  on  those  topics  is  expressed  in  "Violence,
Non-Violence  and  the  Struggle  for  Justice,"  published  in
*Proceedings and Selected Papers of the American Society of
Christian Ethics* for 1977.   An exposition and critique of
"Pacifism  and  the  World  Council  of  Churches"  appeared  in
Thomas Shannon, ed., *War and Peace* (1980).  The function of

the present paper is different. It states what is implied
in this whole collection, a never finished activist
Christian social ethic historically committed to the
permanent task of radical social change as a continuing
ministry of Jesus Christ and coherent with a personalistic
theory of reality. The kingdom of God, transcendent and
immanent, is the ethic's theological criterion; the Church
understood ecumenically is Christ's agent. Yet, God in
Christ through the Holy Spirit is at work in all aspects of
human history.

In the midst of multidimensional revolutions a renewed
Church must once again say "No" to all that represses the
human spirit and "Yes" to all that liberates personal worth
and constructs new institutions in which persons can be
truly free: -- Say "No" to all systems and structures East
and West, North and South that deny justice, universal participation, and which require military domination to maintain order: -- Say "Yes" to the positive moral roles of
government and responsible economic change. The applied
ethic of the churches must combat all political efforts to
annul the state's duty in promoting the general welfare.
Hence they must defend human dignity in terms of the basic
entitlements of human beings to quality of life, not as
"hand outs" or paternalistic charity, but as justice. The
state must assist in developing the resources of people
"from below" through equipping and enabling the most dis-
advantaged persons first, not last as every "trickle down"
program does. Empowerment is the proper response to alienation.

The churches must help re-establish the ethic of communal responsibility for communal resources such as the protection of public lands from the rapacious greed of a profit
hungry and energy-hunting body of entrepreneurs. Until now

the church have not fully assessed their stewardship with respect to a sustainable earth and the needs of unborn generations. Neither social market capitalism nor the various socialisms in the world have adequately planned their economies. The ethical edge of theology is a revolutionary communitarian personalism with a permanent mandate.

It has been my destiny to begin my adult life in the Coolidge era and to spend my mid-seventies in the Reagan era.    Hence my commitment to prophetic Christianity has been bracketed between "the business of America is business" and the slogans of Reaganomics.   From the corruptions of Harding's men to the corruptions of Nixon's Watergate.   From the pre-New Deal old-federalism to the shallow shameful betrayal of the poor and powerless in the "New Federalism." The liberal and radical ethical theology of protest and reconstruction that has developed in the intervening years, as these essays show, has been based not on novelty in theological aspiration or speculation or philosophical docetism, but on constant recovery of the personal theism of a great tradition, the inherent worth of persons, a communitarian understanding of human nature, the redemptive universality of Christ, and the identification of Jesus with the disinherited.   The revolutionary power of this theology is as old as Judaeo-Christian social prophecy and as new as every immediate creative encounter with truth and God.

A special note to those who are devoted to rectifying gender language in theology and ethics:   I have, with few exceptions, retained the generic male language of the original form of these essays in order to be faithful to the era in which they were composed.   Nevertheless, the personalistic tradition has affirmed the full personhood of men and women in church and community and in all positions of power and authority.

## NATURALISM FACES
## PROPHETIC RELIGION
## (1939)


Roy Wood Sellars has recently stated that the most fundamental problem confronting religion today is this: "Can religion adjust itself to naturalism?"[1] Adjust is a word laden with ambiguity. The above proposition might be taken to mean that all religious data must be interpreted within the framework of naturalistic presuppositions. The statement may mean that what is valid in religion must be harmonious with "physical realism." Perhaps the following disjunction is intended: Either the religion of the future will be a "function" of naturalistic philosophy, or religion will decline more and more from now on——at least for truly philosophical minds. However, not all truly philosophical minds are naturalistic, and therefore it may be relevant to reverse the question as follows: Can naturalism "adjust" itself to prophetic religion? The reason that the adjective prophetic is employed is to emphasize the element of social justice in religion, which is the element most closely related to the social idealism of many naturalists.

The two basic concepts in religion are personality and value. Can naturalism do justice to these concepts, as they reveal themselves in prophetic religious experience, within the frames of reference of natural science, social behaviorism, and non-theistic social idealism?

What is prophetic religion? What is naturalism?[2] From the time of Amos prophetic religion has been an integral part of Judaic and Christian civilization. Concern for social righteousness within the nation and justice among the

43

nations under the governance of God and his righteousness
have been central in much Christian preaching. Since apostolic times there has, to be sure, been a fluctuating interest in the social gospel and in dynamic revolutionary salvation.    But in periods of great social change there has
always been a remnant that has resisted all priestly accommodation to the status quo and all cheap escapes into a
nonsocial religion from the real struggles and needs of the
common people. The remnant has recognized that the church
and all secular institutions stand under the judgment of
God.    There have always been those who have sustained the
creative ethical monotheism of the eighth-century prophets
and Jesus, in the face of exploitation, war and secularism
of every kind.    Today[3], also, in America and in the ecumenical gatherings of world Christians, one finds prophets
who view history through religious categories and who are
committed to the inescapable demands of Christ upon history.
In the presence of more-than-human values they work together
with God to reconcile the world to him.    Such is prophetic
religion in general terms.

From a more philosophical standpoint we may say that
prophetic religion is an attitude in which theism leads to
radical applications in personal and social relationships.
Analysis reveals at least the following elements in the
faith of prophetic theism: (1) a personal divine will taking
active part in human history; (2) a holy will which is the
source of all moral and spiritual values, and of human personality; (3) a divine command recognized by the human will
to find the central meaningfulness of life in a righteous
fellowship of persons committed to God; (4) recognition of
the unique selfhood and sacredness of individual personality; (5) freedom to decide in favor of or to reject the
religious demand; (6) radical positive action against evils

which frustrate the coming of a righteous fellowship of persons; (7) recognition of the natural justice of God as judge of the conventional justice of man; and (8) awareness of the instrumental nature of all social institutions.

There are some religious prophets who do not embrace a full personal theism. And yet, their actions naturally lead to an affirmation of such a philosophical faith. The objectivity of ideals which they affirm requires for its concrete interpretation a purposive divine intelligence who acts creatively and redemptively in human history. Such men (Niebuhr, Wieman, Tillich) acknowledge an order of meaningfulness which either "transcends" present values, or demands complete "commitment," or calls for a "decision" to be loyal to the "center" of history. In each case a dynamic value-seeking order is implied which requires philosophically a divine holy will that is personal.

What is naturalism? It is difficult to find a clear-cut definition which will be inclusive enough to take in all the chaos and competition within the circle of those who call themselves naturalists. A few samples from a variety of writers may, however, point the way for a general definition. Sellars, in *Religion Coming of Age*, writes:

> What, then are the controlling principles of naturalism? Essentially those of science: the beliefs that nature is an all-inclusive, spatio-temporal system and that everything which exists and acts in it, is a part of this system. In short, naturalism is the expression of the desire for explanation in terms of objects which can be handled and studied in accordance with scientific methods.[4]

Naturalism is, therefore, opposed to explanations in terms of super-human agencies of a generally invisible and unlocalized sort. Ernest Nagel emphasizes the following point:

> To a naturalistic philosophy man occupies

> no central position in the flux of events.   He
> is part of the flux, and in that sense nature
> would not be what it is if man were not what he
> is....There is no cosmic plan which aims at
> man's survival or at his achieving his ideals,
> for to his lot the universe is morally indif-
> ferent.[5]

Morris Cohen writes in a similar vein:

> From a naturalistic point of view the whole
> life of the human species is a minor episode in
> the history of a tiny speck of cosmic dust; and
> man's natural fate is determined by forces which
> visit death and destruction upon the just and
> the unjust.[6] I for one cannot see in history or
> in nature any rational proof of "a power not
> ourselves making for righteousness."[7]

In his new work on *Logic* John Dewey emphasizes especially
two features which make his logic naturalistic:

> The primary postulate of a naturalistic
> theory of logic is continuity of the lower (less
> complex) and the higher (more complex) activ-
> ities and forms....What is excluded by the pos-
> tulate of continuity is the appearance upon the
> scene of a totally new outside force as a cause
> of changes that occur.

The second feature of naturalistic logic is this:

> Inquiry is a development of organic-envi-
> ronmental integration and interaction.[8]

For men like Edman, naturalism

> is really a faith in what man, himself an inci-
> dent in natural processes, may do to render his
> existence rich with meaning and possibility
> through generous imagination and ingenious con-
> trivance.[9]

As over against the elements of faith found in prophetic
religion naturalism assumes, we may therefore say, (1) that
science in general is our sole guide to knowledge; (2) that
the "natural" order is all there is; (3) that nature, apart

from persons, is indifferent to ideals; and (4) that the
good life is nevertheless possible for humankind.

Though there is general affinity among naturalists on
these four points, the conflict between so-called "halfhearted" and "broken-backed" naturalism has never been
resolved. This issue refers to differences between
Santayana and Dewey and their followers. On the one hand,
the "halfhearted" bring the ends, aims, and values which man
cherishes directly into nature. On the other hand are the
"broken-backed," who tend to alienate man from nature
because no place is found there for human values and ideals.
Men otherwise as far apart as Russell and Edman stand with
Santayana, while the New Humanist and the social revolutionary groups stand with Dewey. For these, nature gives
some kind of undefined "support" to human striving and
provides "possibilities" for social improvements, though
nothing approaching a theistic principle is affirmed.
Nevertheless, this social action group is closer to prophetic religion than the "broken-backed" naturalists. The
latter find in life ultimately only an heroic despair or an
escape into aesthetics.

Distinctive as theism and naturalism are, the terms are
nevertheless not completely disjunctive. There are many
phases of naturalism which are congenial to prophetic religion, inasmuch as they more adequately deal with personality
and value than the older materialistic naturalism did. The
tendency in modern philosophy has been for materialism to
confine its philosophical tenets to the crude presuppositions of mechanical natural science. Reduction to physics
has been the order of business. The tendency for idealistic
and spiritualistic philosophies, on the other hand, has been
to plead the cause for recognition of richer understandings
of reality congenial to the highest aspirations of

personality.    Modern  naturalism  has  developed  methods  and
principles much more congruent with the demands of religious
experience  and  the  uniqueness  of  personal  selfhood.   In  the
following discussion we shall point out "adjustments" favorable to prophetic religion; after which we shall point critically to present lacks in the assumptions and doctrines of
contemporary naturalism.

    1.   Rejection of reductionism.   Reductionism means the
identification of  higher  forms  with  lower  forms  of  being  of
which  they  are  supposed  to  be  reorganizations.   Art,  religion,  thought,  and  imagination  are  today  affirmed,  however,
to  be  "functions"  of  nature,  just  as  much  as  are  breathing,
digestion,  and  the  movements  of  molecules  and  stars.    A
third  of  a  century  ago  William  James  protested  militantly
against "medical materialism." Today most naturalists insist
that  they  are  not  reductionists.    They  do  not  reduce  all
natural relations to physical relations—they say.

    2.   This shift from reductionism has partly come about
through  the  general  adoption  of  emergent  evolution  with  its
stress  on  the  doctrine  of  levels  and  the  unique  quality  of
mind  in  man.    Emergent  evolution  has  tended  toward  a  more
organic  conception  of  reality.   The  universe  is  approached
as  a  whole  of  wholes.   Lloyd  Morgan  himself  has  accepted  the
theistic  interpretation  of  the  emergence  of  mind,  though
others, like Sellars, still urge a non-theistic view.

    3.   Along with a recognition of the doctrine of levels
has come a gradual awareness of some of the implications for
philosophy of the presence of persons in nature.   The interpretation  of  nature  is  qualitatively  affected  by  this  fact.
While  some  concede  that  the  view  of  nature  as  a  whole  is
involved,  others  stress  the  merely  local  significance  of
man's appearing.

    4.   A new appraisal of the significance of the human

presence in nature has influenced both scientific method in general and contemporary psychology in particular. There now exists a more critical attitude towards behaviorism in its Watsonian form and a readiness to attempt more independent work in the field of personality. Along with better work on personality has come a shift away from what might be called "scientific fundamentalism." A broader empirical method, unashamed of introspection, aware of purposive categories, open to other data than sense data, aware of the role of faith in knowledge, and more appreciative of the coherence criterion of truth, has in part liberated some naturalists' investigations.

5. Another philosophical gain in the direction of a favorable handling of prophetic religion is growth in the use of historical categories. Scholars in all schools of thought tend today more and more to stress the reality of time. Indeed, more understanding of time in nature and history is indispensable for an adequate philosophy of religion. Formerly, naturalists tended to absorb or lose persons in a non-temporal, undeveloping mechanical order of nature in which there was motion but no history. On the other hand, theists also thought unhistorically. They set non-temporal mechanical nature sharply over against history. Today, as a result of many influences—including Hegel, Marx, Bergson, Alexander, Dewey—the universe is viewed as a process genuinely temporal, developmental, and historical. But if the universe is genuinely evolutionary with a nisus towards mind, its real historicity and purposiveness in human beings require a proper recognition of the status of value in the cosmic process.

6. Naturalists, on the whole, reject with Sellars the objectivity of value. Some realists like Spaulding affirm the objectivity of value after the manner of Plato. Some

pragmatists imply it in so far as they follow the lead of
Dewey's *A Common Faith*. When pragmatists say that they are
religious because they believe that this is the kind of
world that can be made better, they are affirming an attenu-
ated theism. The cosmic fate of values is a crucial problem
for prophetic religion; and most naturalists will insist
with Max C. Otto and Bertrand Russell that a human being is
the sole custodian of his ideals in a universe essentially
indifferent to them. On the other hand, it is significant
that philosophers as insistent on naturalistic method as
Wieman and Meland make the objectivity of value a basic
tenet.

7. Many naturalists express and practise a concern for
social justice. Sidney Hook and John Dewey are outstanding examples, but so also are Morris Cohen and many in the
New Humanist school of thought. The devotion to social righteousness is conceived by many of them to be the essence of
religion. They display an undoubted zeal for a radical
reformation of the capitalist social order, and much of
their writing is as clear and incisive both in analysis and
in constructive suggestions as any in circulation. Naturalism in America has frequently tended to concentrate much
needed attention on conserving human values. Men like Hook
have cooperated with men like Sherwood Eddy in presenting
social philosophy of a radical type. Prophetic religion has
been materially aided by the cooperative work of
naturalists. This cooperation is an illustration of the
fact that people can and do achieve in practice deeds of
unity which theoretically are inadequately supported. As we
shall see, naturalism as a general theory fails in its
theoretical understanding of personality and value—the
chief concepts in religion—though in practice the actual
work of conserving personality and realizing values goes on

courageously.

All of the above tendencies are congruent with the
practical interests of prophetic religion.   It must be
noted, however, that these doctrines have for a long time in
principle been the platform of most philosophical theism.
In naturalism they are belated ideas.   While they support,
they do not materially add to the fundamental personalism
implied in prophetic religion, the philosophy that has been
their nurturing soil and climate.   Naturalistic philosophies
have inherent defects—both in method and doctrine—which we
now briefly consider.

1.   There is a tendency for naturalists to identify
their type of philosophy with scientific method.   Although
they do make extensive use of science, and though much in
naturalism is appropriate to scientific work, it is presump-
tuous to assume that scientific method as such can resolve
ultimate metaphysical issues or that any one philosophy has
a special claim on scientific work.   To confine philosophical interpretation to the frames of reference of natural
science is a clear indication that reductionism has not yet
been entirely overcome in the naturalist's approach to reality.   The method is still reductionist, as further evidence
will reveal.

2.   We have noted above that Dewey makes continuity the
touchstone of a naturalistic logic.   The tendency in spite
of some evidence to the contrary is to view the continuity
from the standpoint of the lower orders of being.
Continuity, if it is to be a valid principle, must be viewed
from a synoptic point of view.   Moreover, there are other
difficulties.   One of these is to recognize that emergent
evolution and the humanistic sciences imply certain discontinuities which are as genuine aspects of being as is continuity.   The emergence of mind in nature is a novelty and nov-

elty is discontinuous in a real sense from the previous
state of affairs. The evidence reveals discontinuity, and
the method must be humble before this evidence. Dewey recognizes the novel, and yet insists on the primacy of continuity. If there is to be real and inclusive continuity it
must be theistic—we believe. The other difficulty is that
Dewey goes too far in his attempt to overcome all dualism.
The drive to eliminate the dualism of organism and environment, the dualism of higher and lower orders of being, the
dualism of mind and body, and the dualism of man and society, is a part of his method of continuity. The danger in
this method is of submerging the self in its environment and
of losing sight of the unique status of personality as an
active agent. Dewey's social philosophy tends toward perfectionism, and his ethical emphasis has been on the achievement of the unique good in each situation as well as on the
attainment of freedom. And yet his whole method of continuity has militated against a clear and coherent conception
of the self as individuality. On the other hand, it tends
logically to do violence to personality, since it deals with
it behavioristically. The elimination of all dualisms leads
to what Hegel called "the night in which all cows are
black."

     3. The theory of levels, which we have noted above, is
incomplete in the philosophy of naturalism. The emergence
of new levels is still accepted with too much "natural
piety." Lloyd Morgan's immanent theism seems to be the
least that one could affirm on the basis of the evidence for
novelty. The principle of sufficient reason would require
that naturalists consider more seriously the category of
cosmic purpose to account for the creative activity postulated by the emergence of any higher novelty, especially the
novelty of finite mind. It is imperative that naturalists

reintroduce the ideal of productive causality into their
theories. The descriptive scientific and positivistic idea
of cause is insufficient for metaphysical purposes.

4. One of the greatest weaknesses of the general theory which we are investigating is its overdependence on the
almost daily fluctuation of the scientific weather. There
was a time when most naturalists rested their case on what
they believed to be the mechanical metaphysics postulated by
the science of physics. Today, with the rise of "operational" physics and logical positivism, there seems to be hardly
any metaphysical ground left to rest the case on—unless the
naturalists go over to some kind of neo-Berkeleian
philosophy. Sellars, it must be noted, still tries to stand
by physical realism; but the drift in much "scientific"
naturalism is to take refuge in semantics, or Viennese
positivism, eschewing metaphysics altogether as nonsensical.
Such tendencies evade the metaphysical demands presented by
the fact of personality and its value experience. No metaphysics, then no personality; no real values; and no meaningfulness in the historical process—including the attempts of
positivism to have meaning. One of the basic grounds for
the instability in naturalism which we have just described,
is the ambiguity of the term "nature." Idealists, theists
and other devotees of personality have been pressed by the
constant demand from naturalists to "tell what personality
is." Personality is consciousness capable of reason and
ideal values. But what is nature? Its meaning fluctuates
with every wind of scientific doctrine. More and more it
appears that "nature" equals "all there is," and
"naturalism" equals "philosophy."

5. The reduction of philosophy to science is apparent
in a thinker like Ames, whose discussions of God and religion do not transcend the categories of social psychology.

In this he leans heavily on the work of George H. Mead.
Mead introduced into social psychology and into the literature of pragmatism the idea of a "generalized other." The
generalized other, we are told, arises out of the process in
which the self arises.  For example, in conversation a
person must put himself "at the point of view of the other
and see himself as the other sees him.  He reacts according
to the responses he understands the other to be making."
Thinking is held to be conversation with this generalized
other.  Ames finds in this idea a "fruitful enrichment of
the idea of God and of the nature and function of prayer!"[10]
Praying, on this basis, is talking things over with your-
self, and God is simply the posited alter of this conversation.  This analogy breaks down, of course, as soon as one
recognizes that in a real conversation the "generalized
other" has an objective reference to an existent, while the
God of Ames, to use his own words, is only an "honorific"
absolute.  Years ago Pratt pointed out that if the worshiper
ever got on to what Ames' God really means, this insight
would kill the goose that lays the golden egg of religion.
In practice Ames has substituted devotion to the highest
social values for prophetic religion with its objective
reality of God.  There is a basic difference between loyalty
to an ideal and loyalty to God.  Ames is a reductionist in
that religion is reduced to social psychology.

      6.  This leads us to observe that most naturalistic
thinking fails to distinguish clearly between religion and
morality.  Sellars says that "religion is self-conscious
human life functioning in the face of its problems.  It is
the setting up of objectives and courage in their pursuit."
In this definition the differentia of religion is omitted
entirely.  Completer and more empirical understanding of
religious experience would reveal that religion is an atti-

tude towards a super-human power with whom persons must deal and who presides over the fate of values. The identification of religion and morality is yet another illustration of reductionism, for religion is qualitatively different from social morality taken by itself.

7. The ineptitude of naturalism for prophetic religion may be illustrated, finally, from an article by John Herman Randall, Jr., "On the Importance of Being Unprincipled," which appeared recently in the *American Scholar*. He points out that persons of principle are not able to get anywhere in politics without fighting, and they never really achieve anything. Randall defines a principle as a postulate or an assumption; it cannot be proved by anything else, nor verified by an experience different from your own; and since it cannot be proved if questioned, the only thing one can do is fight for it. The case is closed and the argument is over. Such a procedure leads to disaster. The only thing to do, says Randall, is to learn the method of politics and compromise. The principles cannot decide the matter.

This point of view is a travesty on all principles. It confuses dogmatism with principle and never gets beyond the wrangling of competing interests, for it provides no guiding principles for the resolution of conflict. Moreover, it makes of politics and compromise a sheer contest of power. The standpoint of prophetic religion, on the other hand, employs principles without making them absurdly absolute. It regards the will of God as the final judge, and requires all people to seek this will and commit themselves to seeking a fuller understanding of it. This will is not the objectification of one's highest ideals, although they are evidence for it. God is not an "honorific absolute." A person must be loyal to reason, but human thinking is not

the absolute Reason.   The ultimate judge is an active agent,
not an abstract idea.   Randall, like many naturalists, seeks
unity through compromise on the level of interest.   Prophetic religion seeks unity on a level above the competing interests of persons, though these interests are not ignored.
They are transmuted, *aufgehoben*, through rational loyalty
and common committal to the ultimate source of all insights
and intuitions.   Prophetic religion is empirical, rational,
and realistic because Reality, not passing interest, has the
final word.

The foregoing discussion has shown that many tendencies in current naturalism are favorable to the philosophical presuppositions of prophetic religion, and it has also
shown defects and deficiencies in the movement.   The structure of the paper may seem to set seven virtues over against
seven deadly sins, but that is purely accidental.   The virtues and sins do not cancel each other.   If naturalism will
face more empirically and rationally the whole of religious
experience and the larger meanings of its own insights, then
a firmer foundation may be laid for a consideration of
personality and value, an enquiry which will bring new insights into the study of religion.   The future of naturalism
will depend partly on how it learns to face religion.

## NOTES

[1]Roy Wood Sellars, "Religion faces Naturalism," *Religion in Life*, Autumn, 1937.

[2]Naturalism as defined here does not include the theistic mystical naturalism of Wieman and his group; neither does it include the position of J. B. Pratt as recently stated in the Yale Lectures.

[3]1938.

[4]Page 141.

[5]S. Hook and H. A. Kallen, eds., *Philosophy Today and Tomorrow*, pp. 388-389.

[6]G. Adams and W. P. Montague, eds., *Contemporary American Philosophy* (New York: Macmillan, 1930), Vol. I, p. 239f.

[7]*Ibid.*, p. 247.

[8]*Ibid.*, p. 23f. See also ch. I.

[9]Hook and Kallen, *op. cit.*, p. 152.

[10]H. N. Wieman and B. Meland, *American Philosophies of Religion* (Chicago: Willett, Clark and Co., 1936), p. 334.

# TWENTIETH CENTURY DISSENTS TO
# RITSCHL'S THEOLOGY OF MORAL VALUE
# (1979)

## I
## General Introduction

The nineteenth century was one of the great centuries of Christian thought and movements. Many ideas which flourished then have not yet spent their force, though they have been greatly modified in the nexus of scientific and social revolution, war, ideology, and liberation movements of the twentieth. In the case of Albrecht Ritschl one must be highly selective because of the scope and originality of his work. Dissent is linked to continuity. The focus of this communication is his theology of moral value as the final end of his systematic effort.

The procedure will be as follows: first, to lay out seriatim the theological principles which he employed; second, to summarize the relevant major doctrines which follow from his use of value-judgments with respect to Christ and God; third, to specify particularly his notion of the Kingdom of God as the teleology of the Christian religion; fourth, to define the idea of the Kingdom of Sin; and fifth, to show the correlation as well as the distinction between the religious and ethical motifs of his major work, *Justification and Reconciliation*. This will conclude the exposition of Ritschl's theology.

In the presentation of twentieth century dissents, I shall first deal with personal idealism at Boston University. Here the constructive role of metaphysics in

theology will be accented.  The second response will be that
of the social gospel as formulated by Walter Rauschenbusch,
noting the Kingdom of God and the Kingdom of Evil.  Finally,
Karl Barth's criticism will be presented, lifting up common
themes and radical rejections.

Ritschl's work lies on the nineteenth century side of a
great  social  divide  when  colonial  empires  were  still
flourishing and science had put religion on the defensive,
but his intellectual labors on behalf of Christian theology
show him to have anticipated many movements with motifs in
theology  like  positivism,  pragmatism,  historicism,  the
universal  Christian  community,  Christocentrism,  and  the
place of value-judgments in a religious theory of knowing.
His life spanned the heart of the century, 1822-1889, but
Anglo-Saxon influence produced an early twentieth century
literature.  *Justification and Reconciliation* was translated
in 1900.    In 1925 Alfred Garvie summarized his own
researches in the well-known article in the *Encyclopaedia of
Religion and Ethics* and in 1937 H. R. Mackintosh devoted a
whole chapter to him in *Types of Modern Theology*.  The
literature on Ritschl and Ritschlianism is, of course,
enormous.  For a quick characterization of his thought the
labels by Garvie may give the uninitiated a handle on what
is a complex system:  religious pragmatism, philosophical
agnosticism, historical positivism, and moral collectivism.
The appropriateness of these categories will become evident
in due course.

II
Ritschl and His Theological Principles

Who and what determined Ritschl's principles?  Barth
was to say Kant and the Enlightenment.  Critical response to
that must wait until the end of this communication.  His

reading was so vast and his knowledge of the history of
dogma was so profound that one must rather ask, who did not
influence him?   This foremost of nineteenth century German
theologians after Schleiermacher was the son of Karl
Ritschl, a Berlin pastor and later Pommeranian General
Superintendent, or "evangelical bishop."   In his maturity
Albrecht Ritschl was a professor at Bonn and after 1864 at
Göttingen.  For a while he was greatly under the influence
of the Tübingen School as represented by Friedrich Christian
Baur.   Baur was epoch-making in the studies of the New
Testament, church history, and the history of dogma.   The
principal instrument of the school of Baur was the Hegelian
dialectic which was used decisively from a purely scientific
standpoint, a method which sought to be free of theological
or doctrinal presuppositions.   In short, the quest was pure
history and employed the idea of development in church
history, seeking thereby to establish the genesis of the
church and its progression as free of all supernatural or
miraculous causes.   The chief labors of the Tübingen School
were devoted first to the synoptic gospels, with the
Hegelian logic applied to the synoptic problem and the
consequences of this applied to the other writings.

     Ritschl broke with this school in the second edition of
his own epoch-making book, *Genesis of the Old Catholic
Church* (1850, 1857).   No theologian has so robustly opposed
the imposition of speculative philosophical ideas on
theology as Albrecht Ritschl, though not always succeeding.
His most influential work was from the Göttingen period with
the publication of *The Christian Doctrine of Justification
and Reconciliation* (Vol. I, 1870; Vol. II, 1874; Vol. III,
also 1874).   An English edition of Vol. I appeared as early
as 1872, but of the definitive Vol. III only in 1900.

     Turning now to his doctrinal principles, they were

characteristically the following:    (1) The locus of the
systematic theologian is within the Christian community.
This community possesses the fruits of Christ's work in the
forgiveness of sins and shares Christ's faith.   Thus Ritschl
rejects presuppositionless perspectives entirely.   One gains
a true knowledge of God only through the person of Christ.
(2) Natural theology is rejected.   He rejects and combats
every "metaphysics" as a support of dogmatics, though, as we
shall see, there are both Kantian and Lotzean elements in
his arguments.   As a method he attacks speculative philosophy and all mixtures of natural theology and revelation.
(3) The emphasis on the church and the rejection of natural
theology resulted in a primary appeal to the Bible and a
sharp differentiation between canonical New Testament and
extra-canonical writings.   On the whole Ritschl took a conservative position in New Testament criticism and opposed
efforts, then popular, to write "lives of Jesus."   (4) As a
consequence of Scriptural emphases, the sources of doctrine
are held to be not the pious self-consciousness of Christians, as most theologians since Scheiermacher had stressed,
but the Gospel.   In this Ritschl tended to be close to the
biblicists; however, he differed from them because of his
heavy involvement in doctrinal history, particularly of
Lutheran texts and confessional statements.   (5) Ritschl
accents particularly the difference in principle between
religious knowledge and secular knowledge, making use particularly of Kant and Lotze.   In so doing he created a widely
misunderstood Neo-Kantian theory of knowledge.   Religious
knowledge is not affected by the scientific knowledge we
have of nature or the world, but rests on "value-judgments,"
not on what Kant called theoretical judgments.   "Value-judgments" are a hinge conception in his entire theology.   (6)
Underlying these "value-judgments" is an austere voluntar-

istic piety which is directed to spiritual supremacy over
the world, a self-affirmation of personality over against
the brutalities of life, a piety which expresses an ethic of
fulfillment or Christian perfection.  This fulfillment is
found in doing one's vocation, thus furthering the Kingdom
of God, the ethical community of humankind.  The Kingdom of
God is the final end of the Christian religion and of God's
work in creation and redemption.  (7)  By developing such a
system, and correlating religious and ethical motifs, he
sought to demonstrate a genuinely Christian and Lutheran
position, expunging Greek metaphysics and mysticism as well
as Protestant Pietism.  These he believed were derived from
monastic and mystical motifs.  His attack on Pietism was
persistent and even polemical.

## III
## Justification and Reconciliation

Having formulated the theological principles with which
he worked, we are ready to consider the doctrines of justification and reconciliation and their relation to moral
value.  Ritschl used the figure of an ellipse with two foci,
inasmuch as the activity of the Founder of Christianity
issued at once in the redemption of sinners and the historical initiation of the Kingdom of God.  Normative Christian life has a double character, being perfectly religious
and perfectly ethical, both manifested in Jesus Christ.
"Christianity is the monotheistic, completely spiritual, and
ethical religion, which, based on the life of its Author as
Redeemer and as Founder of the Kingdom of God, consists in
the freedom of the children of God, involves the impulse to
conduct from the motive of love, aims at the moral organization of mankind, and grounds blessedness on the relation
of sonship to God, as well as on the Kingdom of God."[1]  Thus,

Christianity is conceived as a culmination of the monotheistic, spiritual and teleological religion of the Bible
in the idea of the perfect spiritual and moral religion.
These two characteristics condition each other mutually.
Since Christ made the universal moral Kingdom of God his
end, he came to know what kind of spiritual redemption he
achieved by fidelity to his vocation through suffering unto
death.   At the same time a correct interpretation of redemption and justification through Christ keeps in the foreground the Kingdom of God as the final end.  Hence we come
back to the figure of an ellipse with two foci rather than a
circle with a single center.[2]   Through this redemption
persons win spiritual supremacy over the world of nature and
are at once autonomous ethically and religiously obedient to
the loving God.  The  argument is both Biblical and Kantian.

     To affirm the divinity of Christ in this redemptive
situation is not so much a theoretical as a practical judgment.   In Jesus his disciples find the ideal of humanity
realized and are conscious through him of the power that
raises them above natural necessity into the freedom and joy
of the Kingdom.  To the church, which is the community of
believers and in which theologians do their work, Christ has
the value of God, for, religiously speaking, God means the
practical power to help and deliver.  The religious question
is not the metaphysical speculative one, God as the Absolute
or even as the Logos.

     By relating justification to the Kingdom Ritschl holds
the religious and the ethical poles of the theological ellipse together and affords his system  great  cohesiveness.[3]
He says, "Justification, reconciliation, the promise and the
task of the Kingdom of God, dominate any view of Christianity that is complete."[4]  The telos of the Kingdom is a
dimension of justification.   On this point David Mueller

observes: "The ensuing transformation of individuals within the community of Jesus' followers is tied up with their obedience to the Kingdom of God as the highest good. Forgiveness, therefore, is always correlated with the Person and Work of Jesus as it relates to the Kingdom of God and the community that he established."[5] The connecting links here are twofold, the church and Jesus' vocation. Jesus' total ministry is viewed by Ritschl as disclosing Christ's self-understanding of his vocation, his self-end, namely the establishment of an ethical fellowship among men and women. This self-end of Jesus is at once and the same time the fulfillment of God's purpose and the highest destiny of humankind. In such a conception, Jesus' ministry and that of the Christian community are viewed as ministering to the salvation of humankind as a whole.[6] Christians have a universal vocation in religion and ethics. The vocation is lived out in one's professional secular life.

In essence, then, reconciliation is the teleological fulfillment of justification. And faith, understood as trust, relates the forgiven sinner to God's own work. Reconciliation connotes that the person who is pardoned actually enters upon the relationship which is to be established.[7] The relationships designated by the term teleological are in contrast to those which are in other theologians regarded as deontological. In other words, God is interpreted more as Father than as Judge; Ritschl emphasizes the metaphors of the family rather than those of the courtroom. "Faith," he says, "is emotional conviction of the harmony between the Divine purposes and the most intimate interests of man." Yet, trust is an active and voluntaristic relationship, the opposite of mistrust and withdrawal. "Faith, regarded as trust is no other than the direction of the will towards God as the highest end and the highest good."[8] Again, Ritschl

says, "If justification by faith is the basal conception of
Evangelical Christianity, it is impossible that it can
express the relation of man to God and Christ without at the
same time involving a peculiar *attitude of the believer to
the world* founded upon that relation."[9]  Conversely, this,
of course, means that Christian ethics is conditioned by the
idea of redemption.  In turn this gets us back to the first
of Ritschl's theological principles, the context of the
Church.  "We are able to know and understand God, sin, conversion, eternal life, in the Christian sense, only so far
as we consciously and intentionally reckon ourselves members
of the community which Christ has founded."[10]  Barth and
Lehmann could not, later, be more explicit about ethics in a
Christian and churchly context.

                                   IV
                   Religious Positivism and Value-Judgments

        It follows from the above that Ritschl rejects the idea
of religion-in-general and has, instead, a method which
affirms Christianity as both historical and revealed.  This
means that all real religions are positively concrete.
Religious conceptions are always the possession of a community.  Ritschl is very explicit about this: religions "express not merely a relation of God and man, but always at
the same time a relation toward the world on the part of
God, and those who believe in Him.  All religions are social."[11]  "There is no religion that is not positive, and
there never has been; natural religion, so-called, is an
imagination.    Every    social    religion    has    been
instituted....The general ideas of God——that He is not the
world, that He is absolute Power, that He is mild, indulgent
Will, that He is the lawgiver who imposes universal
duties——are products of scientific knowledge, which as such

are also subject for their production to special conditions,
and have gained a special currency through the consent of
men; but they are neither innate in each human mind, nor
necessary results of reflection upon our position in the
world."[12]

This historical positivism has an important relationship to Ritschl's rejection of speculative philosophy and of
metaphysics whether of the materialistic or of the Hegelian
sort. It entails also his pragmatism, his philosophical
agnosticism, and his appeal to value-judgments. Here, however, his thought reflects the dualism which pervaded
philosophy of science since Descartes and which was not
overcome by Kant. Indeed Kant's theory of theoretical knowledge as it related to the phenomena of nature only heightened the opposition of strict causal determinism in the
material world and the realm of will or spirit which rooted
its judgments in the primacy of the practical reason. In
his value-judgments Ritschl gives this dualism a new direction. The quest of religion is to find a solution, with the
help of the superhuman power reverenced by persons, of the
contradiction within the human situation of both being a
part of necessitarian nature and a spiritual personality
claiming to dominate nature.[13] Thus not only the doctrine
of Christ but also the doctrine of God are value oriented.
It can be shown, Ritschl argued, that religion is in harmony
with reason, but there is always the reservation that the
"knowledge of God embodies itself in judgments which differ
in kind from those of theoretical science" and it is "the
duty of theology to conserve the special characteristics of
the conception of God, namely, that it can only be represented in value-judgments."[14] Theology is, nevertheless,
scientific in the sense that it comprehensively shows the
unity of knowledge of nature and the spiritual life of

persons.[15]

The road to a Christian's knowledge of God is through
the value-judgments of Christology. Every point of religious belief is guided solely by the revelation of God in
Christ. However, valid Christological judgments are not of
the speculative kind found, for example, in the Chalced-
onian formula, but in judgments which evoke faith and commitment    and    are    made    in    the    community    of    Christians.
Value-judgments    provide    Christian    knowledge    evoked    by
revelation. Epistemologically speaking, we must distinguish
particular ideas which have correspondence with reality as
statements of fact from religious judgments of worth that
are unconditionally valuable for us. Thus the statement
'Jesus died on Calvary' is a judgment of fact, whereas 'We
have redemption through Him' is a value-judgment. Religiously speaking, we know the nature of God and Christ only
in their worth for us. Consequently, such judgments lead to
acts of obedience and are the sufficient cause of direct
acts of will and hence of morality. The parallelism of this
whole manner of arguing and the Kantian style of ethics has
frequently been pointed out, the Christian's freedom with
Kant's moral autonomy and the Realm of Ends with the Kingdom
of God. H. Richard Niebuhr, for one, uses the dualisms and
the parallelisms to designate Ritschl as belonging to the
Christ-of-Culture type.

Scholars have pointed out difficulties in such a method
of arguing. The starting point is Christological statements
rooted in the ministry and work of Jesus and attested in the
New Testament by the Church. One proceeds from the historical to the suprahistorical, Ritschl preferring the Synoptic
to the Johannine portrait of Jesus. This starting point, as
Mueller points out, "necessitates that the ethical estimate
of Jesus precede the religious evaluation. Christological

statements that do not grow out of the awareness of Jesus'
redemptive activity as founder of the Kingdom of God are
speculative and of no interest to faith."[16]    There is,
accordingly, an anthropocentric bias at work at the expense
of a metaphysically transcendent initiative.

Ritschl's rejection of a metaphysical dimension is,
however, not absolute.    He identified three types — the
Platonic, the Kantian, and the Lotzean — and agrees with
Lotze.   Indeed, he wrote a little treatise on it, *Theologie
und Metaphysik*.   Yet he attacked any reliance on speculative metaphysics in theology, and very specifically monistic
Idealism.[17]   "We can know what God or Christ is *to us*; we
cannot grasp what God is in Himself, or what Christ reveals
Himself to be in His relation to God."[18]    Therefore,
value-judgments become part of Ritschl's historical positivism, for when he says that Jesus is "the historical Founder of Christianity" this is for him equivalent to saying
that He is the revelation of God.   H. R. Mackintosh argues
that Ritschl makes Jesus homogeneous with the texture of
human events and agrees with Brunner in *The Mediator* that
his logic implies that "there is no rent in the life of
history as such, which could not be healed by the historical
process itself."[19]   Although Mackintosh commends him for
expelling Speculative Rationalism from systematic theology,
he feels he went too far:   "Ritschl asked for more than
could be conceded, and as it were drove the nail in so hard
as to split the wood."[20]

Further questions about the use of value-judgments must
be raised.   Is the standpoint finally too anthropocentric?
Is the standard of value merely moral, according to our
need, or is it also transcendent?   What is the relation of
revelation to history?   Do we argue in a circle by forming a
judgment of faith with ready-made standards for the Person

of Christ?   Does He create faith in us or is Jesus one of
whom we can only say that He is morally indistinguishable
from God?[21]   From these questions we can see that historical
religious positivism invites theological trouble.   Ritschl
affirms the historical revelation in Jesus, and he assumes
the objective reality of Scripture, but he fails to distinguish the actions that are historical in the sense in which
any historical event is interpreted in an historical nexus
from the transcendent reference which makes that event or
person divine in the sense of the objective being of God.
Many things in the life of the church Ritschl assigns to the
phenomenal realm of nature, but his failure to provide the
distinguishing marks of history and transcendence affects
his phenomenalism, his pragmatism, his method of value-judgments, and his way of relating moral vocation to the teleology of the Kingdom of God.   The critics in question do not
doubt his personal belief in Christ's deity or His divine
value for us; what is in doubt is the logic whereby redemption is clearly God's action and not just our personal experience of overcoming distrust and unbelief.   It would appear
to thinkers like Garvie, Mackintosh, Schäfer and Mueller
that Ritschl does not avoid the error of making a value-judgment a subjective or private projection, when what is required is God's self-disclosure and self-attestation as the
starting point, not the conclusion.[22]   A theologically valid
value-judgment in their estimation requires that it be an
*acknowledgement* of the objective meaning and truth in Jesus
Christ.

   The conflicting claims of historical enquiry and systematic theology have been pointed out by Mueller in this
way:   Jesus' sense of vocation is helpful in depicting his
historical ministry, but the early church did not primarily
interpret Jesus in terms of that ministry which was per-

formed prior to the cross and resurrection. On the contrary, the church's confession of Jesus as Lord was based on
the latter events. Mueller follows H. Richard Niebuhr in
observing that as an historical theologian Ritschl is forced
to say that the early church saw Jesus as victorious over
the world in the light of the resurrection, but as a systematic theologian the model presented is the remembrance of
Jesus' patience in the face of suffering and death.[23] On
the other hand, Paul Lehmann goes too far when he says:
"Fundamentally, the most appropriate critical superscription
with which to adorn the portal of Ritschl's theological
reconstruction is this: *Man wants forgiveness; and man
forgives himself.*"[24] Yet the point of these criticisms
sticks. If whatever fails in God's revelation to relate to
a person's problematic situation as already defined must be
set aside, then it would appear that his use of Kant's metaphysics and epistemology caused him, despite all disclaim-
ers, to determine apriori what God can and must say and do
in his situation.[25] In this predicament Ritschl was very
much a child of the nineteenth century philosophy, scientific method, and cultural ideals, Christological value-judgments to the contrary notwithstanding.

V

Evaluation by Some Boston Personalists

We have noted some twentieth century dissents to
Ritschl's theology of moral value, but we have cited them
primarily to sharpen issues which are involved in his methodological principles. We now turn to three substantive
ones. Boston Personalists belong in one sense to the
Ritschlian tradition; Walter Rauschenbusch is bracketed by
H. Richard Niebuhr with Ritschl in the Christ-of-Culture
typology partly because both commit Christians to fulfill

their vocation through basic social institutions. Karl
Barth, by contrast, is polemically opposed to the whole
Ritschlian tradition.

Of the Personalist group I shall mention Sheldon,
Brightman and Knudson. Brightman wrote his doctoral dissertation on "The Criterion of Religious Truth in the Theology of Albrecht Ritschl" and Knudson commented on him extensively. In his *System of Christian Doctrine* (1903) Henry C.
Sheldon makes some of the same criticisms as we have noted
in Garvie and Mackintosh regarding the importance of transcendence. Like Schleiermacher's theory, Ritschl's view has
a grave defect in proceeding on the basis that the whole
ethical nature of God is absorbed in His loving will, for
this pays inadequate respect to the claims of divine righteousness.[26] The objective element is foreign because the
teaching insufficiently treats God's holiness and ethical
intensity in terms of which suffering and death were required of Christ. Sheldon also criticizes the treatment of
the Apostle Paul's view of the Christian community. He
says, "Ritschl's theory that justification is the property
of the religious brotherhood or communion, as the recipient
of the revelation of God in Christ, and that the individual
partakes of justification in virtue of one's inclusion in
the Communion, finds no support in the apostle's language."[27]

Knudson and Brightman studied in Germany under such
famous Ritschlians as Harnack (Berlin) and Herrmann
(Marburg). Like Bowne and Ritschl they drew heavily from
Lotze. Interestingly, Barth also studied under Herrmann and
probably read Ritschl through his eyes. Brightman comments
on Ritschl only briefly in his published works, but strongly
rejects the view that religious faith is independent of
metaphysics and also that the truth of religious judgments

is independent of our judgments about the nature of experience and reality as a whole.[28]   Knudson treats Ritschl as a
religious empiricist, of the type that completely differentiates theology from science and thus seeks to make it
immune from attack.[29]   Knudson further rejects the idea that
theology can be given an assured place in the modern world
by making it independent of natural science and philosophy.
The way of Personalism is that of empirical coherence with
no special immunities of experience or reason.

Knudson appreciated much of what Ritschl tried to do:
correcting the one-sidedness of subjectivism by emphasizing
the objective and historical character of Christianity;
making the norm of revelation correlative with faith; and
verifying claims in the history and present experience of
the church.  Knudson regarded the program which was thus outlined, together with the theory of value-judgments as "one
of the most clearly defined, one of the most original, and
one of the most significant in the entire history of Christian theology."[30]   Still, the originality presented grave
difficulties.   Knudson's appraisal follows the outline of
the program of value-judgments, the negation of metaphysical
speculation, and the rejection of mystical piety.

First, religion moves entirely within the field of
value-judgments.  These furnish, Knudson seems to agree, as
valid a basis for knowledge as does perceptual experience.
As in Kant, practical reason is primary, but Knudson adds
agreement with Troeltsch's theory of the religious apriori.
"Religious value is not an arbitrary and unreal fact; it is
itself a part of the real world, and the only key to ultimate reality."[31]   Yet, we must avoid false claims to immu-
nity from scientific and other criticisms.

Secondly, with respect to metaphysics, Knudson parted
company and assigns to philosophy a constructive supple-

mentary role in theology. This has a bearing on mysticism because Ritschl saw a Neo-Platonist in every Christian mystic and a monk in every Pietist. Knudson rejected the sharp antithesis between evangelical and Roman Catholic piety. The fear of a pantheistic equivalence between the worth of spirit and nature was unfounded. On the contrary both Protestant and Roman Catholic piety emphasize the character of God as revealed in Christ and assert that communion with God is possible only as we enter into God's purposes and obey God's laws. Brightman also has a positive attitude toward piety and mysticism and stresses religious values as experienced and having objective reference. Knudson agreed with Harnack's appraisal that with respect to Pietism Ritschl's views were "one-sided, narrow and partisan."[32] Faith, for Ritschlianism, is too exclusively ethical. Moreover, it failed to take into account sufficiently the fields of history and psychology of religion.[33]

One further reason that Knudson refused to accept the anti-philosophical part of Ritschl's program was that religion and Christianity must justify themselves to the world as well as to themselves. Christianity cannot avoid entangling alliances with metaphysics and historical science. And for this reason he favored Troeltsch.[34] Even more he felt that Bowne's personalism, growing out of Lotze, had taken the right anti-positivistic line.[35] Ritschl himself, as we have seen, favored Lotzean arguments over those of the Platonic and the Kantian traditions. In the *Doctrine of God* Knudson urges the distinction made by Bowne between phenomenal reality and metaphysical reality, assigning the former to science and the latter to theology, rather than the distinction between existential judgments (*Seinsurtheile*) and judgments of value (*Werthurtheile*). Admittedly, Ritschl did not mean two different realms, but

approaching the world from different perspectives. Both
thinkers would agree that value-judgments imply objective
reference, but the term value-judgment as opposed to "judgments of being" has a subjective restriction which should be
avoided. Both values and the phenomenal order of science
point to the unity of ultimate reality.

With respect to the social idea in Christianity,
Knudson lifted up four aspects of the social gospel that
have affinities or roots in the German theologian: its
predominant interest in the present earthly life, its ethical emphasis, its democratic tendency, and its accent on
social solidarity. The focus on the Kingdom of God and on
ethical vocation apply to all of these. As a correlative is
the idea of the solidarity of sin or the Kingdom of Sin,
later developed with distinctive applications by
Rauschenbusch. Ritschl had rejected the traditional interpretation of "original sin" and made the principal characteristic of sin as lack of reverence and trust in God. Hence,
sin is not the same as wrong-doing; it is a value-notion
which relates wrong to indifference to God. Since all of
humanity has a habitual propensity to act in this way, the
Kingdom of Sin is the aggregate of evils in society which we
help to produce or to adopt. The interaction of all sinful
individuals, in so far as they are selfish acting, involve
each in the common evil of all in an illimitable way.
Rauschenbusch, as we shall see, lodged sin also in social
customs and institutions and noted that individuals absorbed
them from the social group.[36] Ritschl had hoped that the
idea of the Kingdom of Sin as the "web of sinful action and
reaction" would substitute for "original sin" and would
bridge "the dilemma which hovered between Pelagius and
Augustine."[37] Knudson felt that many more factors than
these are required to account for the universal sinfulness

of humankind.  While the Kingdom of Sin admittedly presupposes the selfish bias in everyone and has as "the sufficient ground" of this bias "the self-determination of the
individual will," to use Ritschl's words, the latter did not
sufficiently address "the constitution and community of
man's conative nature."  Knudson always stressed the enormous difficulty in the task of moralizing the nonmoral impulses, desires, and interests with which we are endowed at
birth.  We are born nonmoral and the moral sense dawns only
slowly.[38]  This leads us to the final observation that the
Kingdom of God for Knudson is not only correlative with that
of the church, but the church is in fact subordinate to the
Kingdom, and this is one of the profoundest truths in Christianity.  It is a major theological dissent in the personalistic ethic to the Christ-of-Culture trend in Albrecht
Ritschl.


                              VI
                   Ritschl and Rauschenbusch


     Walter Rauschenbusch, according to H. Richard Niebuhr,
presents like Ritschl the Christ-of-Culture interpretation
of Jesus and the gospel, though with greater moral force and
less theological depth.[39]  Niebuhr may have overlooked the
fact that Rauschenbusch was consciously writing corrective
theology.  It is difficult to find an American theologian
who was more intent on the transformation of culture and its
basic institutions.  He drew heavily on the liberal course
set by Schleiermacher, Bushnell, Ritschl, Wellhausen and
Harnack.[40]  The idea of the Kingdom of God became for him
the great unifying power for theology, the teleology of the
church and Christianity.  After his social awakening he said
in 1891:  "It (the Kingdom) responded to all the old and all
the new elements of my religious life.  The saving of the

lost, the teaching of the young, the pastoral care of the
poor and frail, the quickening of starved intellects, the
study of the Bible, church union, political reform, the
reorganization of the industrial system, international
peace—it was all covered by the one aim of the reign of God
on earth. That idea is necessarily as big as humanity, for
it means the divine transformation of all human life. It
alone can say without limitation, 'Nothing that is human is
alien to me.'"[41]

The similarities to Ritschl should not be minimized,
for Rauschenbusch, too, conceived of Christianity as an
ellipse with two foci: redemption and the Kingdom. Many
American followers of Ritschl stressed religious experience
more than doctrine, but in Rauschenbusch doctrine played a
large role. That role was ethical more than metaphysical.
As compared with the Personalists, the latter insisted on
more of a balance between philosophy and ethics. In ethics
many followers of Bowne wedded personal idealism to
Rauschenbusch's social gospel, but few moved close to his
outright socialist position until the 1930s. Handy says
that he minimized the importance of the church in history
and theology,[42] a view which sharply differentiates him from
Ritschl. Yet, when he wrote his most widely circulated
book, *The Social Principles of Jesus* (1916), he drew heavily
on the evangelical scholarship typified by Ritschl and
Harnack in concentrating on the Kingdom rather than the
church.[43]

Analogous comments may be made in the treatment of the
"Kingdom of Evil." The solidaristic conception of sin underlies this idea. Rauschenbusch conceives it not only as a
web of relationships of sinful people, but also as corporate
and institutional power, as exemplified in industrial
capitalism. Moreover, the role of tradition, custom, group

pressures, and the whole panoply of cumulative social causation had been overlooked by systematic theologians in
their preoccupation with biologically inherited corruption.
Rauschenbusch stressed the superpersonal forces of evil and
drew on Royce's conception of objective community to drive
home the point of the power of collective life.  He spelled
out in extensive historical detail and current empirical
description how evil collective forces operate, not sparing
the institutions of the church.  Though he recognized individual sin and its aggregate reality, his social gospel
addressed particularly the many facets of the social kingdom
of evil.  It helped sharpen the neglected aspects of the
doctrine of salvation in relation to power conflict.[44]  Like
Knudson he emphatically placed the Kingdom of God religiously and ethically above the church, while making it the true
end of the church.

VII
Karl Barth's Dissent from Ritschl

In turning to Barth's critique we should, first of all,
note the points at which they make contact:  the churchly
character of theology; the normative grounding of this
through Scripture; the basic Christocentric reference; the
definition of sin through the perspective of Christ; the
referral of ethics back to its proper context in dogmatics;
the correctives in the doctrines of providence, reconciliation, the sacraments and last things; and the polemics
against natural religion, metaphysics in theology, pietism,
the Enlightenment, and Catholicism.[45]  These show Ritschl to
have dealt with many themes which some twentieth century
thinkers regard as typically Barthian.  Here we can touch
only on Barth's general posture and appraisal.  Despite such
points of contact the radical dissent is noteworthy in the

overall estimate. Barth like Brightman studied under
Herrmann. Some current East German theologians find a major
root of present problems in Herrmann and feel that Barth did
not fully overcome these weaknesses, but that issue is not
in the present discussion.

First, Barth trims Ritschl down to size by noting that
the Ritschlian school was more that of a reaction than that
of the beginning of a new epoch in theology. "Ritschl has
the significance of an episode in more recent theology, and
not, indeed not, that of an epoch."[46] Next, in substance
his theology is built on his own ideal of life. "With
Ritschl reconciliation, to put it baldly, means the realized
ideal of human life. It is the intended result of justification. All Ritschl's thinking springs from this result."[47]
Third, Barth makes of him a culture Protestant of the
Bismarckian era. "He stands with incredible clearness and
firmness (truly with both feet) upon the ground of his
'ideal of life,' the very epitome of the national-liberal
German bourgeois of the age of Bismarck. That distinguishes
him from those who went before him and from those who came
after him."[48] Fourth, the historical roots of this ideal
and method are traced to Kant and the Enlightenment almost
exclusively. As an anti-metaphysical moralist and as a
proponent of a certain practical ideal of life he is attrib-
utable to Kant. "Nobody," says Barth, "either before or
since Ritschl...has expressed the view so clearly as he,
that modern man wishes above all to live in the best sense
according to reason, and that the significance of Christianity for him can only be a great confirmation and
strengthening of this endeavor."[49] So vigorously does Barth
push this line of attack that he asks "whether the entire
theological movement of the century resulted not at all in
an overcoming of the Enlightenment, of its decisive interest

of man in himself, but in its fulfillment."[50]

Thus we can summarize Barth's dissent under a fourfold
schema.  He sees Ritschl as a product of the Kant revival of
the latter half of the nineteenth century; as a detour from
Schleiermacher, for whom he had respect, to Troeltsch; as
one who took for his point of orientation the nineteenth
century idea of the 'modern man,' whom as a positivist
Ritschl took far too seriously; and as one who was under the
extraordinary influence of Schleiermacher in stressing the
ethical aspect of Christianity.[51]   Barth's attack is so
polemical that we must surmise that it served his own purposes to interpret him in this way.   We may, therefore,
bring this communication to a close by noting corrections
which some scholars have made of the Barthian broadside.

Schäfer points out that nowhere else is Ritschl so
singlemindedly presented as placing the Christian faith in
the service of the bourgeoisie of the period of Bismarck and
as an Enlightenment thinker.  Barth's prestige as both knowl-
edgeable in the history of doctrine and as a thinker in his
own right has  aided and abetted the persistence of this
negative criticism.   It is not quite fair to equate the
concepts of reconciliation, ideal of life, and the Kingdom
of God with each other or these with the modern person's
desire to lead a rational life, thus putting Christianity in
the service of modernity.[52]

Mackintosh points out that Barth was too harsh in saying that Ritschl simply went back, behind Idealism and Roman-
ticism, to the essential tenets of the Enlightenment.  He was
really a very serious student of the Reformers.  "Never was
there a life more completely absorbed in scientific theology."[53]   In fact, Barthians have a true forerunner in him
in that like all the Reformers he held to the objective Word
in  the  Bible  and  begins  not  with  general  Christian

consciousness but with the 'Gospel' given in Jesus Christ. H. Richard Niebuhr points out that Barth is close to Ritschl in insisting that "the Scriptures must be read through the eyes of a living community, the church."[54]

It is easy to caricature both Ritschl and Barth. Yet we must take soberly the serious observation of Pelikan that Barth was not quite fair to Ritschl in the essay in *Protestant Thought*. Pelikan says in his introduction: "The chapter on Ritschl must, it seems to me, be a disappointment to any reader who has been led by the preceding chapters to expect both fairness and clarity alongside the polemics. It has been said with some justification that in this chapter Barth has treated Ritschl as Ritschl treated the Pietists. But perhaps H. R. Mackintosh's *bon mot* of twenty years ago is still valid: 'Ritschl at the moment belongs, like Tennyson, to the 'middle distance'—too far for gratitude, too near for reverence.'"[55]

The last word of appreciation and the last word of dissent have obviously not been expressed. Disciples and dissenters stand in a new situation with respect to the relation of theology to science, to biotechnology, to world social reconstruction, to philosophy, and to world religions. We would do well to struggle theologically with the same freedom to be original and relevant as Ritschl did a century ago.

## NOTES

[1]Albrecht Ritschl, *The Christian Doctrine of Justification and Reconciliation* (New York:   Charles Scribner's
Sons, 1900), III, 13.

[2]*Ibid.*, III, 10-11.

[3]David L. Mueller, *Introduction to the Theology of
Albrecht Ritschl* (Philadelphia:   Westminster, 1969), 85.

[4]Ritschl, *Ibid.*, III, 35.

[5]Mueller, *Ibid.*, 89-90.

[6]*Ibid.*, 90-91; Ritschl, *Ibid.*, III, 443.

[7]Ritschl, *Ibid.*, III, 78.

[8]*Ibid.*, III, 103.

[9]*Ibid.*, III, 168.

[10]*Ibid.*, III, 4.

[11]*Ibid.*, III, 27.

[12]*Ibid.*, III, 539.

[13]*Ibid.*, III, 199.

[14]*Ibid.*, III, 225.

[15]*Ibid.*, III, 226.

[16]Mueller, *Ibid.*, 169-170.

[17]Ritschl, *Ibid.*, III, 20.

[18]*Ibid.*, III, 178.

[19]*The Mediator*, 138  in Hugh Ross Mackintosh, *Types of
Modern Theology* (London:   Nisbet, 1937), 177f.

[20]*Ibid.*, 142-143.

[21]*Ibid.*, 155.

[22]*Ibid.*, 148.

[23]H. Richard Niebuhr, *Resurrection and Historical Reason*, 41ff. in Mueller. *Ibid.*, 174).

[24]Paul Lehmann, *Ethics in a Christian Context* (New York:  Harper and Row, 1963), 81.

[25]Mueller, *Ibid.*, 169.

[26]Henry C. Sheldon, *System of Christian Doctrine* (Cincinnati:  Jennings and Graham, 1903), 103.

[27]*Ibid.*, 448.

[28]Edgar S. Brightman, *A Philosophy of Religion* (New York:  Prentice-Hall, 1940), 108.

[29]Albert C. Knudson, *Present Tendencies in Religious Thought* (New York:  Abingdon Press, 1924), 138.

[30]*Ibid.*, 165f.

[31]*Ibid.*, 168.

[32]*Ibid.*, 173.

[33]*Ibid.*, 174.

[34]*Ibid.*, 220-221.

[35]*Ibid.*, 227.

[36]Walter Rauschenbusch, *A Theology for the Social Gospel*, 60, in Knudson, *Ibid.*, 309.

[37]Ritschl, *Ibid.*, III, 334-350.

[38]Knudson, *Doctrine of Redemption* (New York:  Abingdon, 1933), 264-265.

[39]H. Richard Niebuhr, *Christ and Culture* (New York:  Harper, 1951), 100f.

[40]Robert Handy, ed., *The Social Gospel in America* (New York:  Oxford, 1966), 154, 159, 255.

[41]Walter Rauschenbusch, *Christianizing the Social Order* (Boston:  Pilgrim, 1912), 93-94.

[42]Handy, *Ibid.*, 261.

[43]*Ibid.*, 371.

[44]Rauschenbusch, *A Theology for the Social Gsopel* (New York:  Macmillan, 1918), chs. VII, VIII, IX.

[45]Walter Klaas, "Ritschl's 'Unterricht in der christlichen Religion' und Karl Barth's 'Abrisse der Dogmatik'.  Ein Vergleich" in *Antwort. Karl Barth zum siebzigsten Geburtstag am 10 Mai 1956* (Zurich:   Zollikon, 1956).

[46]Karl Barth, *Protestant Thought. From Rousseau to Ritschl* (New York:  Simon and Schuster, 1959), 390.

[47]*Ibid.*, 393.

[48]*Ibid.*, 392.

[49]*Ibid.*, 391.

[50]*Ibid.*, 391-392.

[51]*Ibid.*, 190, 191, 225, 227.

[52]Rolf Schafer, *Ritschl* (Tübingen:   J. C. B. Mohr, 1968), 11-13.

[53]Mackintosh, *Ibid.*, 141n.

[54]H. R. Niebuhr, *The Meaning of Revelation* (New York: Macmillan, 1946), 52.

[55]Jarislov Pelikan, "Introduction" to Karl Barth, *Protestant Thought*, 10.

# Personality and Christian Ethics
## (1943)

Personality is the most concrete category of existence and value. This means that the richest synoptic grasp of existential wholes and the highest value in the axiological hierarchy are both apprehended in personality. Since personality refers to both the quality of ultimate reality and to real finite selfhood, the problems of ethics are circumscribed by the finite person's relation to himself, to other finite persons, and to ultimate personality. What is given is a society of persons human and divine together with the ends of conduct and the problems of their realization. The ideal ends are aspects of ideal personality. Christian ethics is an expression of the impact of Jesus on our appreciation of the nature of ideal personality in its relations to all other persons. Jesus emphasized personality. He made people aware acutely of the significance of the individual. His conception of God was such as to give to all individuals infinite value in a life of brotherhood or true community. A recent writer has said, "Christianity has one central truth, one abiding contribution to make to the religious life of the world, and only one. That contribution is Jesus Christ himself. The gospel *is* Jesus Christ."[1] We may dismiss for the purposes of this discussion the validity of the claim that Christianity has only one abiding contribution to make. But it is of utmost significance to recognize that the central contribution is an actual personality, full, mature, concrete.

The category of personality sustains an important relationship to ethical principles or laws. The Christian

ethic has generated many ethical laws.  Without normative
laws of conduct a science of ethics is finally meaningless.
Each law embraces a significant portion of human experience
and relates it to problems of conduct.  It emphasizes what
it regards to be important.  Some laws are richer, i.e. more
concrete than others, and each can become the guiding principle of an ethical system.  Unless systems of ethical law
are subordinated to the law of personality, they become
abstract and command types of conduct which violate to some
degree the nature of persons.  There are many ways in which
the demands of a truly personal Christian ethic can be
frustrated, but none is more injurious than the carrying to
absurdity, or the making absolute, of any moral law which
embraces but one aspect of loyalty or but part of the field
of value.  When personality is made the highest law of
ethics the various moral laws hold each other in check and
bind each other in the service of that which is more than
law and more than ideals, concrete human existence creatively seeking perfection.

    Personality is not a static category.  Human experience
is temporal and hence is implicated in the historical process.  While the ideal of true personal fulfillment transcends every historical epoch, each person reflects
concretely some aspects of the time in which he lives.
One's philosophy of the historical movement is intimately
involved in his conception of responsibility towards his own
age.  At this point ethics and philosophy of history con-
verge.  In the Christian tradition Jesus is conceived as a
revelation of the true meaning of history.  Since that which
is thus conceived as having been revealed through him is
never achieved in any one individual, the notion of Christian personality is one of perfectibility in both its
individual and social expressions.  Christian ethics is thus

properly viewed as historically dynamic. In no era of
Christianity do we find *the* Christian individual. What we
do find is a judgment upon persons and society and a quest
for personal and social redemption.

Personality is thus an exploratory principle. This
exploratory principle may be used for purposes of historical
interpretation and for purposes of moral construction. We
shall first indicate its fruitfulness for the former end.
Personality as the highest axiological concept is a
corrective of narrow historical or one-sided views of the
Christian ethic. When Christian ethics becomes reflective
it is embraced in philosophical ethics. Yet frequent
attempts are made to set them in opposition to one another.
In some such attempts the Hebraic and Greek tendencies in
ethics are sharply defined for purposes of purifying Christian ethics of Greek tendencies and of rendering the ethic
truly "Biblical." Classical ideas about man and the good
are viewed as alien to Christian doctrine. The next step is
frequently to place the great movement of idealism in the
stream of classical thought and by implication to set
idealism in opposition to the Hebraic-Christian position.
Moreover, since the idealistic tradition is both one in
which philosophical method is predominant and one in which
reason plays a significant role, the tendency of the critics
is to set philosophy in opposition to theology and to
subordinate reason to some non-rational principle of ethical
interpretation. Such attempts, however, involve arbitrari-
ness of thought and a blindness to the principle that the
full richness of personal possibilities is never adequately
or completely caught up in any cultural tradition. Try as
we will the Christian heritage is so interfused with the
many strains of philosophical and other cultural influences
from many lands, that only disunity, confusion, or dogmatism

result, when we employ a disjunctive analytical method in
history to determine the nature of the personal good or the
normative essence of the Christian ethic.

Two expressions of recent Christian ethics illustrate
the need for a corrective against the disjunctive method.
Reinhold Niebuhr sets the "Biblical" conception of man over
against the classical Greek and the philosophical idealistic
tendencies of modern times. He assumes the validity of the
Biblical trichotemy of body, soul, and spirit and repudiates
reason and experience in favor of myth and revelation. In
developing his "Biblical" view, however, the basic categories which he employs are those which were developed by
philosophical idealism: self, consciousness, self-consciousness, self-transcendence, will, freedom, and reason. His
treatment is an excellent commentary on the fact that
reflective ethics requires philosophical categories in order
to clarify and define its meanings. It is a commentary also
on the truth that an awareness of the nature of personality
(Niebuhr more frequently says the individual) in its
concrete complexity invites elucidation from more than
Biblical perspectives. Unfortunately in Niebuhr's thought
Biblical figures of speech, theological myth, and philosophical categories are not harmonized or reconciled. Fortu-
nately, the disjunction of the "Biblical" and the philosophical is unnecessary.

The second illustration has to do with the use of the
conception of *agape*. Waiving the question of historical
accuracy, the issue as developed by Nygren and Ferre is
whether the Christian conception of *agape* is reconcilable
with *eros*. The former emphasizes a movement from the divine
in an expression of spontaneous uncalculating devotion,
while the latter emphasizes the search and aspiration for
fuller satisfaction and well-being. The tendency is to

regard these views as irreconcilable and to hold that *eros*
is irrelevant to the Christian ethic. The issue is not one
of linguistics or of historical and cultural accuracy. The
issue is, however, whether personality is concretely think-
able without both conceptions of love? A Christian ethic of
sex and labor requires the equivalent of *eros* in its
appreciation of the person, and neither can be omitted from
a complete account. The final decision of the comparative
emphasis on *agape* and *eros* cannot be laid down by Biblical
criticism or theology aside from a philosophical
understanding of coherent and integrated personality. Here
personality as an exploratory category is fruitful when used
synoptically.

When the category of personality is fully accepted by
Christian ethics it will give much needed freedom. The
great streams of culture which have their confluence in
Christianity will each be more sympathetically studied.
Also cultural tendencies like mysticism, rationalism,
moralism, and humanism within the ethic will be viewed more
as experiments in types of personal experience and as
neglected aspects of personality than as rival heresies or
even rival competitors for the central position of authority. There is a final advantage which the whole-hearted
appropriation of the conception provides, namely, a more
understanding approach to the ethical values of non-Christian world religions. For these, too, are explorations of
the meaning of personality within cultural contexts of great
significance.

The history of Christian ethics is an attempt to
realize the meaning of human vocation. It seeks to understand and achieve real individuality in persons. What is
the correct gestalt of the component factors structurally
and culturally? We are presented in retrospect with the

anchorite, the bishop-king, the knight, the catacomb slave,
the reformer, the monk, the Puritan, the philanthropic
capitalist, the circuit-rider, to mention but a few. None
of these types can be strictly universalized. Even in the
case of the matchless personality of Jesus we must distinguish between the concretely universal and the man as
expressing what was historically particular and eccentric,
though characteristic of his time. Every person is historically conditioned but the principle of personality always
transcends what is merely immediate. In ethics the
culturally immanent and the transcendent ideal meet in
dialectical tension in individual personality. Therefore,
the meaning and nature of human vocation will be clarified
by a study of individuality.

An adequate view of individuality is a major problem in
Christian ethics. We shall briefly view some historical
contributions and failures in this regard. The Christian
feeling for the preciousness of personality was early
offended by the Greek tendency to sacrifice the particular
individual to the Idea or to the species or to what were
called universal intelligencies. Gilson points out that the
early Chruch Father, Athenagoras, first attempts a justification of genuine personal individuality, in connection with
his justification of personal immortality. Man, he held, is
created by God as a distinct individuality; he is conserved
in being by an act of continuous creation; and he is the
protagonist of a drama which involves his own destiny.
Augustine under the influence of the Neoplatonic spiritual
conception of God regarded the soul as immaterial spirit.
He thus added to the metaphysical foundations of ethical
personalism. On the basis of his analysis of mind, whereby
memory, abstract thought, and self-consciousness are regarded as non-material unique acts, he defended spiritual

individuality. Augustine's indeterminism, moreover, gave to
will a primary place. This general conception of man in
Christian ethics throughout western thought has been largely
due to Augustine.

Boethius made a permanent contribution to the position
when he defined the human person as "an individual substance
of a rational nature." Along with Augustine's the view of
Boethius was frequently appealed to by the mediaeval
ethicists. The rational tendency in Boethius' definition
was constantly reinforced by the impact of Platonic and
Aristotelian assumptions in scholastic thought. In the
philosophy of Thomas Aquinas the principle of individuality
and the principle of personality have an identical basis.
This may be stated as follows: the essence of personality
is also the essence of liberty; liberty roots in
rationality; rationality is the basis of the subsistence of
the soul, and, therefore of man. It is the moral duty of
man to live in accordance with reason. By the end of the
mediaeval period long strides had been taken towards an
appreciation of individuality in the Christian ethic. However, a fully consistent expression of Christian personality
had not emerged. An adequate foundation could not be provided for individuality so long as a basic authoritarianism
dominated and subordinated free reason. When the scholastic
ethic made the essence of morality to consist primarily "in
the relation of human activity to eternal law," and only
secondarily "in the attitude of human activity toward right
reason," it betrayed its distrust of finite reason and
appealed to a superhuman law which could not be known unless
the finite reason were first found faithful.

The Thomistic ethic was a faltering personalism because
its strong elements were finally subordinated to a fusion of
patriarchalism and paternalism with organic ideas of

society.     Both  patriarchalism  and  organic  tendencies  in
Christian  ethics  can  be  traced  to  St.  Paul.    The  organic
principle  as  it  expressed  itself  in  the  developing  ecclesiastical  organization  is  inherent  in  the  Catholic  idea.    As
such  it  is  potentially  both  a  radical  and  a  conservative
idea.    It  stresses  equalities,  interdependencies,  the  family
ideal,  the  communism  of  monastic  mutuality,  and  at  times
social  activism  and  the  social  welfare  state.    When  linked
with  paternalism  the  organic  idea  becomes  conservative  and
when  combined  with  ecclesiastical  patriarchalism  it  tends  to
confirm  the  class  structure  of  the  status  quo.    The  organic
idea  as  modified  in  Thomism  held  that  the  lower  classes
should  evince  the  virtues  of  humility  and  gratitude  while
the  ruling  classes  should  evince  paternal  care  and  love.
The  domination  of  husband  over  wife  and  children  is  the
continuing  model  of  familial  ethics  which  is  also  finally
the  basis  upon  which  the  social  whole  is  viewed  as  a
patriarchalism  of  love.    This  pattern  of  social  thought
tended  to  be  confirmed  by  Old  Testament  analogies  and
authoritarianism.    Together  with  his  assumptions  regarding
natural  and  divine  law  and  his  hierarchical  use  of
Aristotle's  philosophy,  the  outcome  was  to  vitiate  many  of
the  strong  points  of  his  emphasis  on  the  individual.    At  the
same  time,  by  virtue  of  its  personalistic  theism  and  the
conviction  that  the  individual  personality  is  metaphysically
grounded,  the  Thomistic  ethic  laid  a  basis  which  is
substantially  sound  against  all  naturalism  and  pessimism.

     Protestantism    gave    to    individuality    a    profound
expression.    In  revolting  against  the  patriarchalism  of  the
mediaeval  ethic,  it  sundered  also  the  organic  idea,  and  in
its  exaggerated  individualism  laid  the  basis  for  much  modern
anarchy.    In  this  it  influenced  and  was  influenced  by  the
Renaissance  conceptions  of  the  completely  autonomous  man.

Whereas in Thomism the metaphysical foundation was a modified realism, in much of Protestantism an extreme nominalism
prevailed. In this situation the individual is approached
often-times from the perspective of "total depravity," he
loses complete confidence in reason and the natural law of
right reason and is given up to bibliolatry and irrationalism. The revolt against reason was not as great in
Calvinism as in Lutheranism and for this reason the social
order was less easily surrendered in ethical thinking to the
rising secularism of the state and the middle classes among
Calvinists than in Lutheran countries.

The category of personality in modern times has had not
only to contend with a defective doctrine of human nature in
certain Catholic and Protestant tendencies, but also with
the individualism of our business civilization. As in the
Renaissance period the hero type of person who struggles
single-handed against insuperable odds and shows forth the
virtues of adventure, daring, independence, intrepidity,
capability, courage, so in the later period the characteristic business man is viewed as exhibiting initiative,
courage, resourcefulness, risk, competitive vigor, and
decisiveness. He is a man who especially in the early days
of this period was thought of shaping destiny to his own
ends. He is a man of power over material goods and over
others. The overwhelming role of both the power idea and
the materialistic ends in molding persons has progressively
tended to eliminate the needed counter-balances. The New
Testament ethic of personality made security to be sought in
love and good-will and rejected security through power, and
it repudiated mammonism. The attempt on the part of
multitudes to embrace both types of ethic at once causes
what Horney calls the "neurotic personality of our time."
The quest for monetary power as a basis of security causes

people to move inordinately among things and to separate
them spiritually from each other in the competitive struggle.    They tend to take on thinghood and, unfortunately,
lose sight of the spiritual bases of the individualism which
gave the modern period its impetus.

Personality tends in our business culture to be lost in
a pseudo-individualism.    This pseudo-individualism is reinforced on its philosophical side by much contemporary
naturalism.    The individual is completely immersed either in
natural processes or in historical processes which he cannot
effectively transcend.    Naturalism repudiates a transcendent
value reference; it repudiates a metaphysics in which a
person has ultimate significance in the larger cosmos and
builds on psychologies which can yield at best, as Hocking
has shown, only "near-minds."    Man is divorced from a
spiritual order to which he belongs and upon which he
depends for the satisfaction of his deepest needs.    In the
final analysis there can be no adequate democratic
personalism in society unless personal theism is granted.
The group of Princeton thinkers at the Second Conference on
Science, Philosophy, and Religion were right when they said:

> Many who hold to this naturalistic view in
> democratic countries are unaware of the dangers
> in their position.    Influenced by the last
> remnants of philosophical idealism, romantic
> transcendentalism, or religious theism in our
> day, they act as if they still believed in the
> spiritual conception of man which they have
> intellectually repudiated....They are loyal to
> their democratic society and culture, but they
> deny the spiritual nature of man and his values
> upon which it has been built.    In short, they
> are living off the spiritual capital which has
> come down to them from their classical and
> religious heritage, while at the same time they
> ignore that heritage itself as antiquated and
> false.

In the foregoing paragraphs we have recognized the

difficulty of attaining a satisfactory notion of individuality without which an ethic is fatally limited. We have
noted certain tendencies in philosophy and the social
process which are related to these inadequacies. Little has
been said about will and to it we now turn for a rapid
sketch of the explorations of it since Augustine which seem
significant in a valid understanding of personality.

Mediaeval theology explored many possibilities
regarding the nature of the will, and its freedom, and
relation to the whole man. One emphasis of freedom was that
of spontaneity of the will, the indissoluble connection of
the act of choosing and causal efficacy. Anselm may be said
to have held this view as also Hugh of St. Victor. In Duns
Scotus the spontaneity of the act of will is clearly
expressed. He held to a radical indeterminism of the will;
its unforseeable decisions, he said, arise from within
wholly undetermined by anything else.

Boethius took quite another view, rejecting
spontaneity, and placing freedom in the free movement of
reason. He roots the will in reason. In one sense this was
not novel, for Christian philosophers and theologians had
not overlooked the part played by knowledge in the production of free acts. But as over against the view held by
Duns Scotus, the significant emphasis in this general
position is that where several spontaneous impulses are
involved, an act becomes free when the critique of reason
compares it with possible alternative actions and judges
which is better. Aquinas stands close to Boethius in the
strong rationalistic bias of his conception of the person.
But he does not eschew the claims of voluntarism. He admits
that free-will is a problem of will willing, not of reason
judging. His fusion of rationalistic and voluntaristic
tendencies is significantly expressed in the formula about

him which Gilson presents concerning the freedom of the
will: "materially, free-will is voluntary; formally, it is
rational."[1]

Aquinas had the benefit of the influence of Peter
Abelard whose *Ethics* or *Know Thyself* marked a new and
notable stage in the history of Christian ethics. One
important aspect of his ethics was an advance beyond
Augustinianism in that the agent was viewed as able to
decide what was good, and could consent to or refrain from
the tendencies which he finds in his mind. In the exercise
of his will to act as reason prompts him to do he can unite
himself to the divine grace which is thus, for Abelard, not
the sole ground of right conduct but a means of help which
man may accept from God. Abelard here moves in the direction of personal moral autonomy without which there is no
escape from external authoritarianism which vitiated so much
mediaeval ethics. This position is closely related to the
greater emphasis on motive, both formal and teleological.
In each person resides the ability to discern and the power
to respond to the divine love as displayed in Christ. By
repeatedly emphasizing that it is not the doing of an act
which reveals its morality but the motive in the mind of the
doer, he anticipates Protestant and Kantian ethical conceptions. Aquinas was not unmindful of the significance of
motive. Indeed, he defined sin as "a voluntary departure
from the law of God." This would seem to be sufficient
except that the law of God is not really self-recognized and
self-imposed by the sinner.[2]

Immanuel Kant first made the autonomy of will a clear
and self-conscious principle, though Abelard, as we have
seen, probably came as close as any to a full recognition of
it. Kant's fundamental principle is the categorical
imperative: "Act only according to that maxim by which you

can at the same time will that it shall become a universal
law." He made it the *sole* principle of all moral law and
thereby vitiated much of the fruitfulness of the principle.
This practically emptied ethics of all axiological content.
In this respect Christian ethicists before and after him
were wiser in their appeal to a criticism of values in
addition to the "pure" will. What was needed was that
Kant's contribution be coherently integrated into an ethics
of concrete personality which recognized a system of moral
formal and axiological laws. This is essential if ethical
personality is to come to completeness. Ethical reflection
since Kant has successfully integrated the most fruitful
thinking in the classical and Christian traditions in combining synoptic empirical method, the coherence criterion of
truth, a dynamic and purposive view of the self, an
appreciation of formal categories, and an openness to the
cultural values of all streams of thought. It has freed
itself from authoritarianism without surrendering to
relativism and it has done this without repudiating a
theistic world view.

An adequate view of personality as individuality requires a social interpretation of person. Oldham has
pointed out an aspect of this requirement when he says:

> This personalism of Christianity must not be
> confused with individualism. True faith is the
> very opposite of individualism. For genuine
> faith means being incorporated into the body of
> Christ. The most personal kind of faith
> involves the most universal responsibility.[3]

Aquinas represents a highly significant achievement in his
organic social ethic despite its limitations of
patriarchalism and lack of adequate individual autonomy.
His social personalism was in some respects much more
satisfactory than most modern Christian ethics. He clearly

conceived every act as a social act. He balanced this
principle by the realization that individual happiness is
the sole reason for living in society. "The collectivity
exists for the sake of the individual, and not the
individual for the collectivity." Thus there is linked in
Aquinas the unity of the group and the inalienable rights of
its members. The unity is that of a "unity of functions,"
not that of a substance.

The communitarian nature of persons is generally
overlooked by both the extreme individualist and the extreme
collectivist. The former is brittle and atomic and makes
for irresponsibility and alienation. Hence it makes for
externalism and impersonalism. The latter loses the
individual in the social whole. This is the danger which
critics have perennially seen in Hegelian idealism and which
Reinhold Niebuhr has recently amplified.[4] As over against
the tendency to vitiate true personality in the breadth of
its view and in the expansiveness of universal mind, he
pleads for a different type of relationship. "The ideal
possibility," he says, "is a loving relationship between the
self and the other self in which alienation but not discrete
identity is transcended."[5] In collectivisms like Fascism
and Naziism and in all social wholes which become ends in
themselves this ideal is violated. In many parts of the
world today human life seems to be growing more and more
impersonal. The state, the cartel, the corporation, the
large undemocratic trade union, to cite typical examples,
tend to deny that personality is the center of meaning and
tend to place it in a position of an impersonal anonymous
unit. Some writers in despair inquire whether an individual
is more than a plaything of collective forces "which he is
powerless to understand, to control or even to resist." The
situation here described is all the more anomalous because

in so-called democratic countries the age of industrialism
which was initiated with so much confidence in individualism has come to a stage in which the individual is reduced
almost to a non-entity.    Individualism destroys individuality.

The lack of a sufficient social perspective in much
Christian ethics results from its individualistic definition
of personality and its consequent neglect of communitarian
characteristics.    Too frequently the bi-polar unity of
person-in-community has been missed.    The social teaching of
Jesus, according to Francis G. Peabody was this, that "the
social order is not a product of mechanism but of personality fulfilling itself only in the social order."    Character is
social and society is a spiritual enterprise.    On the other
hand, when the impersonal factors in society are not subordinated clearly as means to realizing personality, they are
given a status of independence and of positive control which
makes for utopian illusions, as for example that a change in
the environment is sufficient to achieve social salvation.

Social reformers within the Christian tradition who
have been profoundly influenced by Marx's brilliant analysis
of capitalism, have sometimes argued as if a change of
economic and other social institutions would of itself bring
about the redemption of society.    This view rests on a
reaction against individualism which has placed the impersonal on a par with the personal.    It leads to externalism
which is the besetting sin of reformism.    If anyone could be
wholly saved by a change in his material environment alone,
he would not be a person.    Each person is morally a decider;
he is saved by commitment.    Without personal decision there
is no redemption.    This principle roots back in the idealistic tradition to Kant's primacy of the practical reason.    It
is metaphysically grounded in a voluntarism which holds that

"to be is to act and to act is to will." The basic conflicts in society are not between things and persons but
among personal wills in the communitarian whole and among
social minds.

Philosophical Christian ethics needs a more adequate
understanding of social mind than it has generally recognized. Its nature would seem to be as follows. There is a
genuine gestalt which may be called a social mind. It has a
level of existence not above or below personal minds, but on
the same level. The consciousness which it embodies may be
termed objective spirit, but it is not distinct from minds.
It exists in minds. The content of social mind is too rich,
because of its embracing all component minds, for our individual consciousnesses to contain this content. No individual mind has an immediate intuition of this total content,
nor is there an objective finite self-consciousness which is
aware of this content. Individual minds genuinely participate in it; they are aware of each other through it; through
it group decisions and volitions are achieved; and as a
mental gestalt it may act with selectivity and creativity.
On a normative level it constitutes whatever we know as
fellowship or community. But on every level it is the
matrix of all personal decision.

The significance of this communitarian dimension of the
category of personality cannot be too greatly emphasized.
We can come to somewhat of an appreciation of it by taking
into account the emergence of the person from self-hood. No
one is born a person, rather one comes into the world as a
self. Only gradually does personality emerge as self-direc-
tion, reflective self-consciousness, and the capacity to
criticize values develop. These characteristics appear only
within a social mind, only in social interaction. Hence
personality is the product of a socializing process from

which it is never completely free, though the person
develops types of transcendence over it. Personality is a
social whole with an individual center, and therefore it is
a communitarian category. Since the emergent person acts
from a creative center, the personalizing process is more
than what is usually understood as social conditioning, for
this would reduce man to a mere function of his environment.
Personality means freedom, not *persona* as a role or mask or
function of impersonal natural or social process.

The highest virtue of personality is love, by which is
meant the affirmation of personality of complete good-will.
It includes concern also for its potential emergence from
self-hood. It is the most concrete of the values and
virtues because it is a voluntary commitment to fellowship,
and hence social as well as individual. Ideally this
commitment would bring into being a pluralistic socialism
which recognizes social solidarity, objective social wholes,
social justice, forgiveness, and redemption. What we seek
is an individuality which is productive of the highest
social solidarity, objective social wholes, social justice,
forgiveness, and redemption. What we seek is an individual
who is productive of the highest socialism and a socialism
which is productive of the richest individuality. It would
be a democratic collectivity which recognizes that reality
is a society of persons who know their chief task is the
creation of a social mind among human beings responsive
toward and responsible to the Supreme Mind to whom they owe
their existence, their ultimate value ideals, and their
final redemption. On the basis of such a personalism
Christian ethics can with faith face the new future.

## NOTES

[1]F. E. Johnson, *The Social Gospel Re-examined.* (New
York:  Harper and Bros., 1940).

[2]E. S. Brightman, *Moral Laws.*  Abingdon Press, 1934,
p. 110.

[3]J. H. Oldham, ed., *Official Report.  The Oxford
Conference*, 1937, p. 30.

[4]Reinhold Niebuhr, *The Nature and Destiny of Man.*  (New
York:  Charles Scribner's Sons).

[5]*Ibid.*, p. 78.

# Reinhold Niebuhr's
## Conception of Man
### (1945)

The title of Niebuhr's Gifford Lectures, *The Nature and Destiny of Man*,[1] poses a two-fold dimension to the problem of human nature. The *nature* of man invites an analysis of man's personal structure as a self-transcending being and the *destiny* of man invites a study of his end or *telos*. In the analysis of man's nature we are involved in an anthropology of freedom and anxiety. In the study of man's actual and proper end we are involved in the problems of the philosophy of history. One dimension of man is thus the hierarchy of self-transcendence, the other is the relation of freedom to the meaning of the social process.

Christian theology has been challenged, negated, and enriched by modern movements in philosophy and science. These movements have precipitated a felt need for a new statement of the Christian doctrine of human nature. Niebuhr's two volumes are part of a growing contemporary literature which attempts to restate the doctrine of man in modern but Christian terms. In the various traditions of rationalism, naturalism, idealism, and pragmatism which have flourished since the Renaissance, the Biblical doctrines have been put on the defensive and either largely discarded or ignored, or at least profoundly modified. An era of criticism of the ideas of the soul and of spirit has produced not only materialistic rejections of them, in which man is reduced to nature, not only idealistic impersonalizations of selfhood, but also dissolutions as in Freudianism.

Many a Christian leader in the past few decades has

drawn heavily for his ideas of man from Adam Smith, Marx,
Spencer, Freud, Jung, Dewey, Bergson, Kant, Hegel, James,
and the like, rather than venture an authentic restatement
of the Christian faith.  Today it is becoming quite clear
that the Christian faith cannot well survive as a parasitic
growth on a merely secular tree of learning.  The faith
requires an autonomous theology and philosophy of religion.

     The Christian idea of man needs redefining because the
rival views are so active and so powerful in the world.
Capitalism has its doctrine of man; so do Fascism, Nazism,
and Communism.  Niebuhr's first volume is an analysis of
human nature in which he takes the offensive against modern
cultural philosophies of man in defense of what he terms
"Biblical" insights.  It is his thesis that the Christian
faith assesses the spiritual stature of man more highly than
alternative doctrines, both ancient and modern.  At the same
time Christian faith has a lower estimate of man's virtue
than rival doctrines.  In both instances Niebuhr takes pains
to show that the Christian view is more *unique*, and hence is
to be more sharply distinguished from other views, than is
commonly assumed by modern Christian thought.

     If Christian theology has assessed its view of man by
too great accommodation to modern cultural estimates of
human nature on the structural side, it is even more the
case that Christian dogmatics has been blind to the problems
of philosophy of history.  History is an area almost completely ignored by systematic theologians.  On the whole, it
is amazing to note the scarcity of great names among
Christian philosophers and theologians who have dealt with
the interpretation of history in the period just prior to
World War I.  Writers of the stature of Ernst Troeltsch are
lonely landmarks.  But the last twenty-five years have seen
a growing historical concern over the crisis of civiliza-

tion.  A  significant  list  of  writers,  including  Tillich,
Dodd,  Bevan,  Wendland,  Horton,  Lyman,  Dawson,  Flewelling,
Case,  Macmurray,  Piper,  Berdyaev,  are  wrestling  with  the
tragedy  of  historical  existence.  Along  with  such  thinkers
it  is  the  great  achievement  of  Reinhold  Niebuhr  that  he  has
so  intimately  and  organically  understood  the  need  for
relating  the  problem  of  the  nature  of  man  to  the  destiny  of
history.  Like  Marx  and  Troeltsch  his  radical  perceptions  of
social  problems  are  fixed  on  historical  and  transhistorical  ends.  In  volume  two  of  *The Nature and Destiny of Man* he
seeks  to  show  that  the  Biblical-Christian  faith  has  a  more
dynamic  conception  of  history  than  classicism  and  a  less
optimistic  view  of  historical  dynamism  than  alternate  modern
views.  Niebuhr  is  convinced  of  the  bankruptcy  of
contemporary  interpretations  and  propounds  the  new  relevance
of  what  he  chooses  to  call  "classical  Christian  interpretations."

In  commenting  on  Niebuhr's  claims  it  may  be  said  at  the
outset  that  his  views  are  probably  less  orthodox  and
certainly  less  Biblical  than  he  assumes  them  to  be.  He
incorporates  into  the  Christian  faith  many  insights  and
employs  categories  which  have  their  origin  in  Greek  and
modern  philosophical  thought.  He  overhauls  in  terms  of
historical  and  liberal  criticism  such  ideas  as  original  sin,
the  fall  of  man,  original  righteousness,  and  guilt.  He
introduces  into  the  old  wineskins  of  Christology  novel
assumptions  of  fact  and  doctrine.  Thus  he  makes  essentially
symbolical  the  reality  of  the  Christ,  the  sinlessness  of
Jesus,  and  the  resurrection.  Indeed,  the  use  of  myth  and
symbolization  with  respect  to  Christian  doctrine  is  so
thoroughgoing  that  hardly  any  direct  denotative  meaning  can
be  recognized.  The  historical  Jesus  is  lost  in  the
paradoxes  of  abstract  ethical  idealism,  in  transcendent

perfectionism.[2]

In stressing the uniqueness of the Biblical view of
man, Niebuhr attacks and seemingly rejects Greek and modern
idealism.   Yet, it is idealistic concepts and categories
which carry the weight of his argument.   Such ideas are:
self, consciousness, transcendence, self-consciousness,
self-transcendence, freedom, reason, will, universality, and
personality.   Without them he could not analyze spirit and
"soul," and with them he is dependent beyond measure on the
stream of philosophical idealism.   That he does not agree
with some of the tendencies of idealism does not mitigate
the basic idealistic pattern of his theological criteria.
Unfortunately, Niebuhr does not recognize or face squarely
the presuppositions of the idealistic categories, but begs
the metaphysical question by putting them at the disposal of
so-called Biblical presuppositions.

We have already noted that the two volumes handle each
a distinctive dimension of the doctrine of man.   This
arrangement may account for some of the differences in
emphasis and type of criticism in the two volumes.   However,
it appears that the author has modified in the later volume
some of the theory developed in the first. We may list some
of these shifts in treatment.   In the first volume the attitude toward reason is quite derogatory and essentially
negative; in the second volume the attitude toward reason is
more conciliatory and its constructive uses are positively
appraised.   In the first volume the view of human nature is
primarily individualistic; in the second volume more stress
is laid upon social solidarity and community in man's make-
up.   In the first volume social groups are treated essentially as heightened forms of man's pride and egotism; in
the second volume the constructive and redemptive roles of
social groups are recognized.   In the first volume the

discussion of transcendence seems to imply a dualistic
metaphysical opposition between time and eternity; in the
second volume eternity is explicitly defined as not a separate order of metaphysical existence as over against time.
All in all, it appears that the attempt to establish the
*uniqueness* of the Christian view of man distorts the *view*
which the discussion of historical destiny requires. The
reason for this situation may be in part an overemphasis on
essential human nature in opposition to all supposed rivals
to the Christian view.

By focusing attention on the nature of freedom as
self-transcendence the author tends to lose sight of personality as a whole throughout much of the argument. That
Niebuhr places the emphasis on will and anxiety is obvious.
Not so obvious is his belated recognition of the two-fold
character of man's essential nature. He says: "To the
essential nature of man belong, on the one hand, all his
natural endowments, and determinations, his physical and
social impluses, his sexual and racial differentiations, in
short his character as a creature embedded in the natural
order. On the other hand, his essential nature includes the
freedom of his spirit, his transcendence over natural
process and finally his self-transcendence."[3] In trying to
realize fully what these words imply one must note his
insistence on the unity of body and mind and his rejection
of all Greek, idealistic, and naturalistic dualisms. In
this connection it is interesting to note that he assumes
the "Biblical" view to be a triadic unity of body, soul, and
spirit. How he unifies the triad by the manipulations of
self-transcendence and self-consciousness is admittedly
paradoxical.

One is impressed by Niebuhr's inability to recognize
love as the action of personality as a whole in all its

self-conscious beauty and ethical and religious power. Self-
transcendence for Niebuhr is almost habitually related to
sin, not to love, and love is left as an abstract ultimate
demand. Man is regarded as essentially a sinner; this means
that man in his will is rebellious against God. Man is a
creature, and his refusal to admit his "creatureliness" and
to acknowledge himself as merely a member of a total unity
of life, i.e., his pretension, is the occasion and fact of
his sin. Man's essence is his freedom (a term left quite
undefined and ambiguous). In his freedom man is self-contradictory. His essence is free self-determination. On the
other hand, the law of man's nature is love, a harmonious
relation of life to life in obedience to the divine center
and source of his life. This law of love is violated when
he seeks to make himself the center and source of his own
life. Thus sin is a spiritual act. Man's sin is the wrong
use of his freedom and its consequent destruction.[4] One
misses in this analysis of love and sin the recognition of
the self-transcending power of the former. Love as a law of
human nature is power as well as norm.

We shall note that the primary difficulty in Niebuhr's
conception of man resides in the fallacy of abstracting one
type of self-transcendence and making it serve as essential
human nature. This makes Niebuhr an individualist. Man, he
states, is an individuality. The basis of selfhood lies in
the particularity of the body, but the freedom of the spirit
is the cause of the real individuality.[5] Man is the only
animal which can make itself its own object. This capacity
for self-transcendence distinguishes spirit in man from
soul. Self-knowledge is thus the basis of discrete individuality. The author seems to assume that self-knowledge is
necessarily or inevitably egoistic, while love is regarded
as problematical, a law which man cannot fulfill, and a

relationship which is "frustrated by inscrutable mysteries
in the heart of each person and by opaque 'walls of parti-
tion' between man and man."[6]   Here is scant recognition, in
fact none at all, that mutuality and communitarian solidarity may be normal forms of self-transcendence. Egoistic
self-consciousness is oftentimes but an interruption of
self-fulfilling and natural fellowship.

If we assume that man's will is essentially self-contradictory and ego-centric, it is impossible to unite such
inevitably sinful willing in love. Even God cannot get out
of man what is not there. He must work with man's power to
love in self-conscious freedom. If we begin with the isolated will we shall end with the war of all against all.
But if we begin, where empirically we do begin, in the
reciprocity of group life, we shall be able to recognize
that all self-transcendence takes place in a larger whole of
nature and society, and that normal mature living is a
process of moving from one level of communitarian solidarity
to a higher one. The sense of isolation in self-consciousness is a problem, but it is not the essential clue to the
whole communitarian reality of personal existence.   The
communitarian character of personality is not simply ideal;
on one level or another it is the empirical fact.

As there is a notable emphasis on freedom and self-
transcendence in Niebuhr, so there is also a great emphasis
on the consciousness of judgment. A view which regards self-
transcendence as a journey into isolation and into anxiety
naturally regards man as standing under the judgment of God.
When men are isolated they tend to feel anxious and alienated, hence guilty and under judgment. Thus judgment is an
experience of terror. Niebuhr beholds human experience "at
the edge of human consciousness" as aware of being a
creature before the "wholly other," as filled with a sense

of moral obligation and of moral unworthiness before a
judge, and as "longing for forgiveness." Forgiveness, he
emphasizes, is longed for rather than assured.[7] We know we
are judged; we have no assurance of reconciliation.

This conception of judgment does violence to both Christian presuppositions and to empirical group relations, for
example in the family. The context of love, mutuality, and
forgiveness is prior both logically and psychologically to
alienation and judgment. If family judgment (sense of
ethical failure and personal rejection) is stronger than the
bonds of spiritual solidarity, the family will suffer
destruction. Realistic criticism (judgment) must be within
the frame of reference of mutual appreciation and good will
if the criticism is to be constructively meaningful. So
too, if God is *Agape*, the uniqueness of man must not be
sought in his moments of creature-feeling primarily or of
moral judgment primarily. These exist, to be sure, but they
have a frame-of-reference in the Christian faith which is
more ultimate than they, and which gives them constructive
significance. If man has no assurance of the ultimacy of
*Agape* as his religious ground and as the character of Him
who judges him, and if he cannot find in social experience
the analogue and basis which warrants this faith, then
creature-feeling and judgment will be intolerable. Fortu-
nately, a solidaristic conception of man comes closer to the
empirical human situation than the conception which Niebuhr
emphasizes.

Anxiety, we are told, "is the inevitable concomitant of
the paradox of freedom and finiteness in which man is
involved."[8] Anxiety is not sin, but it is sin's precondition. Moreover, anxiety is the basis of all human creativity. Man is anxious because his life is limited and
dependent and he knows it. He is also anxious because he

does not know the limits of his possibilities. "No life,
even the most saintly, perfectly conforms to the injunctions
not to be anxious."[9]   To be anxious is a concomitant of
freedom.  It resides in the inclination of man, either to
deny the contingent character of his existence (in the form
of pride and self-love) or to escape from his freedom (in
forms of sensuality).  Since anxiety is a concomitant of
freedom, sin is not necessary, but since anxiety lies at the
root of all creativity and activity, sin is inevitable.
These paradoxes, we must affirm, arise from a confusion of
moral,    psychological,    and    metaphysical    categories.
Niebuhr's outstanding contribution in this connection is to
wrestle with the dynamics of sin and not to let the problem
rest in mere moralism where many theologians have left it.
But he has not refined his categories and makes, for
example, no clear distinction between sin and evil.  Moreover, by assigning to guilt an essentially objective role as
meaning historical consequences, he confuses the issues
involving responsibility.  Responsiblity must relate to
choices; historical consequences may be, and largely are,
impersonal.  What is impersonal must relate to choice as
foreseeable consequence, if moral qualities are to be
assigned to it.

     In view of the author's general treatment of anxiety
and sin, it is especially noteworthy that he makes an important concession to self-transcendence as an instrument of
good.  He recognizes that there is only one self which sometimes contemplates its actions.  "In contemplation the self
has a clearer view of the total situation and becomes
conscious, in some degree, of the confusion and dishonesty
involved in its action."  This contemplation, we are
belatedly told, carries with it a power not otherwise
assigned to self-transcendence.  "When the self in contem-

plation becomes contritely aware of its guilt in action it
may transmute this realization into a higher degree of
honesty in subsequent actions."[10]   Thus, apparently, there
are actions of freedom, unfortunately not included in the
theory of essential man, which do not produce greater
anxiety, and therefore sin, but which raise the self to a
higher level of motivation and honesty.   On the basis of
this concession, it is theoretically possible at least, to
erect a constructive, though modest perfectionism.   That
Niebuhr has not exploited this possibility in treating the
destiny of man is one of the  failures of the second volume.

It is the destiny of man, according to Niebuhr, that he
can be saved in principle, but never in fact.   Love is the
law of the self, but in practice love is always betrayed
into self-love.[11]   To be saved the self must be shattered at
its center.   This happens whenever it is confronted by the
power and holiness of God and becomes genuinely conscious of
the real source and center of all life.[12]   The shattering of
the self is regarded as a perennial process and occurs in
every spiritual experience in which the self meets the above
conditions.   The real question which is posed is "not
whether we are able to achieve absolute perfection in
history...(but) whether in the development of the new life
some contradiction between human self-will and the divine
purpose remains."[13]   The new life is always implicated in
the corruptions of history which are in turn due to the
anxieties attending upon man's essential nature.

The strength of this position lies in its critique of
the easy conscience and the complacency of some forms of
perfectionism.   But its weakness resides in its inability to
deal adequately with the relative perfection which is the
fact of the Christian life.   How there can be development in
the spiritual life of the self; by what powers are Christian

values conserved in personality; what redemptive forces can
be released into history by committed human beings; and how
the immanence of *Agape* in human nature and history is to be
concretely conceived——all these issues are left unresolved.
The practical assurance of the ultimacy and availability of
the divine *Agape* is not naive and it is not to be dismissed
as extreme perfectionism which misjudges the historical
situation.  There is a Christian perfectionism which may be
called a prophetic meliorism, which, while it does not
presume to guarantee future willing, does not bog down in
pessimistic imperfectionism.  Niebuhr's treatment of much
historical perfectionism is well-founded criticism from an
abstract ethical viewpoint, but it hardly does justice to
the constructive historical contributions of the perfection-
ist sects within the Christian fellowship and even within
the secular order.  There is a kind of Christian assurance
which releases creative energy into the world and which in
actual fellowship rises above the conflicts of individual or
collective egotism.

Prophecy as criticism and judgment plays the central
and leading role in Niebuhr's philosophy of history.  For
him the prophetic problem is not that God should be revealed
as strong enough to overcome the defiance of the evil
against His will; but as having resources of mercy great
enough to redeem as well as to judge all men.  But he finds
redemption only beyond history, for the resources of meaning
are located there.  This means practically that in history
"judgment" is the rule, not redemption.  Human history
stands in contradiction to the divine will on any level of
its moral and religious achievements in such a way that in
any 'final' judgment the righteous are proved not to be
righteous.  The final enigma of history is, therefore, not
how the righteous will gain victory over the unrighteous,

but how evil in every good and the unrighteousness of the
righteous is to be overcome.  In contrast to this view which
is true only as a corrective to utopianism, stands the view
that God calls men not ultimately to judge the world, but
that the world through them may be saved.  Prophecy which is
Christian and mature becomes redemptive and emphasizes the
effectiveness of *Agape* in human history.   If His will be
never done on earth, we would not know or have faith that it
is done in Heaven.

## NOTES

[1]New York:  Charles Scribner's Sons, 1944.

[2]Vol. II, pp. 81-95.

[3]I, p. 270.

[4]*Ibid*., I, p. 16.

[5]*Ibid*., I, p. 55.

[6]*Ibid*., I, p. 294.

[7]*Ibid*., I, pp. 131-132.

[8]*Ibid*., I, p. 182.

[9]*Ibid*., I, p. 183.

[10]*Ibid*., I, p. 259.

[11]*Ibid*., II, p. 102.

[12]*Ibid*., II, p. 108.

[13]*Ibid*., II, p. 121.

## Essential Elements in the
## Christian Conception of Man
## (1947)

## I
## Man is Communitarian

The basic sociological unit is the group. Man is born into a group. He is nurtured physically and spiritually through a group, and he comes to self-realization as a participant in group life. The end for which God has created man is communion; thus the perfection of community, or the Kingdom of God, is the goal of mankind. Thus man and society are symbiotic, for there can be no social being on the human level without persons, and there can be no real persons as isolated individuals. Community is written into the nature of man in such a way that it is proper to think of man as person-in-community.

Man is a participant in many communities. There are face-to-face groups like the family and the neighborhood. In a family the members are not joined together by mere interest, but by organic bonds. The unity precedes the interests of the family. The family lives in a reciprocity of services, loyalties, affections, needs, appreciations, and love. Man is a member of secondary groups as well as of primary groups. In present American society there is the school, the playground, the Church, the trade union, the employer's association, the professional society, the club, and many another. The groups just mentioned are usually communities of like or common interest, the products of man's inalienable interdependence and need for social expression. Such communities have real social being. Some of

117

then are highly contemporaneous and transient, associations
which come into being for a brief period and then disappear
in the social process when their purposes are fulfilled or
found no longer viable.  Such are the migrant workers' camp
or the civil rights defense committee.  Other communities
are expressions of long historical purposes, accumulating
traditions, stable institutions, and a relatively involuntary membership.  Such is the nation and such also is the
church.  Membership in each of these may be voluntary or
involuntary, transient or permanent.  Besides these communities and cutting across them is the great transhistorical
community, the City of God.  We must think of the universe
as a society of persons having its source, ground, and ultimate purpose in the divine personality of God.  Thus each
individual human being is a member of many communities human
and divine, participation in each of which both determines
and expresses his developing personality.

    The reality of social being does not contradict the
ontological reality of individual personality.  The Christian view of man respects both the sacredness of the person
and the solidarity of brotherhood.  Because thought often is
betrayed into a false opposition of extremes, setting the
collective whole in absolute contrast to the solitary individual, it is important to emphasize the bi-polar unity of
person-in-community.  Some anthropologists take so individualistic a view of human nature that society and culture are
viewed as artificial and superficial.  Some take so impersonal a view of culture that the person is reduced to a non-
entity.  There is a "culturistic fallacy" which hypostatizes
culture into an autonomous entity apart from its organic
personal foundation.  Culture is personal and is essentially
experiential.  It depends basically not on the mere
existence of tool, machine, and gadget, but on human

thought, attitudes, and action.

## II
## Man is Free
## and Creative

The conceptions of freedom and creativity are closely related.  Immanuel Kant separated them in his treatments
of man, assigning the creative activity of thought to the
theoretical reason and postulating freedom in the realm of
the practical reason.  Actually this separation cannot be
made in any truly personal experience.  Freedom is as necessary for the finding of truth as it is in the moral life.
In this context it means the ability to say yes or no to any
given content.  It means that there is a creative initiative
which the individual may take in a situation, though
circumstances or other factors outside his control may limit
the range of effective choice.  Thus freedom and creativity
are metaphysical attributes of human nature.  Man may say
"Yes" or "No" to God as well as to his own ideals or to
hypotheses in problem solving.

Reinhold Niebuhr relates freedom to self-transcendence, self-transcendence to isolation and anxiety, anxiety
to creativity and temptation, and hence to the inevitability
of sin.  "Man," writes Niebuhr, "is a spirit who stands outside of nature, life, himself, his reason and the world"[1]
"Consciousness is a capacity for surveying the world and
determining action from a governing center.  Self-consciousness represents a further degree of transcendence in which
the self makes itself its own object in such a way that the
ego is finally always subject and not object."[2]  "The
essence of man is his freedom."  "Man contradicts himself
within the terms of his true essence.  His essence is free-
self-determination.  His sin is the wrong use of his freedom

and its consequent destruction."[3] Temptation roots in
anxiety.  "Anxiety is the inevitable concomitant of the
paradox of freedom and finiteness in which man is
involved....Anxiety is the internal description of the state
of temptation....Yet anxiety is not sin.  It must be distinguished from sin partly because it is its precondition and
not its actuality, and partly because it is the basis of all
human creativity as well as the precondition of sin."[4]  We
dissent from this point of view.  Niebuhr's treatment of
freedom and creativity lacks coherence with the constructive
aspects of personal living, being limited in his overemphasis on human failure.  Self-consciousness and freedom not
only make it possible for man to be a subject, but they also
make communication on the personal level possible.  Self-
transcendence and freedom are powers of conjunction as well
as of isolation and separation from nature.  Freedom from
animal limitations is a precondition of freedom to express
personality in community.  Niebuhr overemphasizes the tendency in man to use freedom sensually and pridefully.  He
underemphasizes the freedom of man to find God.  Without
freedom there is admittedly no horror of aloneness; but without freedom there is no path to the security of the Kingdom
of God.  Without  freedom to redirect the decisions of the
total self there would be no faith, no spiritual life.

     The moral life of man has many essential aspects,
ideals, purposes, values, obligations, rational calculation
of consequences, social context and the like.  But freedom
is fundamental since it underlies the formal autonomy of
each moral choice and the rational control of purposes.
Because of it responsibility has meaning.  It is clear that
"ought" would have no moral significance unless the person
is free to accept or reject an obligation.

     Social relations are not ultimate moral determinants.

We return here to an issue raised in Section I.  Culture as
a super-organic and impersonal whole has only a secondary
metaphysical status.  Culture is not an entity or process
sui generis over and above the participating personalities.
Culture is personal.  It involves the cooperative self-cul-
tivation of free vital agents.  Man is always implicated in
an historical social context, but he stands in principle in
a relation of creative freedom to that context.  Paul
Tillich has rightly observed that no generation of Christians can predetermine the moral choices of the next generation.  There is a spiritual precariousness in all preparation of youth with respect to the choices that they will
make.  But while history shares continually the possibility
of betrayal of its most cherished values, there is always
the glorious possibility of cooperatively undertaken and
more Christlike choices made by the youthful generation.
The proper Christian nurture of youth provides a fellowship
in which virtues are developed.  There is little ground to
accept the pessimistic paradox of Niebuhr between "moral
man" and "immoral society."  David Bidney observes rightly:
"Only by surreptitiously introducing the attribute of self-
directed activity (which pertains only to organisms) into
the notion of the superorganic does one come to regard it as
a dynamic, autonomous force which supersedes human agents.
If we bear in mind that culture, in its primary sense, is
logically and genetically an acquired attribute of human
nature and *that it is for us to determine which cultural
heritage is to be conserved* and which is to be allowed to
wither away through desuetude, then we shall be rid once and
for all of fatalistic delusions concerning the cultural
superorganic."  Human nature is communitarian; it is a
socius with a personal center, and essential to that center
is creative freedom.  There can be no conflict between

freedom and an adequate nurture of youth in group life.


                                    III
                         Man  is Purposive
                           and Rational


        In the development of self-hood freedom, purpose, and
reason are emergent qualities.   The definitions of these
terms as here used are those of personalistic psychology.
Free purposive self-control in the light of imperative norms
and criticized ideals mark a well-developed personality.
There is an important and useful distinction to be noted
between a self and a person.   We may profitably follow the
definitions suggested by E. S. Brightman at this point:
"The word *self* is used for any and every consciousness,
however simple or complex it may be.   A self is any conscious situation experienced as a whole.   Each 'empirical
situation' is a self.   All consciousness is self-experience;
but self-experience is not properly called self-consciousness (reflective consciousness) unless the self in question
has the special attribute of being able to think about the
fact that it is a self in addition to the fact that it experiences sensations and desires.   A *person* is a self that is
potentially self-conscious, rational, and ideal.   That is to
say, when a self is able at times to reflect on itself as a
self, to reason, and to acknowledge ideal goals by which it
can judge its actual achievements, then we call it a person."[5]
        Human life is dynamic, conative, purposive.   Impli-
cated and involved in all the drives of man is the one great
drive for wholeness or self-realization.   The many needs are
facets of the one great need.   Man seeks to satisfy the
restless cravings of the partial needs; he must achieve

total meaningfulness and express coherence in his social
relations. The law of the higher life is to love God with
all the mind, heart, soul and strength, and one's neighbor
as himself. Purposiveness in man demands coherence individually and socially. Most of the fallacies regarding human
nature arise from an essentially analytical approach to the
study of human nature. In the analysis of the segments the
unity eludes the investigator. Man in his wholeness is
actively outreaching. What sets the organism going is the
dynamic "tendency to actualize itself." Actualization is
the drive by which the organism is moved. In other words,
the teleology of the person is to realize the self. But,
admittedly, not all aspects of the organism come into the
foreground at once; and because they seem, superficially
taken, to be directed to diverse ends the impression is left
that these various activities exist independently of each
other. This, however, is not the real situation. In reality, there are various capacities which serve the self-actualization of the organism. This quest for wholeness takes
place in an interdependent inter-personal world, through
reciprocity and fellowship in community.

Man's purposiveness on the personal level is rational. In the current wave of irrationalism the ideas of
reason and the rational are misunderstood. They are viewed
as abstract and formal. Reason, however, must not be confused with mere intellection. Reason is the power to recognize and establish significant relationships, not only analytically but coherently and synoptically. Through reason
the person integrates the chaos of the non-rational into a
cosmos of meaningful experience. When desires and values
are rationally controlled they are autonomously criticized
in the light of a hierarchy of ideals and freely expressed
in harmony with community.

The Christian tradition in its Biblical source conceives of man as having a divine vocation. He is born to
become a son of God and to participate as a spiritual individual in the Kingdom of God. God places an intrinsic value
on each person. All equally carry the dignity of potential
sonship. The symbol of the divine sonship with its clear
sense of purposiveness indicates the dynamic character of
the human situation much better than the symbol of the "image of God." But both stress the spiritual nature of man
and the inherent equal dignity of man as man. This emphasis
on personal worth gives to the idea of freedom a basic equal-
itarian content. Freedom as a metaphysical trait and freedom as a communitarian quality meet in the notion of Christian liberty, wherein man freely accepts the way of love
toward all men as his human vocation. In so doing the Christian does not adopt a doctrinaire equalitarianism, nor ob-
scures the empirical differences among men, but does accept
a radically personal understanding of interdependence. God
has created all men to be interdependent; they can fulfill
their rational and purposive needs only in freely chosen
community. From such a perspective it is wrong to make
man's relation to his fellows a paradox between "moral" man
and "immoral" society. For unless purpose, freedom, and
vocation are regarded as basically or merely abstract, we
must place a positive and constructive value on primary
groups like the family and on secondary groups like the free
associations, the professions, the state, and the church.

## IV
## Man Grows

The term "growth" as associated with the doctrine of
man is suspect among many theologians because of its alleged
naturalistic taint and its suggestion of inevitable human

development towards the good. With respect to the first
point it must be admitted that there is no way of avoiding a
naturalistic "taint," for man is not only a potential son of
God, he is also very much a finite child of nature, an emergent product of cosmic, biological and social evolution. In
this evolution the theologian recognizes the immanence of
God and the rectigradation of His work and willing. Resistance to the idea of growth is especially strong among those
who overremphasize God's transcendence, important as that
doctrine is, to the neglect of His presence in creation.
Men like Wieman have done theology a great service by
stressing the divinity of the processes of growth in meaning
and value. There is in growth no inevitable establishment
of the Kingdom of God. On the personal plane, as on the
subpersonal, one must be aware of discontinuity, though
continuity is the more basic conception. Man grows through
decision and commitment, through facing and overcoming crises, through reciprocity and mutuality, through responding
rightly to the objective order of ideal values as grounded
in God. But in all growth God gives the increase.

The idea of growth stresses genuine development in
man. Without some nurturing fellowship, without guidance,
there is no integrated development. The path from immaturity to maturity is described by many psychologists as a
growth from dependence in childhood, to independence in
adolescence, to adult interdependence. Along this pathway
many persons experience only arrested development. In our
competitive, acquisitive, and sensate culture the sanctions
of society support arrested development at the level of
adolescent revolt and individualism. The confusion of Christian interdependence as the goal of society with the
Church's tendency to sanction individualism is one of the
causes of man's failure to "grow up" spiritually. Man's

growth is so much influenced by the groups which nurture
him, that he cannot be expected to make significant progress
beyond sensate and ego-centric respectability of educating
him in Christian interdependence.

The real development of man is communitarian, at once
inward and outward. Man is not a bundle of conditioned
responses. No mere manipulation of the environment resolves
his basic problems or brings him into spiritual maturity.
What we have said above about personality as free, purposive, creative, and rational has bearing on this point. Each
man must make an inward pilgrimage to the good life and he
alone can make it.

The unhistorical dogmas of the "fall of man" have made
the prospect of spiritual achievement appear gloomy and even
doubtful. The recent mythical uses of the dogmas has scarce-
ly improved the situation. They have been responsible for
the obscurantist confusion of moral responsibility and non-
moral sin, concerning which we shall say more later on.
Psychiatry and clinical psychology are of great service to
us here on the clarification of certain issues. Fritz
Kunkel for example describes the growth in persons as a
development from the Original-We to the Maturing-We. Seen
from the outside the unit is the whole human race; seen from
the inside the unit is the We. "The conscious fact of sharing itself is what we call We-experience or We-feeling."[6]
When a child is born the We-experience which exists between
mother and child is called the Original-We. In this unity
no barriers are acknowledged. But the Original-We is inevitably shattered both from the side of the mother's individuality and from the side of the child's becoming a true
subject. The tragedies of life begin as the unity is broken
from the inside. It is the great problem of human life to
move by invisible steps into a Maturing-We. The Maturing-We

for Kunkel means that though individual differences may
arise and increase, the community increases still more. The
community is vital to the objective personality who participates creatively in the We and expresses itself as love.
Such participation is ethical and involves autonomous ethical commitment. In the transition from the shattered Original-We to the Mature-We lies a great deal of ego-centricity.
In order to become a real subject (person) a self (used here
from the personalistic point of view) must learn autonomy;
and this cannot be done without passing through the throes
of ego-centricity. But ego-centricity must be transcended
if the self is finally to be actualized. To bring many by
an inner development through innumerable crises and conversions from an unavoidable childhood self-centeredness to
spiritual wholeness is a cooperative undertaking involving
both God and society. Because this growth is so terribly
difficult to bring to fruition it has been rightly said that
selfishness (both non-moral and moral) is the central problem of all religion. As a religion of redemption Christianity therefore speaks to our human predicament.


## V
## Man Needs Redemption


In traditional language we say that man is a sinner,
that he must confess and repent, and that through the forgiveness of God he may grow in grace. The apparent
all-inclusiveness of sin has obsessed many writers on the
subject. But nothing is gained by using sin as an omnibus
expression. Some distinctions are therefore in order. In
the first place, it is important to distinguish between sin
and evil. The word evil is the more inclusive term and in
general refers to anything (act, event, thought, entity)
which frustrates the good. Among evils there are two easily

distinguishable classes, natural evils and moral evils.
Natural evil comprises any frustration of the good which is
not directly assignable to responsible choice. Such frustra-
tions may be found in the constitution of man, in history,
in natural events outside man, in the social order, and perhaps even in God's experience. Moral evil is either material or formal. Formal evil refers to the quality of autonomous willing. Material evil refers to the quality of the
values and ideals chosen.

Many discussions of sin confuse moral and natural evil.
The position here taken is that the term sin is appropri-
ately used concerning moral evil viewed in its relationship
to God. Man's responsible choices, both formally and materially, are made in a universe in which God is the source of
all good, in which divine purposes guide and judge all processes, and in which man is dependent on God both for his
being and for his capacity to experience "ought" in relation
to formal and material good.

Strictly speaking, there is no non-moral sin. Writers
who assign to man responsibility for all sins and yet treat
sin in non-ethical ways create confusion. But the tendency
of much present thought is to define sin in such a way as to
include essentially non-moral situations. In a discussion
of man we may allude briefly to those conceptions of sin
which simply identify sin with selfishness and then include
under the latter indiscriminately all non-moral self-
centeredness and self-acting as well as ethical selfishness
as expressed in sensuality and pride.

We have said that man is a growing self, destined for
a God-centered communitarian self-realization. We have
noted that some of the basic categories or traits of personality are emergent creations: self-consciousness, freedom,
purpose, reason. We have noted that man must become an

autonomous self if he is to become a person capable of mature interdependent cooperation. The growth of the self with its emergent capacities to relate its various powers and capacities to a unitary self-consciousness involves innumerable self-centered (i.e. acting from the self as a center) acts. The freedom of an inclusive self-consciousness over all the self's acts is not initially given. In no person is it ever complete or perfect. Man is imbedded in a biological and historical bundle of life over which he never has complete control. The moral consciousness of every child is a relatively late emergent compared with some of his other drives and expressions of wholeness. It is inevitable, therefore, that a natural (non-moral) self-centeredness precedes both logically and genetically his first moral act. In adult life and even in much of childhood it is no longer possible to separate the higher and lower orders of emergence. The self has vital needs which cannot be gainsaid. The moral progress of man is a series of crises and conversions whereby the emerging ethical self-consciousness of man comes to dominate the antecedent ego-centricity of his finite situation. Man's purposes are destined to seek communitarian and divine fulfillment. When man comes to himself as a Christian he comes to the consciousness of God's objective purposes in the world, God's purpose for man's individual life, the resources which are available for the successful accomplishment of his journey, and the way to fulfillment which Christ has pointed out and made available to him.

It is important to repudiate both false pessimism and false optimism with respect to the human situation of sin. To say with Niebuhr that the real situation is that on every level of the moral life man is still a sinner, places the emphasis on the negative side. But the gospel places it on

the side of the "good news" of God.   Redemption is possible.   The human being who is struggling with his own mixture
and confusion of rightful self-centeredness and sinful selfishness finds in the Christian conception of God not only
condemnation for not living up to the "law of Love" but also
forgiveness, grace and power.   The divine judgment must for
this reason be understood within the frame of reference of
the divine love.

Man needs a "saving" knowledge of his own highest
good.   This means more than intellectual knowledge about it;
it means spiritual insight which frees him for it.   The
habits of inevitable self-centered acting genetically condition the growing moral consciousness, but the latter is free
to initiate significant triumphs over the lower levels of
consciousness.   This involves him in much self-deception,
however.   He has to learn among other things that God and
the whole community share in the "divine comedy."   The triumph over self-love and the need of insight into the objective Good is classically stated in the *Theologica Germanica*:

> So long as man seeketh his own will and his own
> highest Good, because it is *his*, and for his own
> sake, he will never find it; for so long as he
> doeth this, he is not seeking his own highest
> Good, and how then should he find it?   For so
> long as he doeth this, he seeketh himself, and
> dreameth that he is himself the highest Good;
> and seeing that he is not the highest Good, he
> seeketh not the highest Good, so long as he
> seeketh himself.   But whosoever seeketh, loveth,
> and pursueth Goodness as Goodness, and maketh
> that his end, for nothing but the love of
> Goodness, not for love of the I, Me, Mine, Self,
> and the like, he will find the highest Good, for
> he seeketh it aright, and they who seek it other-
> wise do err...

In this passage both the responsibility of a morally
autonomous self and the dependence of man on the Goodness
which is objective with respect to the autonomous will are

emphasized. Many pessimistic views of man in current theology confuse the moral autonomy of the person with an
alleged metaphysical autonomy. The former must be affirmed
if man is to be a responsible creature and the latter must
be denied because man is a creature.

## VI
## Man Has a
## Divine Vocation

Two figures of speech in the Bible as we have seen are
commonly related to man's divine vocation, the "image of
God" and the "divine sonship." The latter is the richer
conception for it embodies not only the thought of man's
divine origin, but also the thought of his communitarian
solidarity with other men and God, and moreover the idea of
divine destiny. The transhistorical destiny of man includes
his historical mission or vocation. In the idea of the
divine sonship we combine both the thought of the inwardness
of man's spiritual ties with God and the outward community
freedom of creatively and responsibly serving one another.

The Christian insight unites the faith that Jesus
Christ is the Son of God with the vocation of every man to
be a son of God. Therefore both the interior quality of
Jesus' loyalty and God's consciousness and the outward
expression of brotherhood and unlimited responsibility for
"the sins of the whole world" became normative for the Christian. Jesus was the Son of God; we are called to be sons of
God. At this point the historical fact of Jesus Christ's
life among men is of the utmost importance, for it links the
vocation of man to concrete historical expression while it
points to a cosmic destiny beyond human history. His life
also links in concrete form the participation of man in both
present community responsibility and a transcending City of

God or divine community. When the Christian takes Jesus as
the Christ to be "the way, the truth, and the life," he
affirms that the central meaning of history has already been
given concrete expression and that history has a divine
purpose. The Christian life thereby becomes a spiritual
growth in personal self-realization, at once both inward and
social, through participating in the continual historical
actualization of the Kingdom of God.

Participation in the historical struggle for the Kingdom of God involves man in innumerable moral compromises.
The moral compromises here referred to are material, not
formal. For no one ever has a right to compromise formal
goodness, sincerity, integrity. Materially, however, every
significant moral choice involves a mixture of good and
evil. The mixture of good and evil may be so complex that
the situation seems ethically ambiguous. For example, to
many conscientious Christians the present state of property
rights and the waging of war are ethically ambiguous. But
in any case the Christian is not absolved from responsibility to act conscientiously. He may not retreat from the
predicament.

Although participation in the historical predicaments
involve man in compromise (material relativity), the Center
of history affirmed in Christ is not itself a relativity.
The Kingdom of God as man's vocation is a concrete historical commitment. Some Christians have come to believe that
the affirmation of Christ as history's central meaning
involves negatively a repudiation of war in principle and a
repudiation of absolute private property, and involves positively unyielding loyalty to non-violent good will and
relative (partial) private property. These are but illustrations of what we mean by saying that Christian vocation
means more than the affirmation of high ideals. In every

situation man is bound to respect the fundamental dignity of
every Child of God and the solidarity of the human community.

Concrete historical responsibility implies and involves constructive creation of social institutions and
participation in them. No one believes truly in justice who
does not believe in courts of justice, or in nurture without
schools, or in religion without churches or temples, or in
children without the family. Man's Christian vocation is
therefore linked to institutions, but to institutions judged
by their communitarian contributions to human life. For,
while man is communitarian by nature, and while the Kingdom
of God is a community, the institutions of man have a secondary place. The collectivity expressed in institutions is
made for man, not man for the collectivity. The Kingdom of
God is therefore always a meaning which transcends any historical accomplishment and points to a destiny for man
beyond death. And yet, the historical groups in which man
participates are the nurturing centers of his personality.
The manner of his participation in them conditions largely
his spiritual growth. No man finds God in isolation. Apart
from fellowship and mutuality there is no salvation. Therefore, it is incumbent upon man to accept responsibiilty for
the moral character of the total social order, in order that
men may come to that fulness of divine sonship to which God
has called the whole human race.

## NOTES

[1]R. Niebuhr, *The Nature and Destiny of Man* (New York:
Charles Scribner's Sonc, 1944), Vol, I, p. 4.

[2]*Ibid.*, I, p. 13f.

[3]*Ibid.*, I, p. 16.

[4]*Ibid.*, I, pp. 182-183.

[5]E. S. Brightman, *A Philosophy of Religion* (New York:
Prentice-Hall, 1940), p. 350.

[6]Fritz Kunkel, *How Character Develops*  (New York:
Charles Scribner's Sons, 1940), p. 160.

Norms and Valuations
in Social Science
(1951)


I
Social Science and Citizenship

As the social scientist looks out upon his world today
and seeks to make his contribution to the solution of its
most pressing personal and group problems, he finds changing
presuppositions and the quest for valid universal norms the
order of the day. In their capacities as citizens religious
leaders and social scientists have developed a marked consciousness of responsibility. Indeed, the conception of the
responsible community is a touchstone both in religious
circles, such as the World Council of Churches, and in scientific associations. Definitely discredited, though not
entirely eliminated, is the dilettante. To some extent
cultural relativism is still a factor to be reckoned with.
A deep sense of seriousness has settled upon the community
of scholars and with it more understanding and rapprochement
between religion and social research. Values have become
not merely curious entities to be described in various
settings but are viewed as powers capable of creating an
emerging world culture and providing tolerable justice and
satisfaction the world round. Such values are pressing the
scientist to go beyond his traditional Comtean positivism
into more adventurous and difficult perspectives. He is
moving from anti-religious presuppositions into a realm more
friendly to Christian faith.

Thus social science reflects in part its own social

135

environment and the world cultural crisis.  In America the
past twenty-five years have seen three major challenges
which have profoundly affected social studies: the Great
Depression, World War II, and the United Nations.  In the
paper which follows we cannot hope to outline all the great
developments in contemporary social research.  We are select-
ing those changing perspectives and conceptions of human
nature, social responsibility and value-norms which are
especially relevant to the function of religion in American
education.  There is to that extent an admitted bias in the
selection of material and pointing up of issues.  The bearing of the discussion upon the responsibilities of instruc-
tion and research in our institutions of higher education
will be evident to the reader throughout.

American social scientists have long noted the critical
dilemmas of the nation, but not until the Great Depression
did they come into their own as citizens and public persons.
The caricature of the professor in government with his
academic cap presiding over a bureau, pulling fantastic
ideas out of the air while practical men of affairs looked
on with helpless despair, is a familiar symbol of this
sudden new role.  Though initially the butt of sarcasm and
even of angry jokes the specialist was there to stay.
Economists, sociologists, anthropologists and political
scientists came into their own, with the campuses of the
nation turning attention somewhat from physical technology
to social engineering.  Since the significant and critical
problems of business cycles, unemployment, morale, racke-
teering, labor organization, industrial violence, public
works, social security, agriculture and the like took the
center of the stage, social science was forced into new
directions.  There were not only the special problems of
limited interests but the problem of the economy as a whole.

From the static assumptions of a complacent "neo-capital-
ism" men turned more to social dynamics and to logical tools
adapted to conflict and social planning. The theories of
Keynes and Marx and Lenin made an abrupt entry into the
classroom and gained the public ear. They represent here a
shift in all fields.

If the Great Depression with its predominantly economic
and emergency governmental emphasis gave to the social
scientist new roles and to social engineering a new significance, World War II made heavy demands on psychologists and
anthropologists in addition because of the challenge of
racism and the defense of democratic values and ideals.
Scientists were called upon to commit themselves and their
science. Is one racial group inferior to another? What of
the dignity of person as person? Is democracy merely a
conditioned response, a mere social relativity with no
claims transcending nations? Is democracy practical or is
it merely a luxury for wealthy free-enterprise nations? Is
freedom merely what Americans want or ought it have a rightful place in the lives of men and groups suffering from
totalitarian regimes? The problem of universal norms could
no longer be side-stepped in what many had tried to keep as
value-free domains of scientific enquiry. Significant
social problems drove the scientist beyond traditional positivism. We shall develop this conception more fully below.
Gunnar Myrdal's book, *An American Dilemma*, may be taken as
symbolic of the frank commitment to certain personalistic
values on the part of innumerable social scientists.

The legacy of World War II has challenged social
thought to envisage and guide humankind into some viable
world community. To set nations, religions, economic patterns, languages and the like side by side in a neutral row
of differentiated entities, or even to show their interrela-

tions abstractedly, no longer suffices except in purely
preliminary phases of study.  Today the anthropologist is
called on to state, if he can, what culture patterns will
work in a universal frame of reference.  What of cultural
pluralism?   What of the future of minorities?   As the
present writer views the problem we must all ask:  Are the
values and social goals of the United Nations' Charter
anthropologically sound?  Is the "Universal Declaration of
Human Rights" adopted by the General Assembly of the United
Nations really to be the group of social purposes canalizing
the social energy of the whole world?  Social scientists had
their share in drafting this Declaration.  Anyone who reads
it recognizes its Western slant.  Social science in all its
branches has much work laid out for itself if it is committed, along with the General Assembly, to the following:

> The General Assembly proclaims this Universal
> Declaration of Human Rights as a common standard
> of achievement for all peoples and all nations,
> to the end that every individual and every organ
> of society, keeping this declaration constantly
> in mind, shall strive by teaching and education
> to promote respect for these rights and freedoms
> and by progressive measures, national and inter-
> national, to secure their universal and effec-
> tive recognition and observance, both among the
> peoples of member states themselves and among
> the peoples of territories under their
> jurisdiction.

The question which religion on the campus and the social
scientist alike face is whether they really regard these
values as the basis of a new world culture.  In any event
the situation emphasizes the role of social goals and value
norms in social science.

From the standpoint of religions like Christianity and
Judaism the personalistic values of the Universal Declaration of Human Rights may well appear to be only natural
implications of the ethical monotheism of the Bible.  The

special significance of the situation is that these values
and ideals are now projected as inductions from anthropology
and other social sciences or as social engineering goals
which anticipate their confirmation in further social
research.

II
Bias in Social Science

There are explicit and marked indications that social
scientists have a concern for induced social change today.
When sociology and economics made their debut as organized
scientific societies in America late in the nineteenth
century, they expressed concern for social reform. Indeed,
there was an intimate connection between their aims and
those of the rising social gospel. Richard T. Ely, for
example, viewed economics as an application of the Second
Great Commandment of Jesus. Early papers in the journals of
sociology often favored quite explicitly some form of Christian Socialism. It was not out of keeping with the general
spirit of much social science for the first encyclopaedia on
the field to be edited by a clergyman, W. D. P. Bliss, and
to be called *Encyclopaedia of Social Reform*. But soon the
dominant laissez-faire spirit of the nation and the desire
to emulate mathematical and physical sciences made themselves felt. Non-normative, purely descriptive objectivity
was the ideal. Purposes and values were eschewed. Interest
in social reform was for moralists, preachers and philosophers who had not yet reached the maturity of scientific
insight into law. Thus, the naturalistic presumption of
strict continuity of the human presence with physical nature
was in vogue. However, this perspective gave way substantially in 1929, when, as some say, the nineteenth century
came to an end. That year President Hoover appointed a

committee to make a study of social trends in the United
States.   In the report which was issued in 1932 this major
query was posed:    "How can society improve its economic
organization so as to make full use of the possibilities
held out by the march of science, invention and engineering
skill, without victimizing many of its workers, and without
incurring such general disasters as the depression of
1930-32?" The answer was implied that only through planning
and conscious control could a better adjustment between man
and his material culture be achieved.

Some leading scholars were quick to point out that the
previous training of the scientist included "no awareness of
the social consequences of his work," while the training of
the statesman and administrator had no provision "for the
potentiality of rapid scientific advance" with "no prevision
of the technical forces which are shaping the society in
which he lives."    Not only public officials but certain
learned societies and foundations turned attention to the
relation of science to society.   The Social Science Research
Council, the American Council on Education, the National
Academy of Science, the Carnegie Corporation, the Laura
Spelman Rockefeller Foundation, the Falk Foundation and
others, played important parts in assisting in the new direction of research.    In 1937 at the American Association for
the Advancement of Science the current movement was described as "an effort to shift from science for science's sake to
science for the sake of humanity."

The concept of social engineering has largely replaced
the earlier notion of social reform.   Scholars now recognize
that there has been a bias in social science against induced
change, especially against all attempts to assist social
change through legislation.    The supposed validity of
Sumner's conceptions of "folkways" and "mores" has been

challenged. Gunnar Myrdal argues: "By stowing the commonly
held valuations into the system of mores, conceived of as a
homogeneous, unproblematic, fairly static, social entity,
the investigator is likely to underestimate the actual
differences between individuals and groups and the actual
fluctuations and changes in time....Summer's construction
contains a valid generalization and offers a useful methodological tool for studying primitive cultures and isolated
stationary folk-communities under the spell of magic and
sacred tradition....The theory is, however, crude and misleading when applied to a Western society in process of
rapid industrialization....It conceals what is most
important in our society; the changes, the conflicts, the
absence of static equilibria, the lability in all relations
even when they are temporarily, though perhaps for decades,
held at a standstill. The valuation spheres, in such a
society as the American, more nearly resemble power-maga-
zines than they do Sumner's concept of mores."[1] In much
past social research the ideological tendencies have been
biased in a static, laissez-faire, do-nothing, and conservative direction. Such valuations which are masked behind
descriptive objectivity really serve to injure the
disfavored groups in society.

With the increased use of social engineering the
fact-finding, the scientific concepts, and the theories of
social causation will themselves be instrumental in planning
social change. Because of the New Deal, the War and the
challenge of the present crisis the scientist will more and
more become familiar and competent with planning concepts
and with practical action. He is himself an actor in a
drama in which he wishes to be participant observer. He
will never again be given the opportunity, says Myrdal, "to
build up so 'disinterested' a social science" as he once

conceived to be his ideal.   In the search for knowledge and
control of social causation the environmentalist trend in
science is bound to continue.   Along with it will continue to go the traditional American faith in human beings.
Accompanying it also is the view, which we shall elaborate
later, that 'human nature' can be changed and the confidence
that human deficiencies and unhappiness are, for the most
part, preventable.

     In developing a concern for normative sociology and for
social engineering, the social scientist completes the full
cycle and returns approximately to the practical position
held by the leaders in the Christian social gospel movement
of fifty years ago.   The theological frame of reference is,
of course, absent.   There is, moreover, no well articulated
metaphysics of value, no Christian theism, which provides an
ultimate ground of norms and persons.   Neither is there a
fully developed philosophy of social science with a system
of theoretical ethics coherently integrating these sciences
into a moral whole.   Yet there is some evidence that social
scientists are working with norms consistent with a Christian philosophy of society.   There are, of course, resources
and insights in Christianity which have not been fully
exploited by scientific hypotheses.   Our concern, here, however, is with the internal development in social science
according to its own autonomous and practical logic.   It is
this internal logic and the interactions of research
projects with the social situation which drive the scientist
beyond spectator description to participant decisions.
Social scientists differ radically as to what is involved in
responsible participation from the scientific viewpoint:
some holding that the scientist may depict the social consequences of possible decisions, others going so far as to
include valuational commitments into science itself.

There are dangers in the emphasis on the practical applications of science and social engineering. Some of these will appear more fully later in our essay. It should be noted here that in social engineering one cannot emulate the exactness of the physical technologist. The social engineer cannot assess with any such assurance as the latter the strains and stresses, the reactions of human beings to the measures he may advocate as can the civil engineer. "Should he therefore," asks MacIver, "as social scientist, refuse to advocate any?" MacIver replies, "That would be the denial of the validity of the knowledge he possesses." "If the social scientist does not use (his knowledge), having first acquired it, is he not denying his social responsibility without thereby vindicating his title of social scientist."[2] The risk of inexactness must be taken.

A second risk also is unavoidable. The objective of action is itself the product of a value-judgment. MacIver along with Myrdal rejects the old stereotype that the social scientist must eschew value judgments. Here are two vital considerations: (1) "The danger of bias besets the social scientist in every kind of investigation and his problem is to guard himself against it; in short to maintain his scientific-mindedness, and not to shun areas of knowledge where he may be susceptible to bias." (2) "Applied science is in all fields the concomitant of pure science, and to it we owe all the civilization that man has built—why should it not be so in the social field? In this respect the social scientist is in precisely the same position as the chemist, the bio-chemist, the biologist, the physicist, and all the rest."[3]

Beyond these negative considerations there are on the positive side serious scientific considerations emphasized also by MacIver, Myrdal and others like Linton and

Kluckhohn. "The social scientist who seeks to avoid bias by
complacently refusing to investigate issues that are infect-
ed by it is not thereby saving his scientific soul. He is
like the saint who would guard himself against temptation by
abjuring the world where temptations abound—and then is
beset by new and more insidious temptations in his retreat.
His boasted objectivity is apt to develop into indifference
or into a not too secret satisfaction with the *status quo*."[4]
There is frequently a bias in refusing to deal with biases.
Moreover, the scientist may shut himself off from large
fields of social reality which are of the greatest
importance to his fellow-men. That is a puny type of social
science which does not grapple with axiological issues in
the value-loaded and emotionally charged areas of human
experience. Avoidance of bias is self-defeating. "His
disinterestedness is likely to be or to become the
expression of an interest, and he cannot protect himself
against *that* bias because he proudly proclaims it to mean
the absence of all bias."[5] Moreover, bias is not inherently
bad. If there is truth about values, such truth deserves to
be known. The truth in Christianity may be difficult to
establish scientifically, but the value which biases
argument may be true, nevertheless.

There are also certain ethical considerations which the
scientist has to face in a democratic culture. The anthropologist as citizen, says Kluckhohn, is morally obligated to
look at the world. "For the essence of democracy is that
each individual offers to the thinking of the group those
insights that derive from his special experience and training."[6] Thus beyond the fact of involvement in bias is the
necessity of making a choice among ends and programs based
on research to be promoted. There is thus the need to go
beyond traditional science to philosophical study of the

norms. Even scientifically speaking it is better to accept
this ethical dilemma than to evade it.  "Research workers
should realize," says MacIver, "that their large preoccupation with such subjects as housing, public opinion, crime
and delinquency, unemployment, tariffs, and so forth, is
itself directed by the social importance of these areas of
investigation and that if they refuse to draw inferences
regarding preferable policies they are like investigators of
public health conditions who refrain from recommending what
should or should not be done about them." Social responsibility links research of the most critical and objective
sort with profound ethical choice.  If the social scientist
"refrains from making practical applications he is the more
apt to divorce his particular ethics from his scientific
faith and to make judgments as a layman, as a human being,
without the regard for evidence he insists upon as a scientist."  MacIver concludes:  "The social scientist cannot
move the world, but he may be able to learn the secrets of
how the world is moved and so furnish aid and special direc-
tives to the forces on one or another side of the eternal
struggle to move it this way or that."[7]

MacIver[8] takes issue with Myrdal on how the ethical
valuations are to be related to the factual knowledge which
science provides.  Myrdal emphasizes the aim of practical
research to be that of showing "precisely what should be the
practical and political opinions and plans for action from
the point of view of the various valuations if their holders
had also the more correct and comprehensive factual knowledge which science provides."  Myrdal thus wishes to make
bias explicit.  He would show what values imply by way of
consequences.  He would expose the assumptions behind and
the conflicts between social ideals and practices.  This
pragmatic approach has many supporters among social scien-

tists.  MacIver would go somewhat further, for the cause is
not won when rationalizations are simply exposed in the
light of social science.  The exposure of prejudice and its
consequences alone does not assure the triumph of the larger
ideal.   Prejudice and rationalization are too fecund for
that.   In relation to the study of the Negro in the United
States in *An American Dilemma*, MacIver asks, "Why need he
(Myrdal) study the nature and social consequences of intergroup discrimination exclusively in the light of certain
presumptively dominant creeds of the discriminating group?"
The investigator may find that the consequences of discrimination are detrimental to social well-being, as he understands it.   "If in the judgment of the investigator the
consequences are undesirable it becomes for him a task
wholly consonant with the principles of science to examine
in turn the available methods for mitigating or removing
their source." [8]

     The social scientist can also contribute much by moving
analytically into the center of social movements and showing
how old values are linked with new behavior, how leaders can
manipulate the people with old symbols filled with new content.   The methods of social science are able to show
whether the adaptation of behavior to presumed demands of
value systems is based on a valid or false linkage. [9]   Moreover, once published and publicized, research becomes one of
the social forces making for change along with changes in
the techniques of production, of communication, and of
consumption, to name but a few.   Like these, scientific
ideas force individual and group revaluations.   The spread
of knowledge, moral discussion and political propaganda are
integral factors in an interdependent system of causation.
Ideas have a momentum of their own and enter often into the
breakdown of old myth-patterns and the emergence of new

complexes of value-impregnated beliefs. It makes a significant difference therefore whether the social scientist
believes in the efficacy of social engineering, of democracy, of the American Creed, of Christian brotherhood, or
whether he is a cynic, a fascist or a mere ethical relativ-
ist. In the sense of commitment to ultimate values the
question is thus both ethical and religious. Religion as a
valuational process which rallies mankind to universal
ideals and to the possibility of social amelioration guided
by the objective love of truth and respect for personality
is thus not only a live option for the development of social
science, but a fruitful prospect. And meliorism, the belief
that this is the kind of world that can be made better—a
view natural to the social engineer—rests on a teleological
assumption which opens the door to metaphysics of religion.
Other papers in this volume explore this aspect of the
problem more fully than can be done here.

The rationalism and moralism which are presupposed in
the faith which holds to the possibility of induced social
change are not to be confused with the older doctrine of
progress which played so large a part in the eighteenth
century and which thrived in the optimism characteristic of
much social Darwinism. Meliorism and automatic progress are
poles apart, if indeed they can be placed in any common
scale of social causation. Anthropologists at work among
the many cultures of mankind, sociologists of religion
analyzing primitive and historical communities, economists
at work on the business cycle and on comparative economic
systems have largely liquidated, out of scientific necessity, any view of inevitable progress. Cultures do not
recapitualte each other. Religions have no fixed sequence
of evolution. No unseen hand guides self-interest and cut-
throat competition into the haven of the general welfare.

Social engineering and social planning for freedom amidst a
world where democratic and spiritual values are admittedly
precarious are holding out to mankind a more serious assignment in social responsibility than proponents of necessary
progress ever conceived of doing. Indeed the 'old' doctrine
of 'progress' is today so dead in social science as not even
to be a whipping boy of the innovator in social theory. At
the same time the general term progress is not entirely
outmoded, except among those who deny any standard of value.
There can, for example, be no question that the potential
resources of human culture generally and of most cultures
have steadily increased. Anthropologists incline to view
the triumph over human misery and degradation as having a
spiral character rather than that of an unbroken climb.
There are discontinuities. There are troughs and crests.
Cultures are always in the making. The possibilities for a
significant life for mankind are exceedingly great, but not
predestined. Christian and scientific criticisms of the
dogma of progress present stimulating challenges to the
social theorist and to the social engineer. Higher
education is thus today at a stage where conflicting frames
of reference in religion and science illuminate the problems
of social change.

### III
### Values and the Integration of Social Sciences

Social engineering requires the integration of many disciplines. The T. V. A. was as significant for its inclusive
approach to the problems of a region as for its use as a
yardstick by which to measure the exploitation of utility
companies. In the social sciences there has grown an appreciation for multi-casual and cumulative causation methods as
over against the mono-casual schools of thought such as

economic determinism. This has meant that anthropology as
an inclusive cultural science has been coming into its own.
Its marvelous progress has made an important impact on all
the special sciences. Whereas the sociologist and economist, for example, had carried on their investigation
almost entirely within the narrow frame of reference provided by Western and American culture and society, the ethnolo-
gist was compelled to view societies and cultures as a
whole. Whereas the special disciplines took for granted the
presuppositions characteristic of Western life in the last
few centuries, it has been necessary for the anthropologist
to realize that these are not an invariable accompaniment of
social living. Such presuppositions are of relatively
little value in a period of rapid social change and conflict
and in a period when world community, embracing all previous
histories of nations and societies, is the assignment of mankind. An economist whose generalizations were based on the
American business cycle of one hundred years can hardly use
these as a basis of world trade. Much wider ranges of data
are needed in a day when generalizations must be coherent
with global movements. The "correlation of the social problem" states the contemporary issue.

In one science after another there has been a shift
from the assumption that the individual is the cultural unit
and that society is composed of a sum of identical and inter-
changeable units. Anthropology is dependent on the work of
special sciences but has had to modify them in the process
of meeting wholistic demands. As Ralph Linton has pointed
out with respect to personality psychology: "It concentrat-
ed upon the individual and at first, under the influence of
the natural sciences, tried to explain all individual similarities and differences on a physiological basis. Although
the importance of environment in personality formation soon

became apparent, this was used, at first, simply to explain
individual differences....The discovery that personality
norms differed for different societies and cultures came as
a shock and one which necessitated a basic reorganization of
many of their concepts."[10] The interaction of psychology
and ethnology has been very fruitful.

There has come about a reconsideration of the integrative factors of heredity, physical environment, the family,
the small group, social values and institutions.  Whereas
the nineteenth century social philosophy was still largely
determined by the hereditary point of view, and whereas
under the impact of the American scene an extreme environmentalist viewpoint sometimes made itself prominent, there
is ample evidence today for an equilibrium between these two
opposing standpoints.  Moreover, cultures must be approached
not only from without descriptively but in terms of their
inner meanings.  Anthropology is no longer an assemblage of
curious differences among the habits and artifacts of primitive men, but a holistic discipline seeking comparative laws
with predictive values.  Kluckhohn writes:  "Each culture is
saturated in its own meanings.  Hence no valid science of
human behavior can be built on the canons of radical
behaviorism.  For in every culture there is more than meets
the eye, and no amount of external description can convey
this underlying portion of it.  Bread and wine may mean mere
nourishment for the body in one culture.  They may mean
emotional communion with the deity in another."[11]

In bringing together the representative problems and
generalizations of anthropology in the volume called *Personality in Nature, Society and Culture*, the editors, Kluckhohn
and Murray, take what they call the 'field' approach.  "We
regard," they say, "the conventional separation of the
'organism and his environment,' the drama of 'the individual

*versus* his society,' the bi-polarity between 'person and culture' as false or at least misleading in some important senses. Knowledge of a society or a culture must rest upon knowledge of the individuals who are in that society or share that culture. But the converse is equally true. Personal figures get their definition only when seen against the social and cultural background in which they have their being....Although those who study culture and society are primarily interested in the similarities in personality and those who practice psychotherapy and investigate individual psychology have their focus of attention upon differences, the two sets of facts are inextricably interwoven. One defines the other. In actual experience, individuals and societies constitute a single field."[12]

This field concept, as outlined above, does not eliminate any of the factors biological or cultural, but it does bring them into a new relationship. Franz Alexander's criticism of Freud may illustrate in part the need to be self-critical in these matters. Freud, he says, was too biologically oriented. "He postulated a too elaborate, biologically predetermined instinctual structure which, in its main features, unfolds in a more or less autochthonous manner, like a flower. He recognized, possibly even over-emphasized, the importance of those early experiences which arise in family life, but he overlooked the fact that the parental attitudes themselves are strictly determined by cultural factors. This neglect is the basis of a significant error...Freud declared the personality structure of the European and American of the nineteenth century to be the universal human nature."[13]

There are limits to the adaptability of the biological constitution to cultural demands. To put it absurdly, there are no cultures in which the men bear the children. In no

society do the cultural pressures override and eliminate all
aspects of personal individuality.  On the other hand, no
society is a mere *Und-Summe* of individuals.  The first and
basic task of a child's ego anywhere is accomplishing the
continuous adjustment to those biological changes which
rapidly succeed one another in the processes of maturation.
And yet, cultural factors, including parental attitudes
powerfully influence the child's readiness to accept the
ongoing maturation.  Moreover, cultural constellations reinforce or bring to the foreground certain emotional mechanisms, though they do not introduce any basic dynamic
principles into human nature.

     In cultural conditioning there are, then, both continu-
ities and discontinuities.  "The anthropologist's role,"
says Ruth Benedict, "is not to question the facts of nature,
but to insist upon the interposition of a middle term
between 'nature' and 'human behavior'; his role is to
analyze that term, to document local man-made doctorings of
nature, and to insist that these doctorings should not be
read off in any one culture as nature itself.  Although it
is a fact of nature that the child becomes a man, the way in
which this transition is effected varies from one society to
another, and no one of these particular cultural bridges
should be regarded as the 'natural' path to maturity."[14]

     The reciprocity of individual and cultural factors as
noted in contemporary sociology is enriched by the contributions of psychiatry in case work and by the newer sociology
of the family.  Case methods and clinical relationships
point up the sources of individuality differences.  Family
studies indicate that the immediate group environment
composed of parents mediates largely the demands of the
culture.  An intimate study of family life brings to light
the need of recognizing the specific influence of the par-

ents and not to neglect this while concentrating on the larger cultural whole. There is a dialectical interplay of biological heredity, family life, and the dynamic patterns of culture in the bio-psycho-social whole. On the one hand, the fundamental directions of childhood training do not derive from the inborn nature of persons but anticipate the roles which men and women will eventually play as they fulfill society's ideals. Methods of child rearing and education which are divorced from the general emphases of the culture will finally alter the emerging adult personality. The spirit of the culture is permeative. Desired changes in adult personalities require an inclusive approach to all phases of social life. "No man is an island." No family is an island.

On the other hand, personality structure cannot be deduced from general social ideals alone. The child's inherited constitution reacts and responds to an enormous range of individualities as represented by many personalities along with their parents in the many relationships into which they enter. Especially in a changing civilization like our own, with a great variety of trends and pressures, intricately interwoven in complex patterns, the child selects what it needs. What is selected depends largely on emotional needs developed in family life under the influence of the particular personalities of the parents. There thus emerges a profounder appreciation of the family 'its function and destiny' than has been the case several decades ago. Ruth Nanda Anshen, summarizing the views of a number of leading authorities in *The Family: its Function and Destiny* says: "The contributors to this book have further attempted to show that the family is an integral and indispensable entity in the life of man; that the present collapse of marriage and the family is a perverted triumph

of a profaned passion which in truth now largely consists in
a reversion to abduction and rape, divested, however, of the
ritual that surrounded such violence in some primitive
societies; that the dissolution of the modern family is
tantamount to the gradual profanation of the fundamental
myth which at one time bestowed meaning and sanctity upon
family life now converted into mere rhetoric, and finally
dissolving the rhetoric itself through the complete vulgar-
ization and secularization of its contents; that *eros* is
love which demands to be loved, whereas *agape*, the all-
embracing, descending principle of love, is the redemptive
good will which asks only the joy of selfless service to the
beloved, and that it is for lack of this latter love that
the world is dying; that morals and politics are identical
and are embraced by the same rules which govern the organization of the family and the organization of the state."[15]
In other words, the family is not only an essential cultural
unit within culture as a whole, but social scientists view
its conservation as one of the principal tasks confronting
our civilization.    Adequate family life is a functional
necessity for a healthy culture.

     The 'field' approach, then, includes due recognition of
the intimate relationships obtaining in the person-family-
culture continuum.    John Gillin has shown that definite
correlations exist between the socio-cultural constellations
and the type of person one becomes as an adult.   He credits
Malinowski with probably being the "first to recognize that
the influence of the family configuration and social organization determines the form of the conflicts and resulting
'complexes' of the personality and that, since social
structures differ from society to society, psychological
complexes do also."[16]    Malinowski also laid the basis in
comparative ethnology for much of the "neo-Freudian" theory

today which sees "the source of many neuroses in the socio-
cultural situation surrounding persons in their formative
years." In all of this work today it must be emphasized
that the person is not dissolved into the culture continuum.
This is of the utmost importance for the religious conception of the sacredness of personality. This present
emphasis can be traced from several angles, as we shall see.

David Bidney, combining philosophical and anthropological competence, points out that logically "there need be no
contradiction between the organic or personalistic and the
impersonalistic or superorganic views of culture, provided
it be kept in mind that we are dealing with different levels
of abstraction and that organic or personal culture is
logically and genetically prior to superorganic culture."[17]
Culture as a concept is not to be hypostatized into a transcendental force. Bidney believes that George Mead, John
Dewey, Charles H. Colley, Ellsworth Faris, August Comte and
Ernst Cassirer overemphasized the thought that the nature
and mind of the individual can be understood only through
the society of which he is a member. Hypostatization of
culture, he thinks, is an error in Hegel, Comte, Marx,
Spengler and Sorokin all of whom allegedly made culture the
primary, impersonal 'agent' and man a passive vehicle.
Bidney may go too far here in some of his negative criticisms but he is right in cautioning against "the fallacy of
'misplaced concreteness.'" He brings out a valid relationship of personality to culture when he concludes: "If we
bear in mind that culture, in its primary sense, is
logically and genetically an acquired attribute of human
nature and that it is for us to determine which cultural
heritage is to be conserved and which is to be allowed to
wither away through desuetude, then we shall be rid once for
all of fatalistic delusions concerning the cultural

superorganic."[18]

That the determinate nature of man "is manifested functionally through culture but is not reducible to culture" is
illustrated and partially verified in the study made by
Allport, Bruner and Jandorf of a number of cases of persecuted persons under the Nazi regime. It was a study of how
the persecuted adult defends himself psychologically against
catastrophe; of how far catastrophic social disorganization
disrupts basic personality integration; of how political
attitudes change under the impact of catastrophe and the
like. We are here concerned to show what the psychologist
found it important to emphasize as psychological mechanisms
came into play to protect against catastrophe. Gordon
Allport says "(1) *Persistent goal striving* is the
indispensable postulate. Families to defend, children to
educate, business to foster, friends to help—in short, the
conservation of personality structure and all the major
values of life call for tenacity. (2) Such differentiated
goal-striving demands the *retention of a structured field*.
Migration into a new and strange life-space removes the
'behavior supports' essential to the pursuit of long-estab-
lished goals. In adulthood, our data show, such a catastrophic change in frames of reference, values, and support-
ing habits meets with active resistance."[19] Very rarely, he
goes on to point out, does catastrophic social change
produce catastrophic alterations in personality. "Neither
our cases nor such statistics as are available reflect any
such number of regressions, hysterics, or other traumatic
neuroses as the gravity of the social crisis might lead one
to expect. On the contrary, perhaps the most vivid impression gained by our analysis from this case-history material
is of the extraordinary continuity and sameness in the
individual personality." Thus, while induced social change

is frequently stressed by social scientists, while the
possibilities of planned and manipulated personality development are very real, the adult has a persistent basic structure of personality. Despite disaster the established goals
striving, the fundamental philosophy of life, skills, and
expressive behavior are amazingly the same. "When there was
change in our subjects," writes Allport, "it did not seem to
violate the basic integrations of the personality, but
rather to select and reinforce traits already present."[20]

We can bring this section of our survey to a close by
mentioning the person-in-community or individual-group
discoveries made in a very different field by Elton Mayo,
namely that of industrial relations. Here we note again the
basic shift from an earlier automistic individualism to the
communitarian personalism of the present stage of research.
Much of the social insight found in Mayo was already present
years ago in the social gospel writers and theorists like
Gladden, Stuckenberg, Peabody and Rauschenbusch, but it did
not have much of a place in social science. Clinical
research in industrial relations as reflected in the studies
by Mayo over a quarter of a century may be symbolized by
noting the shift in emphasis from *The Human Problems of an
Industrial Civilization*, published in 1933, to *The Social
Problems of an Industrial Civilization*, published in 1945.
In the first study methods were developed of analyzing and
securing better understanding of individual workers in
relation to their jobs and of ways to improve their sense of
well-being in industry. Later research revealed the importance of social groupings and of team-work as well as of the
individual. Though not excluding the individual, Mayo
stressed the importance of groups and methods of understanding the behavior of groups, whether formally organized and
recognized by management or self-constituted, informal

organizations.  He  showed  that  it  is  within  the  power  of
industrial  administrators,  amidst  technological  changes  in
the  plant  and  social  chaos  in  the  community  outside,  to
create  within  industry  itself  a  partially  effective  substitute  for  the  old  stabilizing  effect  of  the  neighborhood.

Mayo  rejects  what  he  calls  "the  Rabble  Hypotheses"
which  grew  out  of  the  Manchester  School's  development  of
economic  principles.  He  notes  also  that  the  profit  motive
as  a  basis  of  business  organization  failed  completely.  The
conception  behind  individualism  in  economics  that  society
consists  of  a  "horde  of  unorganized  individuals'  misses
social  reality  entirely.  Contrary  to  such  politico-economic  theory  which  would  ground  democracy  on  the  'rabble
hypotheses,'  the  real  outcome  is  that  of  Hobbes's  Leviathan.
Democracy  must  make  group  life  and  adaptive  behavior  a
basically  different  conception  from  all  this.  Clinical  work
in  industry,  with  knowledge-of-acquaintance  of  the  actual
event  and  intimate  understanding  of  the  complexity  of  human
relationships,  "ran  headlong  into  illustration  of  the
insufficiency  of  the  assumption  that  individual  self-interest  actually  operates  as  adequate  incentive."[21]  Given  the
opportunity  of  communication  and  collaboration  amongst  themselves,  the  workers  in  a  "problem"  department  of  a  textile
mill  greatly  increased  their  efficiency  and  the  labor  turn-
over  dropped  from  250  per  cent  to  5  per  cent.  Experiments
led  to  the  conclusion  that  "associative  instincts  overshadow-
ed  material  conditions  as  determinants  of  productivity.
Where  individuals  became  a  team,  not  only  did  their  productivity  increase,  but  their  personal  outlook  and  their
ability  to  collaborate  changed  for  the  better."  Mayo's  work
is  but  one  of  many  new  enquiries  in  the  rapidly  developing
field  of  communication  research.  Without  communication
there  can  be  no  community.  Irrational  hates,  hostile  groups

within industry and among nations, challenge both the theory
and the practice of adaptive society, with the theory and
art of communication and cooperation a central project.

## IV
## The Prospect of Universal Norms

We have not been able adequately to sketch the great
areas of social enquiry being developed along many constructive lines. Especially should more be noted concerning the
newer studies of political units, the state and social
control. Propaganda and the mass-communications problems
are receiving much attention. But we must turn our thought
to the present concerns for values and for norms which transcend nations and cultures, concerns which have been basic
to monotheistic religions for centuries and now confront the
sciences. Over and over again the social sciences bring us
to the threshold of a universal axiology. Without the
critical knowledge of the anthropologist, integrating the
work of special researches, it is presumptive for religion
or philosophy to attempt any concrete or empirical formulations of religious life in the future. But there need be no
longer any disjunctive alternative of 'science' or 'religion.' In all cultures religion's functions are symbolic,
expressive and orientative. It grasps the whole meaning in
anticipation. Every culture has its myths, its value-impregnated beliefs, and must define its ends as well as its
means. Scientific investigation of the technics of society
do not provide the symbolic expressions of ultimate values.
Ultimate norms, moreover, often condemn facts which are
described by science and demand change. On the other hand,
there is no intrinsic reason why ultimate values should be
incoherent with known fact or proven theory. Since, moreover, as J. S. Huxley says, the emancipation of natural

science from considerations of value is a fiction, and since
some of the most important data with which social scientists
deal connote values in some socially approved hierarchical
order, the problem seems to be to find norms which will
provide the most rationally coherent realm of ends
intelligently integrated with the means appropriate to their
realizaion.

In the transition from pure to applied science many
scientists have discovered the inevitability of bias and
values. We have noted how Myrdal and MacIver relate social
engineering to values and social responsibility. Social
psychologists like Weyland Vaughan connect intimately the
"science" of psychology with the "art of living." During
the last fifteen years there has been a marked growth in the
social psychology ot values and of intelligent social
control. E. Freeman, O. Klineberg, S. H. Britt, G. W.
Hartmann, E. C. Tolman, E. L. Thorndike, R. S. Lynd, G. W.
Allport are but a few of the men working in the field who
have come to grips with the problems in the borderland
between traditional psychology, sociology and ethics. G. W.
Hartmann in 1939 speaking to the Society for the Psychological Study of Social Issues argues for "Values as the Unifying concept of the Social Sciences." He held that "Values
are both the basic data and the explanatory tools of all the
social sciences." In 1940 before the same group, E. C.
Tolman, who has devoted many years of study to animal
behavior pled as follows: "Our fellow human beings today
all over the world are giving up their lives in the name of
new loyalties. And, if we psychologists here in America
don't preach our own sermons, we shall be caught by theirs.
If we don't say our say, not merely as to how to detect and
measure and tabulate social change, but as to what good
social changes would be, then we shall deserve no better

fate than the one which otherwise undoubtedly lies in store
for us."[22]

The values to which the American social psychologists
quickly turned were those of democracy and personality. The
moral kinship between science and democracy is natural to
the scientist. Democracy fosters a process of open discussion which exposes more and more of the interests, facts and
valuations of the community. Democracy and science foster a
free, open and critical participation of the members of a
group. Democracy brings under the light of mutual criticism
the varying perspectives of the participants. Public discussion properly conducted has a purifying effect and is part
of the moral education of the people. Science fosters a
community of disciplined thought and criticism in which
enlightened proposals of experimentation and hypotheses for
the solutions of problems are subjected to public examination under commonly accepted postulates and tests in continuous intercommunication among researchers. The exploration
of values by social scientists seems on the whole to have
driven them to greater loyalty to democratic values. Our
multi-group society and the wide range of interests plays
its part too. For democracy stresses not one single
absolute value but thrives in the interpenetration of a
subtle and intricate multiple of values. It finds its path
of least resistance, intellectually and morally speaking, in
an adaptive process in which interests and institutions are
wont to be balanced in a dynamic equilibrium. It may not be
going too far to say that democracy is a way of life in
which personality builds itself ever new institutions more
suitable for its own self-realization.

America feels herself to be humanity in miniature and
hence almost takes for granted that the perfecting of
democratic ideals and values here has universal applicabil-

ity in the long run.  As a matter of fact there is genuine
continuity between the American Bill of Rights and the
Universal Declaration of Rights adopted by the General
Assembly of the United Nations.

In this quest for general valuations, we note a significant shift from much early anthropology to present practical and theoretical concerns.  No longer is the emphasis on
curious differences, on demonstrations that 'anything goes
somewhere in the world.'  The older work frequently fed not
only cultural relativism but moral relativism.  Today we may
say that it is not *relativism* but *relativity* which is
central.  Cultures are meaningful wholes.  The objective
behavior differences of one culture as compared with another
are not grounds for irresponsible conduct in one's own
culture.  Cultures have internal logics.  The economic
theory, the political theory, the art forms and the religious doctrine of each society are expressive of coherent
elementary presuppositions.  The amoralism of ethical relativity finds no support in the serious study of cultural
relativity.  That value to which cultures are relative from
a comparative point of view is the actualization of personality.  Knowing how personality develops in its various
cultural settings, and knowing the vast potentialities of
personality expressions, and the means of social control and
education,one sees how the future depends indeed on a genuine
personalistic axiology.

The convergence of the social sciences on the questions
of intrinsic values and objective norms is new.  But the
coherent convergence is becoming philosophical in spirit and
in method.  There is much to be gained in this new development.  Instrumental values can now increasingly be tested.
Intrinsic values and universal values are only slowly
emerging from the inductive and comparative studies of

cultures. One anthropologist goes so far as to say: "Some values appear to be as much 'given' by nature as the fact that bodies heavier then air fall. No society has ever approved suffering as a good thing in itself—as a means to an end, yes; as punishment, as a means to the ends of society, yes. We don't have to rely upon supernatural revelation to discover that sexual access achieved through violence is bad. That is as much a fact of general observation as the fact that different objects have different densities. The observation that truth and beauty are universal, transcendental human values is as much one of the givens of human life as are birth and death."[23] A generation more of cooperative study will greatly enlarge this list in all probability. Some scholars believe that the common ethical findings are already considerable.

We have indicated above some of the high values which must today be placed on the family. As Ralph Linton says, "In the Götterdämmerung which over-wise science and over-foolish statesmen are preparing for us, last man will spend his last hours searching for his wife and child."[24] Has not Ruth Nanda Anshen perhaps anticipated tomorrow's science by her philosophical observation: "When it is conceded that man believes in a universe of law, of reason, of love, only then will half truths, evasions, indirectness, self-abasement, and falsehoods be understood for what they intrinsically are; sickness of the soul derived from that miasma which poisons love and life while it clouds the spirit. Knowledge, the possibility of truth, is a *sine qua non* of every conscious act, and the primary importance of knowledge is proved by the fact that in order to criticize knowledge it must be presupposed. And a knowledge of the good is the foundation of all reality, of society, of the family, since it is the *ratio sufficiens* of existence."[25]

In conclusion we may note that there is an organized convergence of science, philosophy and religion which has been an active process in America for about ten years.   In 1940 there was convened the First Conference, of Science, Philosophy and Religion.    These conferences which are an ongoing process, are centered about the validity of democracy as a social value and on the dignity of the person.    All who participate agree to the aim of increasing appreciation for the supreme worth and moral responsibility of every individual human person.  Social scientists have freely contributed to this normative discussion along with philosophers and religionists.   This is itself one of the major demonstrations of changing presuppositions and anti-positivistic tendencies in the social sciences.    For many have come to realize that the crisis in civilization is in large part capable of being phrased in these terms:   whether we are to have a world community and a world culture in which untrammelled social science can be responsibly applied to the problems of that crisis.

## NOTES

[1]Gunnar Myrdal, *An American Dilemma* (New York:  Harper and Brothers, 1944), Vol. II, p. 1032.

[2]R. M. MacIver, *The More Perfect Union* (New York: Macmillan, 1948), pp. 173-275.

[3]*Ibid.*

[4]*Ibid.*

[5]*Ibid.*

[6]C. Kluckhohn, *Mirror for Man* (New York:  McGraw-Hill, 1949), p. 264f.

[7]MacIver, *op. cit.*, pp. 276, 279.

[8]*Ibid.*, pp. 276-278.

[9]*Ibid.*, p. 279.

[10]Ralph Linton, ed., *The Science of Man in the World Crisis* (New York:  Columbia University Press, 1945), p. 13.

[11]Kluckhohn, *op. cit.*, p. 202.

[12]C. Kluckhohn and H. A. Murray, *Personality in Nature, Society and Culture* (New York:  Alfred A. Knopf, 1949), pp. xi-xii.

[13]*Ibid.*, p. 330f.

[14]*Ibid.*, p. 415.

[15]Ruth Nanda Anshen, ed., *The Family:  Its Function and Destiny* (New York:  Harper and Brothers, 1949), pp. 426-427; cf. p. 17.

[16]Kluckhohn and Murray, *op. cit.*, p. 167.

[17]L. Bryson, L. Finkelstein and R. M. MacIver, eds., *Conflicts of Power in Modern Culture* (New York:  Harper and Brothers, 1947), p. 183.

[18]*Ibid.*, p. 185.

[19]Kluckhohn and Murray, *op. cit.*, p. 353.

[20]*Ibid.*, p. 365.

[21]Elton Mayo, *The Social Problems of an Industrial Civilization* (Harvard University Press, 1945), p. 59.

[22]W. Vaughan, *Social Psychology* (New York:  The Odyssey Press, 1948), p. 110.

[23]Kluckhohn, *Mirror for Man*, pp. 285-286.

[24]Anshen, *op. cit.*, p. 38.

[25]*Ibid.*, p. 435.

Issues in the Dialogue between Theology
and the Social Sciences
(1966)


I
Representative Instances of the Inescapable
Value Problem in the Social Sciences


In the dialogue between theology and the social sciences we may well begin with some representative instances
of the inescapable value problem in the social sciences.

How big must a city be to get on a map? Do numbers
suffice? On the morning of the horrible earthquake in
Alaska I turned to my atlas and checked the map of the
United States to get freshly oriented on the exact location
of Anchorage. After locating it I checked its size and
found that the city had a population of 44,000, with a total
metropolitan membership of about 80,000. Turning to that
portion of the map that showed my own state of Massachusetts
I found no city indicated which had so small a population.
It was quite apparent that in the science of map making
strict quantitative equivalence was not the criterion of
inclusion or exclusion. Other values are determinative, for
the purposes and significance of the data for map making are
decisive. Selection and recording of data are lockstitched
with interpretation and analysis in the social sciences, as,
indeed in all science.

The "Nuremberg Code." Beginning with the outbreak of
World War II criminal medical experiments on non-German
nationals, both prisoners of war and civilians, including
Jews and "asocial" persons, were carried out on a large

167

scale in Germany and the occupied countries. Conducted as
an integral part of the total war effort, and as a product
of coordinated policy-making and planning at high governmental, and Nazi Party levels, these experiments were not
the isolated and casual acts of individual doctors and
scientists working solely on their own responsibility. The
fact of such experiments raises ultimate ethical and theological questions focused on value considerations. They
show how scientific projects are related to dominating ideologies and faiths which may be rivals to Christianity and
Judaism and how such projects were knowingly ordered,
sanctioned, permitted, or approved.

A whole literature has developed around the value problems precipitated by the trials of war criminals before the
Nuremberg Military tribunals from October, 1946 to April,
1947. Space does not permit a listing of all the points in
the "Nuremberg Code," but its most basic point may be introduced here. Protagonists of medical experiments on human
beings note that such experiments yield results for the good
of society that are unprocurable by other methods or means
of study.

> All agree, however, that certain basic prin-
> ciples must be observed in order to satisfy
> moral, ethical and legal concepts: (1) *The
> voluntary consent of the human subject is
> absolutely essential*. This means that the
> person involved should have legal capacity to
> give consent; should be so situated as to be
> able to exercise free power of choice, without
> the intervention of any element of force, fraud,
> deceit, duress, overreaching, or other ulterior
> form of constraint or coercion; and should have
> sufficient knowledge and comprehension of the
> elements of the subject matter involved as to
> enable him to make an understanding and enlight-
> ened decision. This latter element requires
> that before the acceptance of an affirmative
> decision by the experimental subject there
> should be made known to him the nature, dura-

tion, and purpose of the experiment; the method
and means by which it is to be conducted; all
inconveniences and hazards reasonably to be
expected; and the effects upon his health or
person which may possibly come from his participation in the experiment. The duty and responsibility for ascertaining the quality of the
consent rests upon each individual who initiates, directs, or engages in the experiment. It
is a personal duty and responsibility which may
not be delegated to another with impunity.[1]

The above paragraph from which the other points in the
code follow is replete with Judaeo-Christian perspectives
and values and has implications for many forms of research
other than strictly medical ones. The interpenetration of
legal, medical, and ethical perspectives should be noted.

The doctor-patient, scientist-subject relationships. A
physician is in an "I-thou," a doctor-patient relationship.
Almost anything he does to and for a patient, however, is to
a degree an experiment. When an experiment becomes focal
the relationship may readily be transformed, however
imperceptibly into an "I-It," or scientist-subject
relationship. Such a relationship may often obtain in the
behavioral sciences. There is a general consensus among
physicians that "the confidential relations between doctor
and patient, the personal right of the patient to the life
of his body and soul in its psychic and moral integrity are
just some of the many values superior to scientific
interest."[2]

Before citing other preliminary instances we may note
other issues in passing of interest to both theology and
social science. The first is the social character of both
theological and behavioral disciplines. Basically these are
not lone scholar fields, and perhaps should be even less so
than they are. At least in the medical experiments on human
beings there is a strong conviction that such research is

too hazardous and implies too many responsibilities to be
undertaken by lone investigators.  A person is a solidaristic being both as subject and as object of study.  Advances
in medical research in America at least are due to a greater
and greater degree of collaboration.  Such collaboration has
roots in the Christian and Judaic ethos, in a sense of the
solidarity of the human family both as patient and as investigator.  Playing the role of volunteer research subject
enables some people to express symbolically certain secular
and sacred values that are highly approved in our society.
This value may at times be given heroic proportions.  It is
related to the above ethos and to the high regard for
active, rationally based mastery of life and for any sort of
achievement that blends individualism and a humanitarian
sense of social responsibility.[3]  Along with these are other
assumptions such as that methods of research must
responsibly enhance, rather than destroy, human trust.[4]

        Psychiatry in Relation to Determinism and Freedom.
Turning from the "I-It" and "I-Thou" dilemmas of medical and
behavior research to another facet of values, we may note
the relationship of determinism in the causal nexus to the
moral assumption of freedom.  The psychiatrist-patient
relationship affords an illuminating instance of this problem in science and value.  If psychiatry can accept some
degree of freedom as both operationally feasible and a value
shared by physician and patient, some apparent contradictions may be resolved.  Freedom, free-will, will power and
determinism present one of those areas in which people
behave inconsistently and where it is difficult to reconcile
professed beliefs and operative assumptions.  Because of
conflicts of value in this area between physicians and
patients grave disturbances may arise in therapeutic
relationships.

Many psychiatrists assume causal determinism in human
behavior because it seems to be the modern scientific view
(despite all popular references to Heisenberg, et al.). The
prestige of physical science in the behavioral sciences
centers here through the cause-effect concept. There is
also the humanitarian idea that the patient is sick and his
otherwise displeasing behavior is to be accepted with
equanimity as an expression of his illness. In dealing with
the patient, however, the physician cannot feasibly maintain
the completely deterministic belief about himself. Dr. John
C. Whitehorn observes as follows:

> The physician becomes deeply engrossed in the
> task of understanding the patient and of making
> a wise choice as to how to behave and how to
> speak in a manner that will help the patient.
> Various possible courses of action occur to the
> mind of the doctor and he tries to choose the
> best. Such earnest efforts to choose wisely
> between possibilities is, of course, nonsensical
> behavior if determinism is correct, for by that
> assumption different possibilities are only
> illusions....Meanwhile, out of combined humani-
> tarian and scientific motives, the doctor may be
> envisaging the patient as in a deterministic
> frame of causality....Here is the implicit equiv-
> alent of a caste distinction with a deeply
> emotional connotation, the physician behaving as
> if he possessed freedom while debasing the
> patient to the status of a mechanism....Are we
> dealing here with a necessary conflict?...One of
> the significant human values is some degree of
> faith in freedom. This is a sharable value. It
> appears to me to have considerable practical
> significance, in a psychotherapeutic partner-
> ship, to explore wide areas of experience and
> interest, in order to find and to cultivate what
> freedom of choice does exist, wherein the
> patient can *find himself*, so to speak, and have
> some genuine assurance of being a person, not
> merely a resultant....The ideal human condition,
> toward which Freudian therapy aimed, appears to
> me to have been an ideal of freedom, indeed
> almost of detachment, a state of freedom in
> which a person, through understanding, could

> hold himself free from the coercive prohibitions
> of society and free also from the coerciveness
> of blind biological impulses....[5]

Anthropology in relation to persons and cultural change. With interest in cultural wholes and the inter- actions of changes in one part of a systematic whole with other parts, anthropology has contributed concern and guid- ance to those involved in inducing social change. In 1955 the distinguished anthropologist, Margaret Mead, edited a book, *Cultural Patterns and Technical Change*, which was a manual prepared by the World Federation for Mental Health. Technical change, she noted, was not new nor is the attempt to control technological change new, but there is a new phenomenon in today's rapid social change. "What is new is the assumption, on an international scale, of responsibility for introducing changes which are needed among peoples in areas of the world which can visibly benefit from the knowl- edge which the peoples of other areas have...new also is the recognition and willingness to deal scientifically with the concomitant effects of such change."[6] In approaching these problems Professor Mead makes an assumption drawn from field-work among many kinds of societies, that "a change in any one part of the culture will be accompanied by changes in other parts, and that only by relating any planned detail of change to the *central values* of the culture is it possi- ble to provide for the repercussions which will occur in other aspects of life. This is what we mean by 'cultural relativity': that practices and beliefs can and must be evaluated in context, in relation to the cultural whole."[7]

We may pause to note the stress on central values here. Talcott Parsons, sociologist, considers religion as a phenom- enon relating, and thus in a sense integrating, three subsystems—cultural systems, personality systems, and social systems. Religion is seen as that which is rooted in

the most generalized orientations of meaning.[8]   Though
religion has this basic function of integration, theology
needs social science to come to terms with it.   Parsons
feels that theology as such is not able to provide the
functional differentiation which sociology makes possible.
Science helps theology—and here we anticipate what will be
noted more fully below—to be more sophisticated because
more precise about the way its phenomena and data function.
It helps theology be more relationally self-aware.

If theology teaches people to care because God cares,
anthropology can teach theology now to care in rapid social
change because the "systematic or patterned quality of
culture is a function of the integrated character of human
beings, who, as they incorporate cultural traits, sometimes
very diverse in origin, organize them into viable ways of
life."[9]   It is persons who must make the transition from one
cultural stage to the next.   "In all technical change, even
when it seems to be concerned with tools, machines and other
impersonal objects, the individual person is both the
recipient of change and the mediator or agent of change.
His integrity as a person, his stability as a personality,
must be kept ever in focus as the living concern of all
purposive change."[10]   All changes, therefore, should be
introduced with the fullest possible consent and participation of those whose daily lives will be affected by the
changes.   This observation would seem to be both sound as an
anthropological value and consistent with the norms of the
responsible society.   For a concise and comprehensive discussion of many related problems in which the functional perspectives of cultural anthropology are used see E. DeVries,
*Man in Rapid Social Change*.

Types of Personality theory.[11]   Psychology reflects the
urgent question, "What sort of creature is man?"   The array

of personality theories is vast and complex, but each
theory, it must be noted, is shaped by its view of science,
value, nature, reality whether acknowledged or not.

1.   *Positivistic formulations* represent the empirical,
experimental, chiefly associationist, and increasingly quantitative tradition.   A person is regarded as a reactive not
a proactive being.   Positivism is not synoptic.   Its assignment is to find small facts under controlled conditions.
Attention is given to the partial, the physical, the quasi-
mechanical, the regular, the logical, because these aspects
can be controlled.   Allport observes:   "The only real
difficulty with the positivist formulation is that it does
not know (or rarely knows) that it is a prisoner of a
specific philosophical outlook, also of a specific period of
culture, and of a narrow definition of 'science.'   Positivism seldom defends its deterministic, quasi-mechanical view
of the human person; it merely takes it for granted.   Its
metaphysics is unexamined..."[12]

2.   *Psychoanalytic* formulations present an individual
somewhat like the positivists in seeing him as a quasi-mechanical reactor, goaded by the tyrannical forces of the
environment, the id, and the superego.   One's rationality
counts for little.   Full of defenses and rationalizations,
one's search for final truth is doomed to failure.   If a
person claims to find truth in religion, this discovery is
viewed as an illusion and due to neurosis.   Thus in orthodox
psychoanalytic doctrine there is a deep pessimism.   Many
present-day followers of the tradition, while noting the
dark side of human nature, feel that the image of man dominated by unconscious id forces overweights the role of
libidinal forces in personality and so have made changes and
broadened the perspective.

3.    The *personalistic* formulations   agree   that   the

individual person as a patterned entity must serve as the
center of gravity for psychology. While they gladly assign
to natural and biological sciences the task of exploring
certain ranges of problems, they insist that the task of
psychology is to treat the whole of behavior and this task
cannot be discharged without relating all states and
processes to the person who is their originator, carrier,
and regulator. Personalists are critical of positivism and
see the human being as a creative unity, a purposive, growing individual. There are several varieties of the personalistic viewpoint.

4.    *Existentialist* formulations have some things in
common with personalistic theories. There is the conviction
that positive science alone cannot discover the nature of
man as a "being-in-the-world." Every special science is too
narrow. They tend to rule out the most appropriate tool for
research: phenomenology. "It is not enough to know how man
reacts: we must know how he feels, how he sees his world,
what time and space are to *him* (not to the physicists), why
he lives, what he fears, for what he would willingly die.
Such questions of *existence* must be put to a man directly,
and not to an outside observer."[13]    In a way phenomenology
takes the place of psychology, for the latter, it is felt,
has not oriented itself to the central themes of one's basic
anxieties: fear of death, feelings of guilt, and horror of
meaninglessness. Anxiety, dread, alienation are among the
commonest terms of existentialists. A person thus is a
creature bent on enhancing the value attributes of his
experience. There are many types of existentialism but
there is a common tendency to seek beyond the goal of
'self-actualization' for the one basic intentional theme for
which he takes responsibility. A person is held to be free
to do this——to decide.

5.   An *Eastern* formulation (Hindu).   Gordon Allport
notes a Hindu theory that man has four central desires:
pleasure, success, duty, and liberation.  Pleasure dominates
infancy.   It is supplemented by the pursuit of occupational
and social achievement in youth and the middle years.   Some
people never get beyond this, but with maturity there is a
strong orientation to duty.   Finally, there comes a desire
for understanding, for philosophical and religious meaning—a longing for liberation from the pleasure-success-duty
stages of life.   Allport notes that no major Western school
of psychology includes this whole sequence of four stages
within its view of human nature.

6.   *Interpersonal* formulations.   Why has Western
thought, Gardner Murphy asks, drawn so sharp a distinction
between personality and all else?   Is it perhaps the Judaeo-
Christian religion, enhanced by the growing role of the
individual in the industrial revolution?   Some writers want
to describe personality as interpersonal since it exists
*only* in its social interactions with other people.   Allport
stops short of this point, insisting that there is a neuro-
psychic system "within the skin" and this is the personality
system proper.   He would assign the social and cultural systems, within which the individual is located, as the special
assignment of sociology and anthropology.[14]

In relation to these formulations it is important to
note that it is on *scientific* grounds that the personality
as a system, an integer, a reality "out there" is emphasized.   Positivism is rejected not on philosophical grounds
alone but on the grounds that personality as a whole is the
valid scientific category.   This is an important scientific
given in the confrontation of theology to values in science,
for all values, it is held, are *of*, *by* and *for* persons.

The literature of interpersonal social psychology is

vast. Many techniques have been developed in sociometry, group observation, interview techniques and others which have been useful in studying the structural properties of groups, the relation of larger to member wholes, and the relation of social wholes to their participating members. Social entities have been handled experimentally in field theory, for example. In doing such social research experimenters have learned to take into consideration such factors as the personality of individual members, group structure, ideology and cultural values, economic factors, and the like. Group wholes and individual persons are realities which social science has shown cannot be reduced to each other. The term person is concrete and communitarian. As I have persistently contended, a person is a socius with a private center.

Economics as a behavioral science. Ends and values are pervasive themes in the science of economics. The technical aspects like statistics, quantitative measurement, and mechanical arrangements are often the least interesting parts of economics from the serious economists's point of view. Although economic values are relatively more instrumental than those studied in other social sciences, basic problems of economic decisions arise from the main functions of an economic system. These functions may be conveniently divided into five categories: (1) The first function is that of fixing standards. Whose wants and which wants are to be satisfied and in what degree? (2) The second function is that of organizing production. This has to do with the *allocation* of available productive forces and materials and the effective co-ordination of the various means of production into such groupings as will produce the greatest results. Technological as well as economic questions enter here. Both types of issues depend on the social goals of

the nation and the economic community taken as a whole.  (3)
The third function is *distribution*.   There is a close connection between distribution and the control of production.
Whom shall the economy serve?  Where traditions of "private
property," "free competition," and "contract" prevail, the
emphasis is different from what it is where the dominant
value is sharing production as widely as possible.  (4)  The
forth function is economic maintenance and progress.   This
raises the questions of how much development a society can
afford or cares to have and at the cost of sacrificing what
values and what forms development should take.    (5)   The
fifth function of an economy is to adjust consumption to
production within very short periods of time.  Production
cannot always be adjusted quickly to meet consumption needs
or demands.  Thus, for example, the crop of a given year or
season has to last until the next crop is produced except as
this factor is modified by the world's trade situation.
These functions involve decisions affecting the lives of
many persons and their interrelationships.

     Economics as a science always points toward decision-
making either implicitly or explicitly.   Political and
economic science are therefore interrelated, though the
focus and many of the processes are very different in the
two fields.  Property theory and political theory go hand in
hand.  Consequently Christian presuppositions and criticisms
of the political order must be coordinate and coherent with
Christian criticism and assumptions regarding economic
values and processes.   Questions of freedom, property,
contracts, labor policies, automation, wage-levels, welfare
provisions, etc. are intimately related to one's doctrines
of persona and community, of the individual and of solidarity, of mutual obligation, and of the chief end of human
life.  All basic economic theories bristle with assumptions

about the nature of persons and the social good. In a world of contrasts between poverty and affluence economics cannot avoid ethics. In a world where most poverty can be eliminated, economists have a task which presents hard problems of values to them.

Value judgments in the study of race relations. We may bring this section of our survey to a close by citing some of the kinds of value problems a social scientist confronts when dealing with the field of race relations. The reader will readily note that analagous issues arise in all the behavioral sciences and hence these may serve as a paradigm of the whole.

When Gunnar Myrdal wrote *An American Dilemma*, he spelled out some of the methodological problems in dealing with facts and valuations. "The social scientist is part of the culture in which he lives and he never succeeds in freeing himself entirely from dependence on the dominant preconceptions and biases of his environment."[15] Thus one would expect in a dominant white group that even the scientific biases would run against Negroes most of the time. This, Myrdal found, actually turned out to be the case. Such biases he found in terms of (a) the objects chosen for research, (b) the selection of relevant data, (c) the recording of observations, (d) the theoretical and practical inferences drawn, and (e) the manner of presentation of results. Myrdal proposed ways to detect biases but these fall outside the scope of this paper.

Biases (and therefore value problems) are found not only at the various stages of scientific operation but may be classified in groups, each of which may be noted as a continuum along which specific biases fall. For example, Mydral devised a scale of "friendliness" to the Negro along which one could note the presence or absence of reform-inter-

est, a demand for "fair play," consideration for the
"underdog," and the Negro scientists' leaning over backwards
regarding their own race in an effort to be scientific. He
*also* proposed a scale of "friendliness" to the South,
friendliness to the South carrying with it unfavorable views
towards Negroes. On the other hand a sympathetic attitude
toward the Negro might be taken as a criticism of the social
and moral order of the South. The literature reflects such
a continuum. A *third* continuum is a scale of radicalism-
conservatism. The location of a scientist on this scale has
strong bearing upon both the selection of research problems
and the conclusions drawn from the research. *"In a sense,"*
writes Myrdal, *"it is the master scale of biases in the
social sciences.* It can be broken up into several scales,
mutually closely integrated: equalitarian-aristocratism,
environmentalism-biological determinism, reformism-laissez-
faire, and so forth. There is a high degree of correlation
between a person's degree of liberalism in different social
problems."[16] After discussing this issue in some detail he
adds: "The prevalent opinion that a 'middle-of-the-road'
attitude always gives the best assurance of objectivity
is ...entirely unfounded." A *fourth* continuum is the scale
of optimism-pessimism. Many social scientists are under the
influence of any man or public "not to want to be disturbed
by deeply discouraging statements about the social situation
and impending trends or by demands for fundamental changes
or policy." Technical phrases are coined which reflect an
understatement of the situation or an overstatement. The
common need for a prospective 'happy ending' in race
relations leads to a minimization or suppression of
discouraging facts. Here, to borrow some terms from Robert
Merton we may note the ways *manifest, latent,* and
*dysfunctional* functions are approached or emphasized. The

pessimistic bias may appear, for example, in the accent on factors that are *latent* and *dysfunctional*. On the other hand, unfortunate facts are usually more difficult to observe and ascertain, as so many of the persons in control have strong interests in hiding them.[17] A *fifth* scale would be on an isolation-integration continuum. When the race problem is studied in an isolated or fragmented manner as a Negro problem, bias tends to be greatest. When the maximum integration of this problem in the total complex of problems in American civilization is the frame of reference, there is least bias. "Objectivity is reached the more completely an investigator is able to interrelate the Negro problem with the total economic, social, political, judicial and broadly cultural life of the nation." Synoptic method is one of the highest functions of the life of reason. Finally, Myrdal proposed a scale of scientific integrity. There are variations in the social scientist's willingness to study unpopular subjects and to state plainly and clearly unpopular conclusions derived from his studies. Political inclinations, personal integrity, and relative freedom accorded him by society are relevant factors in this situation.

The methodological observations noted above invite an extended and analytical methodology in order to mitigate the factors of bias in the study of race relations. This cannot be reported or undertaken here. But it must be noted that the end-product of such a quest for objectivity is only a further acknowledgment that the interrelations of fact-value-interpretation continue in all the behavioral sciences. This cursory survey of representative instances and aspects of inescapable value problems in the social sciences by no means exhausts the list of kinds of problems which are encountered. These instances disclose, nevertheless, some

deep lying issues in the contemporary scene. We now turn to
theological perspectives on such valuational problems and
note, what some will treat as obvious, that theology as a
pure discipline has its limitations. In transcending social
science valuations by an appeal to revelation and ultimate
perspectives, theology is less of an independent variable in
the processes of knowing and judging than is often assumed.
The interpenetration of theology and the modern scientific
"mind" becomes evident particularly in the interpretive
dimension of theological theory.

## II
## Theological Perspectives and their
## Limitations as Pure Theology

As theology confronts issues of values and valuations
in the social sciences it does so properly from its own
perspective. Theology operates from a different level or in
a different dimension from that of science. While science
works with the tools of *discovery*, it is said, theology
works from the perspective of *disclosure*. This disjunction
may prove to be useful up to a point, but it may also be
less tenable than commonly supposed. Disclosure and discovery as cognitive problems have a wider bearing than the
central issues raised by values in the social sciences, but
a brief confrontation of the general epistemological and
metaphysical issues may clarify the subsequent discussion of
relationships.

Taken in the large, science is a term for a certain
kind of method of using reason in relation to experience.
As the first section of this essay shows there are, as a
matter of fact, many specific methods in science, and there
is not complete agreement about the appropriateness and
validity of some of them, particularly in the behavioral

sciences. The various theories of personality, noted above, are cases in point. Each of the methods in the various sciences together with its presuppositions, postulates, and interpretations is only relatively autonomous. Thus general scientific method includes a plurality of methods. The situation is methodologically not as pluralistic in theology, though the confusion and ferment in contemporary theology gives much evidence of *unresolved pluralism* there. In theology the major dogmas are deeply implicated in each other. The *kerygma*, or Gospel, implicates and involves a greater whole of thought. In theology one must think all major doctrines through each other, for they involve God-world-man-Christ-Spirit-redemption etc. reciprocally and in dialectical polarities.

By viewing human experience as a whole, theology acknowledges that personal spiritual life is a unity. The elements of spirit do not just lie side by side. There are, conceptually conceived, distinct elements in man's spirit. Yet, as Paul Tillich rightly observes, "all spiritual elements in man are within each other."[18] Thus, for example, faith and reason properly understood do not structurally conflict with each other. They "lie within each other." If reason is used in the sense of scientific method, logical strictness, and technical calculation, it "provides tools for recognizing and controlling reality, and faith gives the direction in which this control may be recognized."[19] At a certain level, or in its own dimension, this analysis by Tillich is useful and we shall follow it a bit further since it is a widely respected view. If reason is used to mean the source of meaning, of structure, of norms and principles, as it has meant in Western Culture, it indicates what is distinctively the humanity of man in contrast to all other beings. And it is important that this

designation not be lost in the midst of merely analytical,
intellectualistic, formalistic, and rationalizing emphases
concerning reason in contemporary society.  Properly understood it is reason that makes a centered personal life and
participation in community possible.   Faith could not
possibly be a principle opposed to this, for then, as both
Tillich and the personalists have insisted, faith would rob
persons of their humanity.  Faith which destroys reason or
regard for reason dehumanizes them.  As Albert C. Knudson
has said, a theological faith based on radical scepticism
will perish thereby.  "Reason is the precondition of faith;
faith is the act in which reason reaches ecstatically beyond
itself....Man is finite, man's reason lives in preliminary
concerns; but man is also aware of his potential infinite,
and this awareness appears as his ultimate concern, as
faith."[20]

When one considers the relation of reason and faith in
the dimensions and at the level noted above, there is no
conflict, and this includes the cognitive function of the
mind.  The preliminary work of science in describing and
explaining the structures and relations of the universe—to
the extent that these can be tested experimentally and
quantitatively calculated—is always limited and incomplete.
Gaps in scientific knowledge cannot, however, be filled by
chunks of ultimate faith, for they do not belong to the same
level or dimension of meaning.  "Science has no right and no
power to interfere with faith (as ultimate concern) and
faith has no power to interfere with science.  One dimension
of meaning is not able to interfere with another
dimension."[21]  When seeming conflicts occur, they do so
because science illicitly posits a particular faith or
because theology illicitly affirms a faith as science.  In
such a situation, as in the struggle of the theory of

evolution and certain theological proposals, "science" affirmed a faith which denigrated human dignity and "faith" was distorted by Biblical literalism.

Sometimes the kind of confusion which once reigned between a philosophical scientism in biology and some literalist theology is re-enacted between psychology and theology. To this conflict Tillich's observations are particularly relevant:

> Modern psychology is afraid of the concept of soul because it seems to establish a reality which is unapproachable by scientific methods and may interfere with their results. This fear is not unfounded; psychology should not accept any concept which is not produced by its own scientific work....This is true of the modern concepts of ego, superego, self, personality, unconsciousness, mind, as well as of the traditional concepts of soul, spirit, will, etc. Methodological psychology is subject to scientific verification, as is every other scientific endeavor. All its concepts and definitions, even those most validated, are preliminary.

> When faith speaks of the ultimate dimension in which man lives, and in which he can win or lose his soul, or of the ultimate meaning of his existence, it is not interfering at all with the scientific rejection of the concept of the soul. A psychology without soul cannot deny this, nor can a psychology with soul confirm it. The truth of man's eternal meaning lies in a dimension other than the truth of adequate psychological concepts....There is no reason to deny to a scholar who deals with man and his predicament the right to introduce elements of faith...[22]

But the faith is a faith and not science, and is subject to criteria of truth appropriate to that level or dimension of theology.

The resolution of the relations between theology and the behavioral sciences, particularly as they relate to values, may be impeccably true and yet too simple on the

above basis.   The purity of the two disciplines, taken
respectively, may be maintained but what of their relevance
and mutual involvement?   Does pure faith (theology) provide
the only way out?   Cannot science correct its biases without
resort to theology?   Is there not perhaps a scientific
methodological corrective to value involvements in the
behavioral sciences?   Can we become content with saying that
"revelation has to do with the mystery of *disclosure*, while
science deals with the mystery which is associated with
*discovery*?"[23]   When theologians speak of the "I-Thou"
relation, do they have a monopoly on it?   Do not the
behavioral sciences show some of the ways to deal with this
relationship, as the personality theories cited above
indicate?   Can the Christian doctrine (doctrines) of man be
translated into operational terms, scientifically and clinically speaking?   Since theological statements are freighted
with value assertions, are they exempt from scientific
review?   Or, are many theological propositions too indiscrim-
inate and universal to be translatable into discriminate
operational or functional terms, such as, "man is a sinner,"
"man is a child of God," "all men are brothers?"   Can
theology effectively remain "pure" in the sense of eschewing
all natural theology in its encounter with valuation in the
social sciences?

        One approach to those questions is the mood that the
unity of knowledge is at best an ideal and at no moment in
history can be made a reality, thus retreating into the
uniqueness of the disciplines.[24]   Another is to adopt a kind
of existential posture.   But when this is done, theologians
sometimes forget that to equate existentialism with theology
is highly questionable.   Theology is in that case not "pure"
Biblical revelation and may, moreover, not be any sounder
than the existentialist philosophy that is imported into it.

The thrust of some existentialism has been against
positivism in science and a protest against making person an
object, an "it." Such protests have come from many fronts,
as with Marx in economics (with his doctrines of value and
alienation) and from many democratic and personalistic
philosophers and even from anthropologists on scientific
methodological grounds. Some theologians have seen the
emergence of existentialism in theology as a recovery of
human beings more congenial to classical theology than the
notion of them as the embodiment of value or as moral
personality, claiming that the latter makes of them only an
idea or ideal object. But theology has no twentieth century
monopoly on man as a real person, a real subject. It would
be arbitrary to say that the choice is between science and
existentialism as theology.

The values and dilemmas of existentialism must both be
faced in terms of the social sciences. Dillenberger properly points out that in Heidegger, Kierkegaard, and
Nietzsche science stands for unauthentic existence. "Science is a matter of indifference, of concern with selected
objects or items, whether of nature of history. It conceals
man in his totality, in his mystery, by a concern with the
multiplication of knowledge essentially indifferent to
himself as an existing subject. Although thrown into being,
man is a mysterious being whose wholeness must be affirmed.
Such affirmation constitutes history, not nature....His
being or his freedom is affirmed as he 'stands out' from any
objective thing which is 'over against' him."[25] In such a
statement theology expresses a thoroughly historical and
personalistic concern for man and protests against any program in social science or society which dehumanizes him.
Yet, the sources of the existentialism which some theology
seems to adopt may be less Biblical disclosure than an

accommodation to some strains in European culture, for
example in Heidegger. Theological existentialism stresses
the human creature as sinner, of course, and notes that
apart from sin he is not on the level of humanity; and in
opposition to some forms of existentialism and naturalism
insists that "the refusal to accept sin constitutes that sin
which is the loss of self, the loss of the risk to be and
therefore of being at all."[26] Yet sin is a category that
falls outside of the social sciences (though some find it
useful in psychotherapy) and, being so universal in its
relevance, tends not to be operationally or functionally
relevant at all. But discriminate judgments are necessary
both in social science and in ethics.

It is in the area of ethics that the problems are often
most clearly seen. The tendency in much theology is to
reject all Biblical legalism in favor of a *kerygma* with
minimal cultural content and maximum insistence on
*disclosure by* and *about* Jesus Christ, preferably about him
as an act of faith. Absolute insistence on authority of
revelation is sometimes linked with maximum relativity in
concrete ethical judgments. When principles are rejected,
the basis of discriminate judgment is highly relative, even
relativistic. What is often left ambiguous is the relationship between the general situation of man's sin and the idea
that there are no common moral answers because there are no
common moral questions and no common verifiable theory of
human nature.

A point to note here is that there are both social
scientists and theologians whose relativism rests in an
ultimate indeterminism. Such relativism sees descriptive
variety, uniqueness in value situations, conflicts of
values, and subjectivity as all in some sense ultimate,
irreducible, and irreconcilable. It affirms or assumes that

there is no pattern or generalization of which the varied or
the unique are but different expressions. Hence the
conflicts can never be resolved and the individual's
isolation can never be resolved. Indeterminacy, Edel
claims, is the heart of the relativism position.[27] A
radical irrationalist type of existentialism whether
Christian or non-theological would seem to leave
indeterminacy in social science dangling in ultimate
scepticism. Dread, anguish, and loneliness would then be
unresolved.

Theological relativism often seeks to overcome the
indeterminacy through an appeal to revelation. But revelation alone only postpones the problem, for it is then only
transferred to the diversity of God's interpreters. The
indeterminacy here roots in the fact, not simply of actual
disagreement, but in there being no mode of decision by
which, in principle at least, the issues can be settled.[28]
Much of the crisis in contemporary hermeneutics is traceable to the irrationalism and subjectivism that underlie
certain of the theories.

The behavioral sciences do not, however, necessarily
imply the indeterminacy and relativism suggested above.
Theology and science can meet each other half way at least
in ethics through what is scientifically known about people.
Edel is probably correct in stating that ethical absolutism
and ethical relativism in their extreme forms have tried
short-cuts to avoid the necessity of empirical investigation
and because they have enshrined as common sense assumptions
the results of earlier chapters of the history of science.[29]
The preliminary and provisional character of the work of
science, on the one hand, and of *all* hermeneutics, on the
other, does not necessarily imply indeterminate relativism.
When, for example, guilt-feelings are appealed to in the

area of ethics, it is well to explore one's assumptions
about human nature, the origin and development of guilt-
feelings in interpersonal processes, and the like.   There
are many tools in the behavioral sciences for dealing with
problems that involve psychological and social reality.

Rationality in science and in theology meet in the
appeal to the person as a whole.   Reason has, when properly
approached, the authority of the whole in ethics where so
many valuation issues deriving from these fields meet.   Edel
notes that

> from today's psychological perspective it is
> established theory that there is a *system of*
> *forces* in the internal economy of the biolog-
> ical individual, even where consciousness shows
> the extreme of a split personality.   In that
> sense it is a lesson of science that rationality
> involves the whole person.   This serves to incor-
> porate at least the whole-person perspective in
> ethical judgment.   The history of the moral
> mandate of unity and system is itself one of the
> most striking cases of the tremendous scope of
> scientific knowledge that is really required to
> justify what on the face of it looks like an
> obvious injunction of reason.[30]

Any theory of ethics, theology, or psychotherapy—and all
existential decision-making—must assume that man (as person
and subject) has a degree of mastery over himself and some
possible insight into himself and his goals.   But if this
degree of rationality is granted, then persons also have
some control in thought about relating means to ends and in
reflecting about alternate ends.   In principle, then,
science can offer a great deal.   Stated ideally the contributions would include at least these:

> It is elementary that a person's whims are to be
> distinguished from his stable and enduring
> goals, and that a rational man who is to be
> regarded as master of himself must have some in-
> sight into himself and his aims.   But once this

> door is opened, the passageway leads on and on.
> Ideally, full advice to the person who asked for
> a cost estimate of the envisaged goals would
> include their scope and function in his life,
> their mode of development, intensity points,
> termination points, possible transformations,
> relation to common ends, possible interaction
> with others and their mutual alteration, and so
> forth—in short all the lessons that a psycho-
> logical, social and historical perspective could
> offer in application to the particular case.[31]

Theology has a tendency to absorb behavioral science theory into itself. This has been notable in the influence of psycho-analytic theory on interpretations of the doctrines of sin and guilt. So, too, the unconscious is often interpreted as evil. On the other hand, the unconscious has also been interpreted as benevolent and akin to what is known as the Holy Spirit.[32] O. Horbart Mowrer proposes that psychologists "have seriously erred in interpreting guilt, clinically, as mere guilt *feeling* rather than as a reality-based state stemming from palpable, incontestable misconduct." He supports the view that schizophrenia is typically a condition in which a person is driven by a sort of progressive terror lest one's sins find him out. But Mowrer is dissatisfied with the view that confession suffices. It may bring transitory relief without, however, effecting a permanent cure. It must, in many instances, be accompanied by some form of atonement or expiation. Mowrer stands with Dietrich Bonhoeffer against the doctrine of "cheap grace" and protests pastoral counseling that has been "taken-in" by secular psychotherapy. He says:

> If one takes the neurotic's guilt seriously,
> that is, if (as now seems likely) 'neurosis' is
> just a medical euphemism for a 'state of sin'
> and social alienation, therapy must obviously go
> beyond mere 'counseling,' to self-disclosure,
> not just to a therapist or counselor, but to the
> 'significant others' in one's life, and *then* on

to active redemption in the sense of the
patient's making every effort within his power
to undo the evil for which he has previously
been responsible.[33]

On Mowrer's view psychopathology, instead of stemming from
unexpressed sex and hostility, comes rather from an outraged
conscience and violated sense of human decency and responsibility. It should be noted for those who are not acquainted
with Mowrer's thought that the presuppositions of his social
psychology are thoroughly naturalistic. "What the scientist
looks for in the realm of religion, if he looks for anything, is a set of principles and concepts which are
universally and eternally applicable and operative."[34]

The quest of behavioral scientists like Mowrer is to
know more about how the universe is constructed and operated
in the psychological and moral realm so that people can
conduct their lives more intelligently and meaningfully.
This approach means to assume that there are principles
which are universal, consistent, and knowable in the domains
of human personality and the social processes which transcend persons. "We can know others and be ourselves, in the
ultimate sense, only in terms of these principles."[35]

A Christian theological view of the relation of
theology and the social sciences must recognize (a) that
persons have a social setting, (b) that this social setting
is historical, (c) that both society and history are lock-
stitched into nature through the human bio-physical constitution, (d) that personality must be approached in terms of
depth, decision, and rational wholeness, (e) that personhood involves self-transcending freedom, and (f) that ultimate "I-thou" relationship mean facing God as creator and
redeemer in direct personal relations as well as through
society, history, and nature.

The historical perspective and dimension are essential

in effecting an adequate conceptual frame of reference for
the problems under review.    The category of history is
complex.  History is not to be absorbed into nature as understood by the physical sciences.    Its significance for
theology must be appropriated by the venture of faith.
History is unique and unrepeatable, though its effects and
many of its characteristics can be described from a sociological, or anthropological perspective.

Most theology today emphasizes that revelation is
basically not propositional, a direct disclosure of truths,
but is an opening of mind and heart in faith that invites,
through enlarged and sensitive awareness, God's self-disclosure, especially through events and acts in history.[36]
Through its emphasis on history and tradition, on revelation
and incarnation, Christian historical understanding enters
into theology's approach to values in the behavioral sciences.    These problems can be signified by such phrases as
"the quest of the historical Jesus," and "the new quest of
the historical Jesus."  The historian's method involves (1)
the establishment of facts and (2) interpretation of the
facts, it being recognized that often these two aspects of
the work cannot be  separated or even distinguished.[37]
"Interpretation," writes Professor Mead,

> is an assertion about some aspect of the past
> stated in terminology meaningful to the histo-
> rian's contemporary audience....An interpreta-
> tion is a translation of a past ideology into
> contemporary ideology....Whatever in the past
> cannot thus be translated into contemporary
> ideology can be no part of contemporary histori-
> cal knowledge.  Hence the historian at difficult
> points is always tempted literally to *create* a
> past....Interpretation of course takes place in
> a modern mind, characterized by presuppositions
> and ideology largely absorbed from the dynamic
> community in which that mind has been nur-
> tured....Thus the historian's value system di-
> rectly conditions his historiography.

Theology compels the thinker to take history seriously; yet the work of interpretation reflects a Zeitgeist, or schools of thought, such as existentialism of various kinds, or scientism, or the mood and value presuppositions of the behavioral sciences which need to be evaluated by theology. There is a circle here. Theology in interpreting its own ultimate "facts" may be reflecting critically or uncritically the "Sitz im Leben" of the theological interpreter. Jesus Christ may thus be viewed as a bare historical "that" and the interpretation of "what" he is and means may be determined by contemporary ideology, phenomenology, and/or philosophy. Professor Mead's view does not face this dilemma in much current hermeneutics. His view is that the Christian historian does not differ from the non-Christian historians in having an allegiance a faith. His conflict with them is more likely to be a conflict of allegiances—of faiths. "This means that the basic differences between historians—or between schools of historians—are theological and/or philosophical and cannot be resolved by historical methods. This suggests at least that theology is 'the Queen of the sciences,' the final arbiter between the claims of the several disciplines and between the schools within disciplines."[38] But if theology is to rule as a real queen she must be certain that the central event of history is the career of Jesus Christ and that God who acted in that event acts continuously in history in a way which is coherent with that event—and consequently there are limits to the ways in which the "modern mind" is logically free, as Christian, to interpret Jesus Christ.

In the dialogue of theology and the social sciences theology has insisted on reclaiming its autonomy and integrity in the modern world. But, as the above discussion indicates, theological interpretation is itself inevitably in danger of reflecting ultimate perspectives which are alien to the historical givenness of Jesus Christ. In opposing culture-religions of various kinds Christian theology may itself be captured by a more subtle culture religion. An ultimate impersonalism, for example, may lurk in an ontology of interpretation and thus subtly deprive faith of the God and Father of its Lord Jesus Christ. Such an ultimate impersonalism may thus become, despite Christian language, a substitute for the real ultimate concern of the Christian faith.

From a theological perspective the social sciences are part of theological activity, for they are engagements of the creature with aspects of God's creation, with humanity in all its personal, interpersonal, and group dimensions. Theology and social science are not on the same level, but theology insists that God is *over* the whole world and over the *whole* world. The problems are logical, epistemological, and axiological. And since purpose is the basic social category, theology must raise the question of one's final end and with this ask questions about the completed ends envisaged or hoped for in all historical purposes. Here again theology is "queen of the sciences" since she affirms God's rulership *over* the *whole* world and considers the *human individual's* and history's *final end*. Theology also recognizes that there is in men not only scientific activity but also a "scientific outlook" and notes that for the nonreligious person the "scientific outlook" has a somewhat different frame of reference from what it has for the theologian, even though and because they both are required to be technically competent in their respective dimensions and levels of work.

In this connection it is relevant to recognize that there are different theologies and that they present differ-

ent postures with respect to culture and cultural wholes, as
H. Richard Niebuhr showed in the typologies of *Christ and
Culture*. These various positions determine the kinds of
"road maps" or "frames of reference" which may guide scientific work as a technical process. They affect the selection of problems, the relevance of data, the significance of
social process and historical events, the interpretation of
the findings, and the way they should be communicated today.
Theological beliefs and attitudes function differently in
various contexts and interact with the work of the social
scientists in ways partly dependent on the latter's perception of how Christian groups understand themselves.

This last comment introduces the problem of theological
self-understanding and interpretation arising from the
various types of Christian churches, sects, and groups. To
use language in such a sociological way reflects the problem
of value in a striking manner. Sociology of religion helps
theology and the Christian churches (however they may be
typed for functional sociological purposes) to a greater
self-awareness of themselves as social institutions and historical entities. The theoretical and the case studies by
the Study Commission on Institutionalism of the Commission
on Faith and Order spelled out many of these issues. They
showed the need to go beyond the earlier typologies of
"church-type" and "sect-type" developed by the methods of
Max Weber and Ernst Troeltsch and showed further how fruitful the combined approaches of theology and a functional
sociology of religion can be. At one level theology is a
queenly discipline, autonomous and sovereign; but at another
level sociology of religion shows how theology is a function
of an institution conditioned by many variables and influenced by a host of often unacknowledged social factors.
Under certain circumstances social science can help theology

be more "objective" in approaching values in society than
she would otherwise be.

Theology may be a reactionary queen. As integrators of
society religious values are conservative. The influence of
conservative theology on the life of the mind is not a thril-
ling story of freedom. Does, then, loyalty to theology give
to the scientific work which it may inspire a conservative
bias? There are many sociologists who think that this is
predominately the case. Is it necessary that it be so? No!
But where the prophet is without honor the outcome for
values in science is likely to be accommodative.

### III
### Ideology, Sociology, and Theology

The social sciences and theology as developed in any
particular historical era tend to reflect the ideologies of
the day. In a world of rival and competing ideologies axiological issues influence both scientists and theologians.
Christian faith and ethics do not comprise an ideology; yet
one of the tendencies of culture is to reduce religion to an
ideology. When Christianity is used to serve the interests
of some social group and thus is robbed of its transcendent
majesty of revelation and comprehensive reason, or when it
is presented as if the Kingdom of God could be identified
with any particular economic, political, or ecclesiastical
order, Christianity is reduced to ideological levels. At
times one is led to think that Christianity is a right-wing
ideology of anti-communism or contrariwise, a particular
kind of peace front.

Karl Marx and Karl Mannheim have done much in developing the category of ideology. Marx recognized and insisted
that in historical and political matters there could be no
"pure theory." Behind every social theory there lie collec-

tive points of view; the interests of a class are involved.
Political theories reflect social situations and limited-in-
terest goals.     The plausibility of finding ideology is
readily discernible in the thought of an opponent; it is not
so easily noted in one's own thinking.    Marx thought of
ideology as a taint, but with the more careful study by
Mannheim and his successors a less sinister meaning is given
to it.  Mannheim's work has had wide influence.

     Karl Mannheim defined ideologies as "more or less con-
scious disguises of the nature of the situation."[39]   This
particular conception of ideology implies that we are
skeptical of the ideas and representations advanced by an
opponent, and even more that, if our opponent or the agent
using an ideology did recognize the truth, it would not be
in accord with his or her interests.   There is another sense
in which Mannheim used ideology in a total conception, i.e.
when "we are concerned with the characteristics and composition of the total structure of the mind of this epoch or
this group."[40]  In either case "the ideas expressed by the
subject are...regarded as functions of his existence.   This
means that opinions, statements, propositions, and systems
of ideas are not taken at their face value but are interpreted in the light of the life situation of the one who
expresses them."  Today ideologies are part of the cold-war,
of racial and national conflict, of the struggles of the
developing nations.  They belong to the arsenal of offensive
and defensive weapons.

     In Europe the period of great change from the 17th to
the 19th century has been called the "age of ideology," in
that it saw an extraordinary outpouring of theories about
the nature of human beings in relation to the present and
future state of society.  Today in the period of world-wide
rapid   social   change——the   revolutionary   shift   from

colonialism to modern nationhood—we have another ideological surge. Despite great differences regarding the
appropriate methods for reaching their goals, the leaders of
many of these nations are united by a group of beliefs that
express common feelings about the past, present, and future.
Paul E. Sigmund, Jr. has pointed out that these beliefs are
ideologies in that they "elicit an emotional commitment by
the leadership and their followers and are directed toward
action—the development of a new society in a certain
direction, in conformity with certain goals."[41]

Sigmund notes that these ideologies cluster around the
goals of modernizing nationalism: "national independence;
rapid economic development; the creation of a nation-state
governed by a regime based on a populist identification of
leader, party, and people; regional federation; and non-
alignment in international affairs."[42] It is instructive
that in many of these countries there is no mention in their
ideologies of liberal pluralistic democracy in the Western
sense. Significantly these are the values which many social
scientists take for granted in the West. This divergence
does not mean that these countries are all deeply infil-
trated by communist ideologies. Quite the contrary. It may
mean that the single party, democratic centralism, and
emphasis on elites should be understood from a deeper dynamic perspective than is customarily done. Ideology has a
function. It draws on various traditions to carry the people through "the period of modernization of traditional
society and to justify the ensuing sacrifices and disloca-
tions."[43] The need to get its own sense of identity is
frequently expressed in the disinterest of a developing
country in becoming involved in the ideological interests of
the great powers.

Theological self-awareness made perceptive by the

critical methods of the sociology of knowledge should assist
Christian social ethics in understanding such dynamic processes.   These combined disciplines should also help scholars understand how the religious beliefs and systems of the
developing nations would inevitably get involved in these
national ideologies.   Religion (including theology) is so
basically entwined in the integrating myth-structures of
peoples that we should expect contemporary thinkers to unite
social criticism with the criticism of religion and to unite
theological criticism with the criticism of social systems
whose myth structures rival the Christian faith at any or
all levels of expression.

From these points it follows that Christian social
ethics is itself not an ideology because it recognizes the
provisional character of all historical embodiments of great
ideas and purposes.   Even when the heritage of values acknowledges the great norms of traditional Christian ethics,
the political, economic, and educational embodiments of
these norms are all provisional.   Hence the Christian social
ethic is able to interact with and respond to the ideologies
of the time.   It may do this through an enlightened church
which has an ecumenical mission of evangelism; through a
community of faith which is in but also transcends nations
and cultures; through a decision not to exploit the new
powers released in the revolutions but rather to serve; and
through the training of persons who make decisions in specific localities and institutions, but who as servants of
Christ humbly seek to transcend ideological perspectives.

When we examine closely the theoretical issues involved
in the sociology of knowledge as developed by Mannheim we
find a number of factors which theology should note.   Do
"facts" and "values" have a common ontological source, or do
they arise out of the unitary life process in which the

individual evolves a knowledge of the world, i.e. life in a
community of persons with a complex of values?  Cognitive
and valuational processes are completely entwined and valuation ultimately offers a basis of interpretation.   Since
facts and values are both integral aspects of knowing, the
problem of validity in one area is reciprocally affected by
the validity of the other.   Mannheim observes:   "The
position of the observer influences the results of thought."
Some sociologists would add that *position means role* and
*role* means one's *status* in action.

The relativity involved in the relationships of "facts"
and "values" does not entitle one to either moral skepticism
or epistemological skepticism.  What sociology of knowledge
should provide is a refinement in our understanding of human
perception and an illumination of the qualifying conditions
of that perception.  Despite Mannheim's constant emphasis
upon the *social* conditioning of cognitive and valuational
processes, there is throughout his work a pervasive emphasis
upon uniqueness, individuality, spontaneity, and self-deter-
mining conscience, and a genuine affirmation of the ultimacy
of the *person*.

Warren Rempel has shown that Mannheim never fully and
formally came to terms *at the theoretical level* with the
*normative* aspects   of   the   science of   human   behavior.[44]
Mannheim's work shows the potential role of philosophy and
theology because of the necessity of integrating, through
interdisciplinary study, both the sociological and the normative, or ethical, dimensions of the study of man, as complementary disciplines.  Social science cannot finally disavow
or eliminate metaphysical issues.  If, as in Mannheim, they
are pushed into the background, this only confirms the
notion that social scientists must at some point become self-
conscious in regard to the metaphysical and axiological

assumptions which they hold and which pervade and guide
their thoughts.


                                  IV
              Theology's Use of the Social Sciences


     Many theologians today express the Church's involvement
in the secular order and a concern for responsible social
change.   There is actually a great deal of work going on in
the field of sociology of religion which draws on the assumptions and methods of both theology and social science.
There is also no lack in the volume of theology which
stresses in general the incarnation, history, and the like
as imperatives and motives in social action.     There is,
finally, through existentialism and various types of Christian ethics an emphasis on decision in social situations.
In all these ways theologians are led to make empirical
claims and to relate values to social science.
     Because of these factors some social scientists like D.
L. Munby lift up "the importance of technical competence."[45]
He legitimately expresses concern when he notes that theologians often do not employ empirical analysis precisely; or
when they make a too simple distinction between means and
ends, allocating means to science and ends to theology and,
in addition, overlooking their complex interpenetration; or
when they are poorly informed in economics and in their
ignorance are unaware of its limitations; or when they
indulge in false searches for 'Christian' answers, giving a
misplaced Christian concreteness to certain schemes and programs; and when they lack relevant expertise.   To emphasize
this latter point he says:   "It is exceedingly rare that one
can find sound theological insight unadulterated with economic nonsense."[46]   The two foundations of effective Christian
social analysis and action, Munby summarizes as the

theological/metasociological assertions about the nature of
man and the willingness to accept wholeheartedly the facts
as they are found to be. There are not shortcuts to responsibility. Whenever a theologian says anything that has
empirical relevance his proposals are logically subject to
empirical verification.

In understanding critically theology's use of the
social sciences, the intellectual processes of moving from
theology to science must be distinguished clearly from those
of going from science to theology. Although the earlier
portions of this paper warned against a too easy disjunction
between *disclosure* and *discovery*, the methodological steps
from disclosure to discovery are different from those
involved in going from discovery to disclosure. Some
thinkers wish to set up a continuum between theology and
science. The unity of selfhood, the unity of God, and the
unity of truth support the idea of an ultimate unity between
faith as response to disclosure and knowledge as verified
discovery. Yet no easy schemas of continuity should blur
the autonomy, the different methods, the contrasting modes
of verification, and the distinct functions of science and
theology. This is one side of the problem. The other side
is that empirical inquiry is able to clarify the operational
meaning of theological concepts and claims. Theology needs
to develop functional definitions of religion and the way in
which religious believing and behaving take place in different settings and cultures. The behavioral sciences have
*discovered* many things about persons and human nature which
Biblical revelation did not *disclose* and these findings are
often important for personal and intergroup relationships.
Theology, like science, should be open to some kind of truth
test if it is to make truth claim. As Frederick Ferre says:
"Any proposition responsibly asserted or assented to must

offer some means of 'verification,' in the broad sense that
some   good   reason   or   reasons   for   maintaining   that
proposition's truth rather than its falsity must be able to
be provided."[47]

   Much more research is needed in the area of continuity
between theology and social science.  Some experiments have
been attempted in the fields of psychology and then applied
analogically to theology.  James E. Dittes argues, "What the
experimentalist has to contribute to the theologian is not
verification or validation of propositions, but rather the
encouraging of more precise definition and conceptualiza-
tion.   It is the empirical operations, not the statistical
outcome, that is of chief importance."[48]    Dittes insists
that " the psychologist can neither measure nor manipulate
the ultimate sources of a person's sense of well-being and
self-esteem.  These are inaccessibly rooted in the outreach-
ings of Divine grace and the religious intuitions of man.
But   the   psychologist   can   deal   with   circumstances   which
approximate these ultimate groundings of well-being.  He can
deal   with   circumstances   on   which   personal   self-esteem
depends   very   highly, if not absolutely   and ultimately."[49]
The   dimension   of   the   transcendent   is   determinative   in
keeping the distinctions clear, on the one hand.   On the
other hand is the question whether ultimate ideas are intended to be empirically relevant.  Professor Harvey H. Potthoff
holds that " science and religion will not go much beyond the
relationship of coexistence...until there is some sort of
breakthrough on the issue of verification."  He would seek
this in the direction of functional methodology.[50]

   But even where no unifying operational method has been
discovered, if it ever will be, there are attitudes taken in
theology which can be fruitful.  These include the view that
theology is vital only when what is held to be valid is also

valuable and hence relevant. Social science can illuminate the context of relevance. Theology can take more seriously the whole order of creation by providing some interpretation of the natural structures and processes "upon which men draw for support, healing, and renewal." Moreover, theology can show a greater willingness to modify its conceptual structures by new scientific knowledge and experience. Even when it is recognized that the methods and models of the social sciences tend to correlate with what is popular intellectual style in a given era, greater openness by theology is indicated, despite this danger.

It is quite evident, as a consequence of all that we have noted above, that one's understanding of the secular forces of society is part of one's obligation of obedience to God, and that technical competence is part of that obedience. Patient co-operation between the theologian and the social scientist is required to build up understanding and develop technical competence. Empirical work requires careful scientific operation in the most diverse situations on earth. There is today a great deal of qualitative as well as quantitiative social research in selected favorable areas of the world, but a hard core of data is lacking on some of the greatest conflict areas of interpersonal and intergroup relations. Conflict resolution has few verified scientific models. The facts are so diverse and society is so complex that only the bare outlines of a synthesis of Christian social thought—or of its middle axioms—is presently conceivable. But since we believe as Christians that a responsible social order will be one where men and women live as their creator intended them to live, all that can be learned about fact, value, and interpretation in theology and social science will be part of responsible living in the secular order.

## NOTES

[1]Irving Ladimer and Roger W. Newman, eds., *Clinical Investigation in Medicine:   Legal, Ethical, and Moral Aspects* (Boston University:   Law-Medicine Research Institute, 1963), pp. 116-117.

[2]*Ibid.*, p. 37.

[3]*Ibid.*, pp. 105, 107.

[4]*Ibid.*, p. 81.

[5]P. H. Hoch and J. Zubin, eds., *Psychiatry and the Law* (New York:   Grune and Stratton, Inc., 1955), pp. 151-155.

[6]Margaret Mead, ed., *Cultural Patterns and Technical Change* (UNESCO, 1955), p. 12.

[7]*Ibid.*, p. 13, italics supplied.

[8]Talcott Parsons, et al. eds., *Theories of Society. Foundations of Modern Sociological Theory.* (Glencoe, Ill., The Free Press, 1961), 2 Vols.

[9]Mead, *op. cit.*, p. 14.

[10]*Ibid.*, p. 288.

[11]In this subsection I have followed the treatment in Gordon Allport, *Pattern and Growth in Personality*, ch. 22, "The Person in Psychology." (New York:   Holt, Rinehart, and Winston, 1961).

[12]*Ibid.*, p. 551.

[13]*Ibid.*, p. 556.

[14]*Ibid.*, p. 570.

[15]Gunnar Myrdal, "A Methodological Note on Facts and Valuations in Social Science," Appendix 2, *An American Dilemma* (New York:   Harper and Brothers, 1944), Vol. 2, p. 1035.

[16]*Ibid.*, p. 1038.

[17]*Ibid.*, p. 1039.   The present writer had more than one occasion to observe this kind of issue as chairman of the

Commission on Institutionalism as part of the Faith and
Order studies (1956-63) of the World Council of Churches.
It was quite impossible to get case studies underway in
certain explosive or threatening institutional situations.
The resultant volume edited by Nils Ehrenstrom and myself,
*Institutionalism and Church Unity,* is therefore biased in its
overall evaluational tone on the optimistic side.  Several
of Mydral's scales could profitably be applied to the
scientific and theological aspects of such research.

[18]Paul Tillich, *Dynamics of Faith* (New York:  Harper
Torchbooks, 1958), pp. 74-75.

[19]*Ibid.*, p. 75.

[20]*Ibid.*, p. 76.

[21]*Ibid.*, p. 81.

[22]*Ibid.*, p. 83.

[23]John Dillenberger, *Protestant Thought and Natural
Science* (New York:  Doubleday and Co., Inc., 1960), p. 283.

[24]*Ibid.*, p. 256.

[25]*Ibid.*, pp. 264-265.

[26]*Ibid.*, p. 265.

[27]Abraham Edel, *Ethical Judgment, The Use of Science in
Ethics* (Glencoe, Ill.:  The Free Press, 1955), p. 30.

[28]*Ibid.*, p. 32.

[29]*Ibid.*, p. 36.

[30]*Ibid.*, p. 59.

[31]*Ibid.*, p. 54.

[32]O. Hobart Mowrer, *The Crisis in Psychiatry and
Religion* (Princeton, N. J.:  D. Van Nostrand Co., Inc.,
1961), Ch. 9, "Psychotherapy and the Problem of Values in
Historical Perspective."

[33]*Ibid.*, pp. 108-109.

[34]*Ibid.*, p. 125.

[35]*Ibid.*, p. 182.

[36]Harold K. Schilling, *Science and Religion. An Interpretation of Two Communities* (New York:   Charles Scribner's Sons, 1962), p. 10.

[37]Sidney E. Mead, "Church History Explained," *Church History*, March, 1963.

[38]*Ibid.*

[39]Karl Mannheim, *Ideology and Utopia* (New York: Harcourt Brace and Co., 1936), p. 49.

[40]*Ibid.*, pp. 49-50.

[41]Paul E. Sigmund, Jr., ed., *The Ideologies of the Developing Nations* (New York:   F. A. Praeger, 1963), p. 4.

[42]*Ibid.*, p. 40.

[43]*Ibid.*, p. 37.

[44]Warren Rempel, *The Role of Value in Mannheim's Sociology of Knowledge* (unpublished doctoral dissertation), (Boston University, 1962).

[45]D. L. Munby, "The Importance of Technical Competence," in D. M. Paton, ed., *Essays in Anglican Self-criticism* (SCM Press, Ltd., 1958), pp. 45-48.

[46]*Ibid.*, p. 58.

[47]Frederick Ferre, "Verification, Faith, and Credulity," *Religion in Life* (Winter, 1962-63), p. 52.

[48]James E. Dittes, "Justification by Faith and the Experimental Psychologist," *Religion in Life* (Autumn, 1959), p. 568.   See also John D. Maguire, "Comment:   Is Experience the Ground of Theology?"

[49]*Ibid.*, p. 570.

[50]Harvey H. Potthoff, "Science and Religion:   Has the Conflict been Resolved?" *Religion in Life* (Winter, 1962-63), p. 27.

## BIBLIOGRAPHY OF SELECTED WORKS CONSULTED

Allport, Gordon W., *Pattern and Growth in Personality*.
New York: Holt, Rinehart and Winston, Inc., 1961.

Balthasar, Hans Urs von, *Science, Religion, and
Christianity*. London: Burns and Oates, 1958.

Chauchard, Paul, *Science and Religion*. Tr. S. J. Tester.
New York: Hawthorn Books, 1962.

Clark, Robert E. D., *Christian Belief and Science. A
Reconciliation and a Partnership*. London: The English
Universities Press, 1960.

Coulson, C. A., *Science and Christian Belief*. London:
Oxford University Press, 1955.

Dillenberger, John, *Protestant Thought and Natural Science*.
New York: Doubleday and Co., Inc., 1960.

Edel, Abraham, *Ethical Judgment: The Use of Science in
Ethics*. Glencoe, Illinois: The Free Press, 1955.

Ehrenstrom, Nils and Muelder, W. G., eds., *Institutionalism
and Church Unity*. New York: Association Press, 1963.

Frank, Philipp, *Relativity, A Richer Truth*. Boston: Beacon Press, 1950.

Hock, Paul H. and Zubin, Joseph, eds., *Psychiatry and the
Law*. New York: Grune and Stratton, Inc., 1955.

Ladimer, Irving and Newman, Roger W., *Clinical Investigation in Medicine*. Boston University Law-Medicine
Research Institute, 1963.

Mannheim, Karl, *Ideology and Utopia*. New York: Harcourt
Brace and Co., 1936.

Mead, Margaret (ed.), *Cultural Patterns and Technical
Change*. UNESCO, 1955.

Miles, T. R., *Religion and the Scientific Outlook*.
London: George Allen and Unwin, 1959.

Monsma, John Clover (ed.), *Science and Religion. Twenty-
three Prominent Churchmen express their Opinions*. New
York: G. P. Putman's sons, 1962.

Mowrer, O. Hobart, *The Crisis in Psychiatry and Religion*.
    Princeton, New Jersey:  D. Van Nostrand Co., Inc.,
    1961.

Munby, D. L., *Christianity and Economic Problems*.  London:
    Macmillan and Co., 1956.

_____, *The Idea of a Secular Society*.  London:  Oxford
    University Press, 1963.

_____, "The Importance of Technical Competence," in David
    M. Paton (ed.), *Essays in Anglican Self-Criticism*.
    London:  SCM Press, Ltd., 1958.

Myrdal, Gunnar, *An American Dilemma*.  New York:  Harper
    Bros., 1944.  2 Vols.

Niebuhr, H. Richard, *Christ and Culture*.  New York:
    Harper and Bros., 1951.

Owen, D. R. G., *Scientism, Man and Religion*.  Philadel-
    phia:  The Westminster Press, 1952.

Parsons, Talcott, et al. (eds.), *Theories of Society, Foun-
    dations of Modern Sociological Theory*.  Glencoe,
    Illinois:  The Free Press, 1961.  2 Vols.

Rempel, Warren H., "The Role of Value in Karl Mannheim's
    Sociology of Knowledge," (Unpublished doctoral disser-
    tation).  Boston University, 1962.

Richardson, Alan, *Science, History and Faith*.  London:
    Oxford University Press, 1950.

Ropp, Robert S. de, *Science and Salvation*.  A Scientific
    Appraisal of Religion's Central Theme.  New York:  St.
    Martin's Press, 1962.

Schilling, Harold K., *Science and Religion*.  An Interpre-
    tation of Two Communities.  New York:  Charles
    Scribner's Sons, 1962.

Sigmund, Jr., Paul E., ed. and Introduction, *The Ideologies
    of the Developing Nations*.  New York and London:
    Frederick A. Praeger, 1963.

Tillich, Paul, *Dynamics of Faith*.  New York:  Harper
    Torchbooks, 1958.

Vries, Egbert de, *Man in Rapid Social Change*. London:
    SCM Press, 1961.

Ward, Leo R. (ed.), *Ethics and the Social Science*.
    University of Notre Dame Press, 1959.

# Religion and Human Destiny
## (1951)

## I
## The Universe a Society of Persons

Religion differentiates itself from magic in many ways, but chiefly in this, that magic seeks to manipulate the world through coercive formulas, whereas religion seeks to cooperate with ultimate reality. Reality has the last word. Prayer, which is at the heart of the religious attitude, places the worshiper in a rightful position of dependence and humility to the will of God. Even when prayers are of the more selfish petitionary sort, they recognize that God has the final determination of the issue. Any realistic or even serious minded religion will conceive its role and function in terms of what it believes the ultimate nature of reality to be.

The universe, metaphysically speaking, we take to be a society of persons. Religion functions in a personal world. God is the eternal person who is the ground and source of all being and value. The term person is of course not to be understood in a crude anthropomorphic way. We mean that the ultimate nature of things is personal. Physical nature is an expression of God's will and purpose and men are created by God to be free persons. God transcends and is immanent in his whole creation. Thus God is beyond as well as in all aspects of physical nature and man's personality. Human wills are dependent on and also transcend in part both that aspect of God's will which is in nature and the will of God more inclusively conceived. The society of humankind is a

213

metaphysical   fact.   But society is only possible community.

God  is  one,  the  unitary  ground  of  all  existence  and
value.   Religion  to  be  realistic  and  humble  must  fashion
itself  according  to  this  actual  situation.   Religious  ideals
and   goals   which   are   contrary   to   the   objective   order   of
divine  intentions,  goals  and  ideals  are  not  only  untrue  in
the  final  analysis,  they  are  futile.   And  persons  who  follow
them  are  of  all  creatures  the  most  pathetic.   Religion  is
the  attitude  of  human  beings  toward  that  which  they  regard
to  be  supremely  worthful  and  to  have  ultimate  control  over
their  destiny.   Hence  religion  must  be  based  on  values  which
are  grounded  in  the  fact  that  the  universe  is  a  society  of
persons  and  that  God  has  the  intention  that  this  society  be
a  true  community.

A  community  is  a  group  of  persons  who  share  and  plan
their  lives  according  to  cohesive  values  in  which  they
participate.    A   community   is   more   than   an   association
wherein  persons  are  united  temporarily  for  the  purpose  of
realizing  some  limited  interest.   In  a  community  there  is  a
hierarchy  of  values,  based  on  the  hierarchy  of  human  needs.
The  common  pursuit  of  these  values  and  the  free  and  responsible  participation  of  interdependent  persons,  raises  society  to  the  level  of  community.   This  community  ideal  we
believe  to  reflect  the  purpose  of  God.   To  do  justly,  to
love  mercy  and  to  walk  humbly  with  God  are  communitarian
values.   To  be  devoted  to  reason  and  love  are  the  highest
values  when  they  are  related  to  humble  acknowledgement  of
God.   Life  devoted  to  the  love  of  God  expresses  the  love  of
God.

Religion  does  not  begin  with  isolated  men  and  women  and
try  to  make  them  less  selfish  and  more  altruistic.   The
world  is  not  that  atomistic.   Reality  is  an  interdependent
system  of  wills.   Religion  has  to  do  with  the  person-in-com-

munity.   Self-determination and mutual responsibility are
aspects of a larger whole.   No person lives to himself biologically, physiologically, psychologically, morally or spiritually.   Persons actualize themselves only in community.
Even when they do not thus express themselves in real freedom, they are still dependent on each other.   Indeed, one of
the great lessons of life is that the precious gift of freedom must be exercised within certain objective limits.   The
higher and the more inclusive that human community and religious relatedness are, the freer persons are.   The more
purely private and self-centered one tries to be, the greater are the internal barriers to integration and actualization and the greater are the external obstacles.   Freedom is
developed in community.   Without the security of community
an individual is too fearful to be emancipated.

Western society places a high value on freedom and associates this value with an emphasis on the individual person.
Therefore, it associates freedom with independence of action
and freedom from external restraints.   Much thinking about
freedom confuses metaphysical, psychological and political
freedom.   Many Americans have their sterotypes about freedom
determined by the myths historically associated with the
colonial struggle of independence and the frontier experience of the self-made man.   Colonial Americans were
oppressed by external legal restraints.   They placed a high
value on the individual resourcefulness of people.   Yet,
historical expressions of freedom do not necessarily define
the nature of true freedom.

Metaphysically speaking freedom means the capacity to
say yes or no to any given content of experience, but it
functions in a context.   It presupposes an order which is a
mixture of determinateness and undetermined possibility.
Freedom and order are thus bi-polar concepts; they belong

dialectically to the same conscious context. Freedom means
the power of contrary choice. This basic understanding of
freedom has important implications for freedom in the community. Freedom is no isolated right; indeed, no rights are
isolated. They are moral claims which the person makes
against the community with respect to some essential need
which must be satisfied if the person is to come to fulfillment. Freedom is always a combination of liberties and
restraints. The liberty to enjoy my own property involves a
restraint on all others. In labor relations, the law which
prevents the employer from interfering with the organization
of the workers makes possible the expression of the workers
to have a union of their own choosing. Thus in all social
relations the problem of freedom is what combination of
restraints and liberties is coherent with a truly actualized person. The problem of political, social or economic
freedom is thus also a problem as to what is the chief end
of man and what are the values in a hierarchy of values
which this chief goal requires. In other words the fundamental social question is a religious one. The liberty with
which Christ sets men free is a liberty to love in such a
way that there is created a barrierless community of justice
and service. Erich Fromm, using the methods of social psychiatry, says that the more the individual is differentiated
from nature and from the group the more he is called upon to
give himself in love and productive service. Liberty or
freedom, then, cannot stop at the level of independence
either in individual or group life. Children are dependent;
adolescents seek to be independent; mature adults realize
that they are interdependent. Communitarian responsibility
which is dominated by love is an expression of the New Testament ideal of coming into the fulness of stature of Christ.

## II
### Religion and the Primacy of Love

The primacy of love establishes the basis for understanding the destiny of man. There is no reason that people should be cynical or pessimistic about human destiny when we realize that God is love. But today they have lost faith in the possibilities of human nature. The loss of faith tends to separate them from the right use of God's resources. Since they are free, they must exercise faith in order to think or act in the best possible way. Faith in intelligent love as the highest expression of personality and as objective reality brings idealism and realism together as the basis for action and community building.

The basic social unit is the group. The group is also essential to religion, for the history of religion demonstrates the centrality of the cultus. It is in the fellowship of the cultus that worship emerges. Without an attitude toward those values which are supremely worthful, in short without worship, there is no religious development. Joachim Wach, the eminent sociologist of religion, is probably right when he says that no act of worship can exist without some conception of the divine, nor can a religion function without at least a modicum of cultic expression. Theoretical and practical factors are inextricabley intertwined. Thus within the worshipping community there is a dialectic of individual and group, of idea and action, of leaders and followers, of dissent and accommodation, of doctrine and ethics, of ritual worship and service. The interaction of these elements accounts for much of the dynamic in the relation of religion to society.

When we survey the history of the Christian Church in terms of its ethic we note that it has several permanent characteristics. This ethic has been produced by the inter-

action of the Christian community through centuries of
struggle with ancient, medieval and modern culture. The
permanent elements of that ethic have been tried by the fire
of innumerable crises in Western and even Eastern history.
Perhaps the greatest interpreter of these social teachings
has been Ernst Troeltsch. He concluded on the basis of his
researches that five elements constituted the essential
traits of the Christian ethic. It is noteworthy that these
traits concern the theological basis of group life, the
nature of persons, the basic elements of human interrelationships and the norms of his destiny both here and beyond. At
a time when men are absorbed by the possible relativity of
all values it is essential to note those which, despite the
many social doctrines which Christianity has produced, have
withstood the purging fires of time. (1) "The Christian
Ethos alone possesses, in virtue of its personalistic
Theism, a conviction of personality and individuality, based
on metaphysics, which no Naturalism and no Pessimism can
disturb." (2) "The Christian Ethos alone, through the
conception of a Divine Love which embraces all souls and
unites them all, possesses a Socialism which cannot be
shaken." Personality and community, then, are theologically
and metaphysically grounded. (3) "Only the Christian Ethos
solves the problem of equality and inequality, since it
neither glorifies force and accident in the sense of a
Nietzschean cult of breed, nor outrages the patent facts of
life by a doctrinaire equalitarianism. It recognizes
differences in social position, power, and capacity, as a
condition which has been established by the inscrutable will
of God; and then transforms this condition by the inner
upbuilding of the personality, and the development of the
mutual sense of obligation, into an ethical cosmos." (4)
"Through its emphasis upon the Christian value of person-

ality, and on love, the Christian ethos creates something
which no social order—however just and rational—can
dispense with entirely, because everywhere there will always
remain suffering, distress, and sickness for which we cannot
account—in a word, it produces charity. Charity, or active
helpfulness, is the fruit of the Christian Spirit, which
alone keeps it alive." (5) "The Christian Ethos gives to
all social life and aspiration a goal which lies far beyond
all the relativities of this earthly life, compared with
which, indeed, everything else represents mere proximate
values. The idea of the future Kingdom of God, which is
nothing less than faith in the final realization of the
Absolute (in whatever way we may conceive this realization),
does not ...render this world and life in this world
meaningless and empty; on the contrary, it stimulates human
energies, making the soul strong through its various stages
of experience in the certainty of an ultimate, absolute
meaning and aim for human labor. Thus it raises the soul
above the world without denying the world."[1] As a normative
historical statement I find these five points essentially
persuasive.

### III
### Social Consequences of Love

The Christian cultus thus has produced an ethic which
undergirds the finest and best in the creation of a universal community. It has provided a sound doctrine of vocation; it has clarified the essential function of property;
it has established the basis for civil rights; it has shown
the proper grounds of voluntary associations and the state;
and it has indicated essential characteristics of the open
community. Before discussing these individually let it be
made clear that there have been many practical errors and

some injustices attending the growth of Christianity. Yet, we must concentrate on our goal which is to show how despite all personal and historical evil, religion has the key to humanity's real destiny.

First, there is vocation. Vocation has to do with work and work is a human reality. From a religious perspective work is more than a job; it is related to a person's fulfillment in the community and to the purposes of God. Here the Bible is helpful. God is a worker; He is creator. Jesus was a worker. "My Father worketh hitherto, and I work." In the Bible work is not a curse, it is part of the order of things. The New Testament relates the work of the Christian to his calling, to his divine sonship. There are realistic aspects about work. "He who will not work, neither shall he eat." Work is related to social responsibility. Another conception which the Christian community developed was one which socialists and the Russians have taken over: "From each according to his ability, to each according to his needs."

The idea of work as vocation in the early Church was not understood as using work to reform the world. Work was recognized as a good discipline, but the idea of serving God through one's work by using the labor to create a new and better destiny did not develop until after the Reformation. Luther stressed the idea of the calling *in* one's work, thus making all callings whether sacred or secular equally sacred. Calvin stressed vocation *in* one's work to the *glory of God*, thus giving work a more positive function. But it has remained for the modern world and particularly for social Christianity to emphasize the expression of work as part of the divine vocation for man to redeem not only the laborer in the job but social institutions themselves. Science and modern industry have given people the positive possibility of generally high standards of living.

The Christian thus brings to the modern world of work three basic ideas which criticize our industrial and technological age of impersonal and anonymous labor patterns and which point the way which social engineering is now going. These three principles are: (a) personality, (b) community, and (c) ultimate meaning. Few will deny that the work relationships under which most people labor today violate these principles. Therefore they are restless, for their inner natures and ultimate destinies are attacked. Yet, there are signs of reform. And modern social science along with social engineering, supported in part by labor legislation, is now recognizing that labor is not a mere commodity, that voluntary association of workers in small groups in factories and in larger units of the trade unions, and in many expressions of community welfare fulfill basic needs in workers, and that if they are to be mature persons they must share responsibly in setting the goals and making vital decisions in the industries in which they participate. The destiny of men and women at work is to create a social order in which labor again has a sense of the ultimate meaning of its own activity. Labor includes, of course, all workers of hand or brain.

In the second place, religion provides a doctrine of economic responsibility with respect to property. In one sense property relates to material or tangible things, with the means of life. As such it is an instrumental value. Money as a symbol of property is a sort of universal means. Thus only a miser would acquire money for its own sake. But property is not only material things; it refers also to immaterial values like credit, ideas, reputation, "good-will," labor skill, know-how, and many others. Strictly speaking, however, property is not the relation of a person to a

thing, material or immaterial. Property is a right relation
of persons to each other with respect to acquisition, exclusive use, or power over scarce values. Even private property is socially created; for it is a right, and rights have
no significance apart from the community. Property is a
legal right and as such is a creation of government. It
thus becomes clear that the political community has the responsibility of jurisdiction over the economic order.

The religious heritage of the Bible and the Church
throws a great deal of light on property. For one thing it
recognizes that God is the real owner. Persons are stewards. They have received God's gifts in an interdependent
world and these gifts are to be used to meet their common
needs. They also have personal or private needs and these
must be recognized and integrated in the whole community of
needs. The idea of absolute private ownership with the
right to do with property as one pleases is unknown in the
Bible and it is contrary to the dominant teaching of the
Church. Jesus recognized private property but he subordinated it to the Kingdom of God. He was aware of the deceit-
fulness of riches, the false status that it tended to
create, and the need to learn non-possessiveness with respect to it. It is not surprising that the early Christians
should have practiced a religious communism of love. However, it was not a Christian requirement, and it seems to
have been quite transient. On the whole the Christian tradition has placed common need and the primacy of *use* over
*possessions* in its doctrine of property. It knows little of
that "gospel of wealth" which modern capitalism has created
in America.

During most of the Christian era the problem of property as power was not clearly faced. But in the last century
this problem has become acute. Property holding of

producer's goods means the power of one person over another or over a whole group of persons. It is in this relationship (usually corporate) that the holding of power is challenged by the doctrine of personal dignity and the needs of the community. With so much property power in the hands of the few, religious leaders are confronted by the challenge of power. The challenge of power must be faced on its own terms and not in irrelevant terms such as merely a wide distribution of goods based on a high productivity. Power like money is a kind of universal means and like it demands responsible stewardship. The concentration of economic power in the hands of a few makes for irresponsibility. Is there need for a widespread distribution of productive economic power? For Christians the answer to this question will not be the same in each nation. Christianity cannot simply endorse any particular economic order or system operative in the world today. Economic systems are instruments of human welfare and must be judged by what they do to persons, to the principle of brotherhood, and to the motive of service. It may be that a mixed economy will today provide, on the whole, the best combination of freedom and security, of creativity and productivity, of opportunity and responsibility for the era through which we are now passing.

A third sphere of social needs which religion undergirds is the realm of civil liberties and civil rights. We have already defined a right above. The most elementary rights are racial rights, for God has given each person spiritual dignity; and differences of color, stature, head form and the rest are at most superficial characteristics. "God has made of one blood all nations of men." They have a common destiny. Racial rights means racial solidarity and hence discrimination and segregation on allegedly racial grounds are morally and religiously wrong. Next to racial

rights  or  liberties  come  religious  liberties.   It  can
fruitfully  be  argued  that  religious  liberty  underlies  all
the  civil  liberties,  for  God  created  men  free,  i.e.  capable
of  denying  or  accepting  his  claims  upon  them.   This  elementary  religious  relationship  of  freedom  between  the  creator
and  the  creature  underlies  the  freedoms  which  people  ought
to  accord  one  another.   In  one  sense  the  civil  and  social
liberties  are  but  a  reflection  of  the  communitarian  freedom
which  exists  in  man's  religious  relation  to  God.   The  greatest  authorities  on  the  cultural  roots  of  civil  liberties
recognize  the  profound  contribution  which  Christianity  has
made  to  this  aspect  of  human  destiny.   Political,  social  and
economic  institutions  are  measured  in  part  by  the  extent  to
which  they  conserve  and  nourish  creative,  critical  and
responsible  participation  by  all  their  members.   One  of  the
great  tragedies  underlying  the  recent  history  of  Germany,
Italy  and  of  contemporary  Stalinist  state  capitalism  is  that
these  nations  have  not  had  the  benefit  of  a  powerful  tradition  of  political  liberty,  not  only  in  theory  but  in  day  by
day  practice  on  all  levels  from  the  village  to  the  state.
The  Christian  ethic,  as  summarized  above  by  Troeltsch,  cannot  accept  any  view  like  Soviet  Communism  which  fails  to
acknowledge  in  person-in-community  a  transcendent  relation
to  other  persons  and  to  God  beyond  the  state.   People  must
be  free  to  criticize  their  governments  from  the  standpoint
of  what  they  believe  objective  right  to  be.   He  who  denies
objective  right  in  effect  debases  the  individual  person.

     Civil  Liberties  have  been  closely  related  with  the
right  of  voluntary  association  which  we  must  briefly  treat
as  a  fourth  principle  of  responsible  community.   Civil  liberties  tend  to  stress  individual  persons.   The  principle  of
voluntary  association  emphasizes  the  primary  principle  of
free  community.   Since  a  person  is  actualized  in  community,

he cannot be free without the exercise of voluntary association. Hardly any greater contribution to Western culture
has been made by the religious sects of the 16th and 17th
centuries than the vindication of the right to worship God
as one felt called upon in conscience to do. Voluntary association has had a difficult time being fully understood or
appreciated, but the idea has been developed in politics, in
education, in the professions, in business, and in labor
relations to mention a few outstanding areas. The principle
of voluntary association requires a doctrine of democratic
and responsible participation. Democracy as a spirit means
the effective expression of persons at the levels where
decisions are being made. In labor unions and in collective
bargaining and in management this conception has its application as well as in the sphere of citizenship. The idea of
voluntary association, of membership in small groups, requires widespread implementation if the evils of mass-mindedness are to be overcome. Human nature behaves at its best
in small groups. Any political or economic pattern of the
future must keep this principle in mind. The state is an
association and should be recognized as that special association to which is assigned all legitimate coercive power. To
emphasize the state as an association is to distinguish it
sharply from the community. States must be kept as servants
of community, not their totalitarian substitutes. On the
world scale states must now be asked to surrender their
alleged national sovereignties and be responsive to the
dynamic need of developing a world community. As there is
no limit to the inclusiveness of the power of love and the
principle of righteousness, true religion today sees human
political destiny in universal terms.

## IV
## Ethical Reality of the Church

Although religion to be realistic must accept reality
as it metaphysically is shown to be, though in its highest
forms it has generated an ethic of responsible love, and
though its power generates many rights and duties in work,
property, voluntary associations, and the state, yet it has
to face, as an organized power, certain dilemmas and problems.   Christians and churches are involved in the sins of
racial discrimination, nationalism, intolerances, and economic institutions not fully responsible.   How are we to
understand this situation and how be delivered from the
"body of this death," for these evils reflect decay in the
body of Christ and deterioration in the community?

The church is a complex ethical reality.   It possesses
the gospel and the personal reality of Jesus Christ with
whom it experiences historical community.   Yet the church as
a social institution is accommodated to society.   Its members participate in many groups and hence in many goals
outside the church.   Their minds and characters are formed
and buffeted by the anarchy of social purposes in contemporary culture.   Every Christian is bound to experience the
tension which exists between the gospel and the "world."
The empirical church is a community which has been created
in part by the gospel and in part by the world.   Thus the
church is bound to experience the tension which results from
the claims of the gospel and the claims of the secular order
on the members and on the institution as such.   This dilemma
or tension we must recognize will continue in some form,
though hopefully on ever higher levels, until the end of
time.

The early church felt a sharp conflict between itself
as a small community of love and the world.   Conflict resulted in persecution.   The ideal of the Christian church
maintaining itself as a community of perfection, in sharp

opposition with the world, has been periodically held by many throughout the long history of Christianity. It manifested itself in the monasteries, in mediaeval and modern sect-type Christianity, and in colonies of the faithful in various parts of the world. This social expression of the Gospel gives up any idea of reforming the world. Human destiny is defined in terms of a sharp contrast between the city of God and the city of earth. In this form religion does not attempt reconstruction or hold out any hope for society in historical terms. Where the Christian's relation to society at large is primarily that of holding one's self unspotted from the world he has really given up the struggle of social redemption.

There is another approach which Christianity has made, and that has been its main line, namely to be the community on its knees, to be an inclusive institution, relevant to every human need, and relating all human struggles to one's ultimate spiritual end. In its sacramentarian form this is what the Church attempted to be in the Middle Ages. And in a very real sense that is what the Church is for denominational Protestantism, but not in its Roman form. But to be inclusive the Church has incorporated much of the "world" into itself; it accommodated itself. in order to influence the world it has to adjust itself. So we see it accommodating to nations, to classes, to wars, to crusades, to political and economic revolutions. The danger of this strategy is clear from the record. The church has often lost the leadership of culture and has then had to submit to the secularism of its surroundings. It became at times so inclusive at the expense of its redemptive power that it became virtually separated from that which created it—its gospel of the righteous reign of God and the Kingdom of love through Christ.

On the one hand, the Christian community may have so
much conflict with its environment that it takes to the
catacombs or is otherwise isolated from the secular order.
On the other hand, the church may become so accommodated to
that order  that it loses its distinctive message and power.

A threefold group of tensions must thus be accepted and
held coherently together:  the tension between the gospel
and the church; the tension between the church and the
world; and the tension which results from the leadership
which the church must undertake in the reconstruction of
society.  It becomes the task of the church to judge the
world even while it seeks to redeem the world; to save the
persons who are caught in the dilemmas of working out their
vocation in the midst of social pressures and change; to
experiment with new types of group life which will give new
motives and new techniques to community building; to cooperate with other institutions that are committed to social
reconstruction; and to provide opportunities for intimate
fellowship and support for those pioneers of Christian community who are especially aware of the contradictions of this
complex situation and who earnestly are striving to bring
into coherence the gospel, the church and society.

The significant fact of prophetic and dynamic religion
is that it is aware of the need for self-criticism and a new
reformation in the church and at the same time is committed
to faith in the Christian community as an instrument of the
divine love to redeem both men and society.  Faith that both
in history and beyond a meaningful existence awaits free
persons is the bridge over which they may travel from the
anxieties of social chaos and despair to the destiny which
God has prepared for those who choose to live according to
the realism of the divine society which is the basic
metaphysical postulate of our enquiry.

## NOTES

[1] Ernst Troeltsch, *The Social Teachings of the Christian Churches*. Two vols. (New York: Allen and Unwin, 1931), pp. 1004-1006.

# Distinctive Characteristics
## of Christianity
### (1953)

The subject assigned to me by Dr. E. E. Aubrey has been
a puzzle. Not having been in on the whole discussion last
year I did not fully grasp the context of the problem to be
attempted. For whatever reasons I did not appreciate until
very recently that the frame of reference was comparative
religion. In this field I have no competence. However,
this predicament should not overwhelm me, for the literature
in the field written by Christians for the most part makes
an apriori claim of finality or absoluteness for Christianity. For many Christians an interest in the distinctive
characteristics of Christianity has final significance only
in relation to this claim. One could spend a great deal of
time arguing over the accuracy or inaccuracy of some alleged
difference between Christianity and one or all of the great
living religions of the world, but that would have only a
provisional significance, since the real issue is not one in
history or comparative religions, but of ultimate validity.
Nevertheless, the predicament referred to above does
overwhelm me for I do not hold to the *apriorism* just
referred to, and I do not have that intimate knowledge of
non-Christian sources, classics, history and culture which
such an undertaking presupposes.

The topic invites exploration methodologically along
several lines: comparative religion, sociology of religion
and systematic theology. Either one of these approaches is
illuminating, but each by itself is limited and creates problems for the others. The methods of comparative religion

231

are unacceptable to some systematic theologians who refuse
to consider Christianity under the broader classification of
religion.  To subsume Christianity under religion would seem
to compromise the uniqueness and finality of the Christian
faith.  This methods affirms loyalty at the expense of all
communication.  A more widespread difficulty in comparative
methods   arises   from   their   essentially   abstract   and
analytical approach.  Aspects of doctrine, ethic, cultus,
and practice are abstracted in each religion and then compared with each other.  This procedure tends to dissolve the
concrete wholeness of the living religions into component
universals.  Although for certain purposes of research and
investigation, this method has values, it violates, when
pressed very far, the concrete realities whose integral
wholeness must be grasped as such.  This observation is today a philosophical and anthropological commonplace.  Analysis must be subsumed under synopsis.

    The effort to find the distinctive characteristics of
religion through sociology of religion alone is often regarded as too descriptive and typological to be finally instructive or determinative.  The method lacks normative validity
when normative judgments are of the essence of religious
loyalty.  The fruitfulness of the typological method is evident from the works of men like Max Weber and Joachim Wach,
but it brings out the universal or common types more clearly
than it does the unique or distinctive elements.  It provides a sufficient answer to the initial objection above
which would refuse to include the Christian faith under the
general class term of religion.  The typological method of
comparative sociology is more effective in delineating
cultic and social forms than it is in comparing doctrine.
It lacks the tools of dynamic analyses and hence cannot
clarify the dynamic elements which canalize the interpene-

trating aspects of a religion.

The standpoint of systematic theology, which has had such a powerful revival in recent decades, raises problems for the disciplines cited above because it tends to over-emphasize the doctrinal characteristics of religion at the expense of equally obvious and important cultural and socio-logical elements. However, it is a significant merit of some recent work in systematic theology that it has appropri-ated the perspectives of various disciplines in its effort to expound the meaning of the essential elements in reli-gious faith and expression. This long explanatory note should invite the reader to expect observations from various disciplines in an effort to lift up the distinctive charac-teristics of Christianity.

## I
## Uniqueness, Social Wholes
## and Personality

The concept of *uniqueness* carries a value judgment for most theologians. We introduce it here, however, as an historical conception free of special pleading for Chris-tianity. The unique may also be the final, but not neces-sarily so. In one sense all historical realities are unique. Historical personalities and events are unrepeat-able. Ernst Troeltsch wrote brilliantly on the contingency, uniqueness and unrepeatable quality of historical events. He related them to the social wholes or *historical totali-ties* of which they were aspects. These individual totali-ties, he noted, were unities of meaning and value and were interlocked with the material conditions of life which Marx and his followers had wrongly made the primary determiners of history. Troeltsch recognized the objective wholeness of all the great world religions and hence their uniqueness.

Indeed, he was so impressed by this quality that he failed
to overcome the philosophical relativism which was implicit
in the idea. At the same time it enabled him to perceive
the distinctive contribution and historical influence of persons. His treatment of Jesus and Luther, for example, in
*The Social Teachings of the Christian Churches* as opposed to
the economic interpretation of Karl Kautsky is a classic
achievement.

The essentially concrete category of *personality* is an
important aspect of our understanding of world religions and
of Christianity. Personality is individual, social and
historical while it transcends both society and history.
Personality is a concrete individuality. Personality is a
particular that universalizes. J. V. L. Casserley appropri-
ately quotes Kierkegaard: "Every man is the universal human
and at the same time an exception."[1] It is the reality of
the concretely personal which tests all abstract universals.
Personality is not a function of sociological laws or cultural laws. Scientific generalizations are aspects of personal
experience. "The person is a concrete and historical reality. We meet and live with persons, know them and love
them."[2] We shall presently show the direct bearing of these
points on the problem of this paper. But it is well to
develop the point a little more fully. There is a large
literature on the issue involved and a brief further quotation from Casserley will suffice: "Personality is an essentially social conception. It can only exist and continue in
constant relationship to the other. There can only be personality where there are persons. There can only be personality in society. Historically speaking, therefore, society
is prior to personality, as the seed bed is prior to the
grown plant. In another, ethical, sense it may still be
true that personality is prior to society, for it is in the

production of persons, or so Christian thinkers would say, that society fulfills its function and justifies its existence."[3]

This quotation from Casserley grounds the scientific concept of personality in the theological concept of person in Christianity. Writers, like E. S. Brightman, have derived the conception directly from self-experience and its emergents. Ernst Troeltsch felt that the idea of personality was so distinctively Western that it could not be used as the basis of a universal axiology. When he came to this conclusion his comparative efforts in East-West religion and culture speedily became relativistic. The idea of personality is directly relevant to Christianity's most central affirmation—the reality of Jesus Christ. Everything of crucial distinctiveness relates to him. The distinctiveness of Christianity is in Jesus Christ and must be understood through his person. This is not to say that modern historical Christianity has not developed many traits which can be fruitfully compared with parallel or analogous traits in other world religions, but a full understanding of their Christian significance is finally dependent on him as the center of the meaning and value of Christianity as an historical totality.

## II
## The Person of Jesus Christ

The centrality of the personality of Jesus Christ in comparative studies cannot be overemphasized. As Rudolf Otto pointed out: "This new religion of Jesus does not grow out of reflection and thinking, out of speculation and philosophy; it is not artfully construed or demonstrated. It breaks forth from the mysterious depth of the individuality of this religious genius." The same point is made by Ernst

Troeltsch.  Christian faith, of course, says much more than
that Jesus was a religious genius.  It says that he was the
Christ and that God revealed himself in Jesus as his Son.
The person of Jesus Christ transcended the first century of
Christianity and he transcends while he helps to form the
centuries of Christian life and faith.  He confronts every
age and every culture with which Christianity comes in
contact and it is in terms of him that every expression of
Christian life is finally judged.

In an instructive work like that of Sidney Cave, *Christianity and Some Living Religions of the East,* we note how in
issue after issue the focal point is Jesus Christ.  On the
nature of the divine Cave first notes the amazing diversity of men's conception of the Divine.  Two types predomi-
nate: the Lawgiver as in Zoroastrianism and early Islam and
the unknowable and infinite Reality of Vedanta and Sufi movements.  By realization of identity with Him, redemption may
be obtained.  Christianity growing out of Judaism possessed
a conception of God as personal and known.  Yet the distinctiveness of Christianity comes from Jesus' own experience
and revelation of God.  The teachings are important but the
concrete personal revelation was definitive.   The life
reveals a divine reality which transcends the finite expressions of the life without repudiating the personality.
Jesus Christ is at once particular and universal.  On account of Jesus Christ the idea of God is radically changed.
God Himself is not thought apart from the event of Jesus.
Christ becomes a standard, on the one hand, and a source of
communion with God.  There are many traits and truths about
God which can be discussed philosophically and compared with
other religions profitably.  Moreover, their philosophical
validity will possess whatever autonomy is appropriate to
such disciplines, but the distinctiveness of Christianity is

not the general idea of God but the concrete historical
totality which focuses God in Christ.

When Cave discusses the manifestations of the Divine he
also finally comes back to the person of Christ. "If, as
Christians believe, God has in Christ revealed His holy
love, then it matters much that men should know of Him in
Christ and by that revelation all lesser ideas of God have
to be tested. It is not intolerance; it is the spontaneous
act of Christian love to seek to pass on to others what to
the Christian is not only his highest religious idea but
certain truth; God made known to men in the life and death
of Jesus Christ."[4] Here, again, there is no repudiation of
philosophy and no necessary warfare of faith and reason.
Yet the simple fact is that Christianity is not itself when
it neglects that personal reference.

The centrality of the person of Jesus Christ is evident
also when other religions are compared with Christianity on
the issue of the relation of God or the Divine to human
needs. Some religions like Zoroastrianism and Islam emphasize escape from the wrath of God through obedience to God's
will. Others, like Hinduism, Buddhism and the Sufi movement
have at times stressed deliverance from the flux and weari-
ness of life. Jesus taught that God loves sinners. God
takes the initiative in seeking out the lowliest and the
lost. The supreme expression of God's love, however, is not
in a teaching or preachment but is found in the optimism of
the Cross. It is an act in the career of Jesus that gives
his teaching a distinctive dimension and makes it personally
concrete in the life of God. The cross is not a teaching;
it is a revelatory act.

It is instructive to trace the various interpretations
of the relation of the Divine to human need in the history
of Christianity. There are many differences from time to

time and place to place. Sometimes the need of man is presented as an eager quest to escape the corruption of the
body. Deliverance from corruption is conceived through the
"deification" of humanity in the Incarnation. Sometimes
Jesus is treated as paying a ransom or again a debt which
man owed to God's honor by reason of his sin. Sometimes the
idea of punitive justice has predominated and Christ's work
seen as deliverance from the guilt and penalty of sin. But
however numerous the interpretations which have prevailed,
the fact remains that the *revelatory personality* of Christ
in his wholeness *transcends* them all as it evokes them all
under various historical circumstances.

For this revelatory reason the main distinction of
Christianity from non-Christian religions is not found in
special *nuances* of his ethical teaching on love, mercy,
righteousness and the like. It may be true, nevertheless,
that Montefiore is correct in pointing out the novelty of
Jesus' teaching on seeking out the lost until the lost be
found: "The summons not to wait till they meet you in your
sheltered and ordered path, but to go forth and seek out and
redeem the sinner and the fallen, the passion to heal and
bring back to God the wretched and the outcast—all this I
do not find in Rabbinism; *that* form of love seems missing."[5]
The real distinctiveness of Christianity here is that Jesus
died for sinners and the faith that God was revealed in his
so-doing and that the work of God's love in the world was
not overcome by evil in the world, but that God's triumph
was being made manifest. What is said of the relation to
Judaism may be instructively extended to other world
religions. Neither Zoroaster, Buddha, the writer of the
Bhagavadgita, nor Sankara seems to have had quite this
quality which Montefiore lifts up for emphasis. However, it
should be noted that Swami Alkhilananda finds in Sri

Ramakrishna and other incarnations the outgoing love for
men.

> "As Sri Ramakrishna tells us, they (the incarna-
> tions) are the connecting link between God and
> man. 'The saviours of humanity are those who
> see God, and being at the same time anxious to
> share their happiness of divine vision with
> others—willingly undergo the troubles of re-
> birth in the world in order to teach and lead on
> struggling humanity to its goal.'"[6] "Of their
> own volition they assume the desire to alleviate
> the sufferings of humanity."[7] "It is love that
> attracts the disciples to the incarnation, as
> the magnet attracts base metal. We have seen
> time and again in history as well as in our per-
> sonal experience that illumined souls have in-
> tense love for human beings. They can inspire
> and transform the people because of their love
> for them."[8] Grace transcends the law of Karma.
> Sri Krishna says in the *Gita*: "Fixing thy mind
> on Me, thou shalt, by My grace overcome all
> obstacles."[9] "A divine incarnation, being a
> manifestation of God, has the power of grace."[10]

Comparisons of the teaching of Jesus with the best in
other religions have led to subtle and overrefined definition and argumentation. The claims for uniqueness of teachings are seldom if ever left undisputed. It is more fruitful to explore distinctiveness elsewhere. As we have tried
to state above Christianity is not the *words* of Jesus, but
the *power* of Jesus in history.[11]

The personality of Jesus Christ has given Christianity
a dynamic quality. Through him the kingdom of God ushered
in a new civilization. Islam is dynamic and produced a
distinctive historical totality. Hindu writers like Swami
Alkhilananda point out that the great incarnations are crea-
tors of civilizations. Certainly there is a Christian civilization and a Christian history. Christianity is an historical totality whose telos has been provided by Jesus as the
Son of God. The dynamic quality in Christianity has been

threefold:   (1) it has been a *ferment*; (2) it has been able
to *use* the materials which surrounded it without complete
accommodation;  and  (3)  it  has  been  able  to  maintain  and
develop its basic ethical eschatology.   The principle of
*ferment* may  also  be  called  its  prophetic  element  or  its
dialectical character.   Christianity is not a sterotype or a
code; it is creative in a profoundly personal sense.   In all
societies which it has entered it has set up a ferment soon
or late.   It has, to be sure, accommodated itself, but it
has always sought to control and to transform.   Richard
Niebuhr's idea of Christ transforming culture points to its
prophetic dialectical element.   The vertical dialectic of
divine-human encounter is always in tension with temporal
horizontal dialectics in history.   In the Christian view of
history the transcendent dimension is as much a factor as
the immanental purposive factor.   At the intersection of the
transcendent and immanent planes is the personality of Jesus
Christ.   Men who are in fellowship with him are likewise
centers of intersection of the historical and the transhistorical.

       The dynamic element is also manifest in Christianity's
power to *use* everything that is usable.   Christianity cannot be identified with the civilization in which it has
participated and which it helped create.   It is not the
Bible, nor the institutional forms of the Bible.   It is
bound neither by the first century, nor the fourth, nor the
thirteenth, the sixteenth nor the twentieth.   Christianity
freely uses all things.   As Bishop McConnell says:  "Everything of the true and good and beautiful will get a better
chance to show truth and goodness and beauty after it has
been  converted  to Christianity than it ever had before."[12]
As an historical totality viewed in any one century Christianity has many of the transient marks of its times.   It

frequently confuses its essence with its historical accidents.  One of its critical problems today is that some
branches of the church identify it with these accidents of
creed, ecclesiastical structures, conceptions of authority,
rubrics of sacrament, and the like.  The churches are
confused because while they recognize their unity in Christ
they do not discern what is historical baggage.  The more
faith the church has in Christ as the center of history, the
more freedom it possesses to use the instruments of its environment and the rich heritages of the world civilizations to do
love's redemptive work.  The capacity of Christianity to
receive new truth into itself and relate it to its center of
meaning is impressive.

The dynamic quality of Christianity is also evident in
its *eschatological* character.  This quality is related to
all that we have so far emphasized.  The Kingdom of God has
been made manifest in history in Jesus Christ and the Kingdom will be made completely manifest.  God has revealed his
universal ethical love and freely given his grace to
unworthy sinners.  The power of his kingly rule has already
entered history and the divine power is overthrowing evil
and is reconciling mankind.  The righteousness of God is the
sanction of the purposes of history.  The purposes of history that are finally to be consummated are only those
"righteous" ones which are sanctioned by the divine nature.

Emphasis on personality resolves many of the antinomies
and paradoxes of ethics.  No ethical principle taken by itself fulfills the requirements of ethics.  Yet in relation
to the concrete reality of person-in-community ethical laws
find their coherence and unity.  The ethical personality
fulfills and transcends codes however lofty.  Through personality the dialectic of *relative* and *absolute* ethics is
resolved, also of *code* and *principle*, of *individual* and

*society*, of *formalism* and *teleology*, of *history* and the
*transhistorical*, of the *empirical inequalities* of men and
their *spiritual equality*, of *justice* and *love*, of *duty* and
*grace*, of *self-realization* and *self-sacrifice*.    The
personality of Jesus has given spiritual and ethical content
to the conception of personality by his disclosure of the
love of God and thus provides a religious sanction for
ethics in the nature of God.    Ethical reality in men as
disclosed by him is theonomous, i.e., neither restricted to
finite autonomy nor heteronomous, but human responsibility
in the context of the energizing of God.


                                III
                The Fellowship of Believers


     A Christian is defined by his loyalty to Jesus Christ.
This loyalty is a personal loyalty.    It is a synthesis of a
dialectic as E. S. Brightman has pointed out between the
thesis:   "Following Jesus is impossible without ideas" and
the antithesis that "following Jesus unitedly is impossible
if we insist on agreement in ideas."[13]    The loyalty of the
individual Christian is an unfinished synthesis that takes
place within a fellowship, within a community.    We have
already noted that Christianity is an historical totality
and as such stands over against other historical totalities
as one whole distinguished from other wholes.
     The fellowship of believers creates a cultus.    Chris-
tianity is not unique in having a cultus.    A cultus is a primary datum for every religion.    Wach defines cultus as follows:    "In a wider sense, all actions which flow from and
are determined by religious experience are to be regarded as
practical expression or *cultus*.    In a narrower sense, however, we call cultus the act or acts of the *homo religiosus:
worship*."[14]    Worship is of the very essence of religion.

The cultus unites and integrates the brotherhood more than
its doctrinal expressions do.[15]   "In actual practice," said
a World Council of Churches Report on Ways of Worship to the
Lund Conference, "ways of worship are never built up in a
theoretical way by drawing liturgical consequences from
dogmatic tenets. Rather is the creed born from worship."[16]
Whether the ecclesiastically organized cultus in
non-Christian religions should be called a church is a
disputed question. Christian theologians hesitate to do so
because the term "church" is not a purely descriptive term
but a normative one, based on definite content of doctrine
and referring to an ideal of life and practice.[17]  In this
sense the Church is a distinguishing mark of Christianity
even though the Church is broken up into a number of bodies,
each claiming the right, some exclusively, to represent the
whole as well as the ideal. Unity and division are social
characteristics of all major religious faiths. It would
carry us too far to compare all the sociological types
(circle, brotherhood, etc.) of the various religions. We
may accept Wach's authority that "there is no parallel to
the unique centralization of government in the Roman Catholic Church."[18]  No Christians outside that church regard its
unique centralization as normative for Christianity, however.

Christianity has been *sociologically fecund.*
Troeltsch's distinctions of church-type, sect-type and mysticism have been fruitful and much discussed. However, many
modifications of his analyses have been urged and attempted,
some with real effect. In any case the focus of the cultus
from which the sociological forms proceed always involves
Jesus Christ. Rudolf Otto's great work on *The Idea of the
Holy* is interesting at this point because he stresses worship as the heart of religion and hence notes the signifi-

cance of the cultus.  The general category of the *numinous*,
the realm of the Holy, reaches its climax and culmination in
Christianity.

    "By the continual living activity of its non-rational
elements a religion is guarded from passing into 'rationalism.'  By being steeped in and saturated with rational
elements it is guarded from sinking into fanaticism or mere
mysticality, or at least from persisting in these, and is
qualified to become a religion for all civilized humanity.
The degree in which both rational and non-rational elements
are jointly present, united in healthy and lovely harmony,
affords a criterion to measure the relative rank of religions—and one, too, that is specifically religious.
Applying this criterion, we find that Christianity, in this
as in other aspects, stands out in complete superiority over
all its sister religions."[19]  The testimony of the early
Church to Jesus Christ and a critical analysis of the
Christian response to him leads Otto to conclude with great
sensitivity:  "We can look, beyond the prophet, to one in
whom is found the Spirit in all its plenitude, and who at
the same time in his person and in his performance is become
most completely the object of divination, in whom Holiness
is recognized apparent.  Such a one is more than Prophet.
He is the Son."[20]

    In the sociological perspective of Christianity there
is an affirmation of both personal worth and social solidarity.  Every culture respects the "thematic values" of
individual well-being and social well-being, but in Christianity they are both metaphysically affirmed and grounded.
In some world religions the status of the person seems to be
ultimately in doubt as their expositions and ideals of the
conception of mystical experience indicate.  Ernst Troeltsch
in summarizing the emergent conclusions of nineteenth centu-

ries of Christian ethics states:

> The Christian Ethos alone possesses, in virtue of
> its personalistic Theism, a conviction of person-
> ality and individuality, based on metaphysics,
> which no Naturalism and no Pessimism can
> disturb.[21]

> The Christian Ethos alone, through its concep-
> tion of a Divine Love which embraces all souls
> and unites them all, possesses a Socialism which
> cannot be shaken.[22]

There is thus an organic pluralism in the communitarian
theology of Christianity. On the one hand is the corpora-
teness of the Body of Christ; on the other hand is the individuality of faith, conscience and sin. The two main sacraments of the cultus illustrate the point clearly. In both
baptism and holy communion the dignity and worth of the person and the solidarity of the church are recognized. Baptism is the rite of entrance into the people of God. Persons do not live in the household of God as isolated
individuals. Both infant and adult baptism lay a demand
upon the person who is entering the Christian community.
The rite also lays obligations on the Church, for baptism
establishes a new status for the person which should reflect
itself in developing Christian character. Infant baptism
normally leads to confirmation. This rite conserves, as
Craig says, "the right of the child to belong at once to the
People of God, and at the same time recognizes the need for
conscious decision in the response to grace."[23] "We are not
isolated individuals who are snatched as brands from the
burning. We are social creatures who are saved through
participation in the People of God. God's grace is usually
mediated to us through a society."[24] This reference to
God's grace is essential for it indicates that we are
members of a more-than-human community. We are members of a
cosmic community grounded in God.

What we have said of baptism is even more evident in
the sacrament of holy communion. Each one comes to
participate in the communion and all belong to each other
and Christ in the eucharistic meal. It is the most solidaristic act in the Body of Christ. "For each one of us our
communion is with God in Christ, and to be in Christ is to
be in the *koinonia* of all who are one in Him. This *koinonia*
is not something added on to our private devotion, a coming
together of privately saved souls: it is the way in which
God reaches man."[25] "The *koinonia* is not of this or that
church, but of the whole Church."

This dialectical polarity and interpersonal involvement
of individual and community is reflected in the characteristic form of mystical experience in Christianity. St.
Bernard and Ruysbroeck have expressed the typically Christian mystical experience. There are exceptions to the
dualistic form of mystical union in Christianity, as Meister
Eckhart illustrates, but he is hardly normative. Ruysbroeck
has a classic passage which is instructive, and I believe
representative, of the principle here involved:

> That measureless Love which is God Himself,
> dwells in the pure deeps of our spirit, like a
> burning brazier of coal. And it throws forth
> brilliant and fiery specks which stir and kindle
> hearts and senses, will and desire, and all the
> powers of the soul, with a fire of love....As
> air is penetrated by the brightness and heat of
> the sun, and iron is penetrated by fire; so that
> it works through fire the works of fire, since
> it burns and shines like the fire...yet each of
> these keeps its own nature—the fire does not
> become iron, and the iron does not become fire,
> for the iron is within the fire and the fire
> within the iron, so likewise God is in the being
> of the soul. The creature never becomes God as
> God never becomes creature....The union takes
> place in God through grace and our home-turning
> love....

The contrasting impersonal type of mystical union, the
ecstasy of identity, which Rudolf Otto compared in Sankara
and Eckhart, is more commonly associated with Eastern religions than with Christianity.   Some Indian interpreters
regard the dualistic communion of the above as a lower stage
of union than Hindu disciplines of the superconscious state
make possible.  It would seem that the personalism of Christian love is its normative form.   Nevertheless, we cannot
overlook the high valuation which Dean Inge gave to Plotinus
and his influence on Christian mysticism.  Nor can we ignore
the fact that mysticism is rejected by some sections of the
Church because it endangers the Lordship of Jesus Christ.
The mediaeval Church insisted on keeping mystical practices
under the discipline of approved spiritual advisers.  Modern
neo-Calvinist protesters against mysticism wish also to keep
Christian experience regulated through the Lordship of
Christ.  Both forms of control imply the mediated and hence
dualistic norm of all worship both private and corporate.

We have noted the sociological fecundity of the historical totality which Christianity comprises.  It is important to stress, in conclusion, the threefold dialectic that
underlies its dilemmas within the organized church, in
relation to the community, and in relation to culture.
Christianity has a thoroughgoing ethical ethos which is
related to it inheritance of the covenant principle and to
its eschatology of divine righteousness.

There is in the first place the dilemma of the Church's
involvement in the world.  There is a permanent dialectic
between the revelatory power of Jesus' ethic and the institutional accommodation of the Church in society.  The
prophetic tension within the Church drives her into acts of
self-purification and social reform.  In the second place
there is the tension between the Christian community and the

social environment.  Though Christianity accommodates itself
to its social milieu it is in a state of permanent dialectic
with that social order.  It must often repudiate the order
which   succors   it.    This   eschatological   situation   is
generally not understood by those who have fully accepted
ecclesiasticism within the Church or by those who wish the
Church to supply the moral cement of the status quo.  It is
also not understood by the secularized eschatology of its
Communist enemies.   In the third place, there is the
permanent revolution of Christianity in relation to all of
culture.   This means that Christianity cannot tolerate
surrendering cultural leadership to any other power.  Where
it has lost the leadership in culture transformation it must
regain the initiative by becoming again what it most
profoundly is, a community of loyalty to Jesus Christ.
Worshipping God through his revelatory act initiates the
permanent purgation of culture and the renewal of
civilization.  This function of Christianity I believe to be
characteristic and *unique* in a *normative* sense.

## NOTES

[1]*Either-Or*, vol. II, p. 277, quoted in *Man and Morals in the Social Sciences*, p. 39.

[2]*Ibid.*, p. 213.

[3]*Ibid.*, p. 214.

[4]Sidney Cave, *Christianity and some Living Religions of the East* (London:  Duckworth, 1949), p. 111.

[5]C. G. Montefiore, "The Spirit of Judaism," *The Beginning of Christianity*, vol. I, p. 79, quoted in S. Cave, *op. cit.*, p. 137.

[6]*Hindu View of Christ* (Boston:  Branden Press, 1949), p. 23.

[7]*Ibid.*, p. 33.

[8]*Ibid.*, p. 37.

[9]*Ibid.*, p. 39.

[10]*Ibid.*, p. 40.

[11]See E. S. Brightman, "The Essence of Christianity, *Crozer Quarterly*, April, 1941.

[12]*Human Needs and World Christianity*, p. 217.

[13]*Op. Cit.*

[14]J. Wach, *Sociology of Religion* (University of Chicago Press, 1944), p. 25.

[15]*Ibid.*, p. 141.

[16]Faith and Order Commission of the World Council of Churches, *Ways of Worship*, p. 8.

[17]Wach, *op. cit.*, p. 145.

[18]*Ibid.*, p. 153.

[19]Rudolf Otto, *The Idea of the Holy* (Oxford University Press, 1931), p. 146.

[20]*Ibid.*, p. 182.

[21]E. Troeltsch, *The Social Teachings of the Christian Churches*, conclusions in Vol. II.

[22]*Ibid.*

[23]Clarence C. Craig, *The One Church in the Light of the New Testament*, p. 93.

[24]*Ibid.*, p. 94.

[25]*Ways of Worship*, p. 11.

# Christ Transforming Culture
## (1957)

The phrase "Christ Transforming Culture" comes from H. Richard Niebuhr.[1] My task is to show how it relates in general operating terms to the mission of the Church. He regarded the idea as one of the basic types of relationship to culture with which Christians have defined the meaning of Christ. It expresses the type of Christian theology and social ethics which is persuasive in conception and compelling in action for me and coherent with the kind of communitarian personalism in whose tradition I stand. For Niebuhr it was one of several types which have characterized Christian thought. Some Christians *oppose* Christ to culture: others place him in a transcendent relation *above* culture; still others make him the Christ *of* culture. When mission and evangelism affirm him as the Christ who *transforms* culture it is acknowledged that one must sometimes place him against some culture pattern or value, that he is always above culture in so far as he is Lord, that he is in culture but never of it, and that at all times he is savior and revolutionary redeemer.

The thesis of this presentation is that the Gospel purposes to set goals for society—all society—and that Christ intends to reform all the people and institutions in the light of those goals. I believe that the Church is mission and that Jesus Christ who is at work in all cultures, often before the missionary arrives, purposes to convert all per-

251

sons, nations, and cultures and to transform all their institutions by his spirit.  Given the thesis of this theological, ethical and evangelical concern I shall analyze in
broad terms what it means to transform a culture and world
culture.  I mean this to be understood in a radical but not
a triumphalist sense.  Outcomes are in God's hands, not in
the hands of ecclesiastical authorities.

In such a conception just outlined the so-called "personal" and the so-called "social" gospel are but aspects of
one organic whole.  The gospel of the Kingdom of God addresses persons individually, in groups, and in institutions, including the institutional structures and processes.
About 1890 Walter Rauschenbusch expressed this dynamic integral meaning of the Gospel and it has informed my own career
in Christian social ethics.  He wrote:

> Most people look only to the renewal of the in-
> dividual.  Most social reformers look only to
> the renewal of society.  We believe that two fac-
> tors make up the man, the inward and the out-
> ward, and so we work for the renewal and Chris-
> tianization of the individual and of society.
>
> Most Christians demand the private life for God
> and leave business to the devil.  Most social
> reformers demand justice in business life, in
> order that private life may be given to plea-
> sure.  We plead for self-sacrifice in private
> life, in order to achieve justice in business
> life; and for justice in business life that
> purity in private life may become possible.
>
> Most Christians say:  Wait till all men are con-
> verted, then a perfect social order will be pos-
> sible.  Most social reformers say:  Wait till we
> have a perfect social order, then all men will
> be good.  We say:  Go at both simultaneously;
> neither is possible without the other.
>
> They all say:  Wait!  We say:  Repent, for the
> Kingdom of God is at hand.[2]

II

The analysis which follows is essentially sociological
and historical in form, but its norms and principles are
clearly theological and Christian. What is a culture? What
holds it together? Why do cultures disintegrate? How are
they transformed?

In a technical sense the concept of culture is relatively new, but it is important. During the past fifty years it
has proved to be increasingly fruitful as a scientific tool.
For our purposes we may use a definition by David Bidney
that: A culture consists of the acquired or cultivated
behavior and thought of individuals within a society, as
well as of the intellectual, artistic, and social ideals and
institutions which the members of the society profess and to
which they strive to conform.[3] Analysis of this conception leads to several observations. First, culture is a
whole of interacting, interdependent parts, no one of which
is changed in isolation. There are three emphases here. It
is a whole whose parts interact and therefore are partly
dependent on each other. No aspect or part of culture under-
goes a significant change without affecting all the other
parts. The initiating change can take place in any part.
Sometimes it is like the invention of the cotton gin, or the
steam engine, or the atom bomb; sometimes it is a new religious community like the Early Church; sometimes it is a new
system of education like the public schools in America; sometimes it is a political or economic philosophy like democracy, or capitalism, or communism. Major changes in one phase
of culture have repercussions in the others. Aframerican
music has penetrated many societies.

The major institutions of a culture are related to its
economic or technical activities; to political or legal pro-

cesses; to family and other authority structures; to educational procedures; to language and communication; to art and
aesthetic expression; and to religion, ethics, or philosophy, the interpretive side of life.  These institutions have
proximate and ultimate values.

Secondly, culture is held together by a value-struc-
ture, a body of meanings and values, largely self-enforcing.
Some call this complex a myth-structure.  it is a cluster of
beliefs, meanings, and norms.

The parts of culture can be adequately understood only
in terms of the common meanings that pervade the whole.
About thirty years ago Margaret Mead prepared a book for the
World Health Organization and UNESCO to guide persons who
would be working to effect changes in some of the areas of
rapid social change, entitled *Cultural Patterns and Technical Change*.  She pointed out that only by relating any
planned detail of change to the central values of a culture
is it possible to provide for the repercussions which will
occur in other aspects of life.[4]  The transmission of
influence from one part of culture to another must come to
terms with the dominant values that hold that culture together.  For example, one does not increase the food supply of
some countries by a shipment of pigs.

It is a serious error to view cultural differences as
collections of curiosities.  Years ago, when social scientists studied marriage and family practices throughout the
world, they sometimes compiled and catalogued a wide range
of diverse customs, mores, and folkways.  Some of these
seemed quite opposite and even contradictory to one another
when compared as abstract beliefs.  Some drew the ethically
relativistic conclusion that somewhere in the world "anything goes."  Were there, then, no universal standards or
norms?  Even that question could be out of context.  With

the concept of culture as a system held together by a myth-structure, such diversities are approached from within a unified system. Cultural relativity does not entail ethical relativity. Indeed, unless the inner meanings and values of a people are understood in relation, it is not possible to deal scientifically or responsibly with their beliefs and practices. The missionary enterprise has learned that such understanding has profound implications for the study and introduction of a new religion and for an appreciation of how Christ changes or transforms culture.

Thirdly, the ultimate concerns within the values of a society constitute its functioning religion. Religion is, therefore, no superficial or expendable element, but is rather the key to and the very heart of culture. In Christian societies the church is the bearer and earthly guarantor of their cultural unity; it is not simply the "people of God" as an enclave. Its survival depends on how it addresses rival ultimate concerns where cultures clash.

In summary, religion functions in culture in two basic ways. Religion comprises the ultimate elements in the pervasive values of all the institutions of society. It refers to the dimension of depth of all the basic institutions. It is in this way an integrater of society, a prerequisite of there being a cultural whole. It is the ultimate expression of the nisus toward consistency among the penultimate values by pointing each to the ultimate ones. In the second place religion as objectively institutionalized, with its distinctive orders and organizations, exists alongside other basic institutions like schools, courts, legislatures, artists' studios, factories, banks, homes and the like. Characteristically, the majority of Christians think of Church as the church on the corner. They do not have a strong sense of responsibility for the preservation and enhancement of the

common meanings and values which hold the world together.
For them the church on the corner serves the needs of individuals.  These two basic functions of religion are dialectically essential.  Therefore, if Christ is not acknowledged
as Lord of all aspects of culture he cannot be truly Lord of
the localized church; and so the mission of the localized
church must be directed not only to individuals but to the
spiritual integration of society as a whole.  The Church as
the Body of Christ is more than a human institution; it is a
"colony of heaven;" its historical form is provisional but
its ultimate values are grounded in Christ, in the Kingdom
of God.


                              III


      The power of Christianity to create and shape a culture
and a civilization is historically demonstrable.  At one
time the word 'Christendom' had a definite meaning, and
although Christian Europe, for example, was never as Chris-
tianized as some romantically suppose, nevertheless, a coherent Christian ethos effectively penetrated law, education, government, art, commerce, and literature as well as
church and family.  Today, some writers speak of a post-
Christian era, of the ghetto-church, or in other terms that
reflect defeatism and pessimism.  It is, indeed, curious
that in the contemporary self-criticism of the Church there
is a down-grading of the function of religion in culture.
At the very moment when Christian self-criticism is most
prevalent, social scientists are regarding religion and
church with a new functional seriousness.  Though preachers
lose their prophetic tongues, are prisoners in their own
pulpits, and are conspicuous by not addressing socially
controversial subjects, wordly writers are using biblical

themes and secularized versions of Christian norms to casti-
gate the failures, corruptions, and cheap values of contemporary life.  On the one hand, while Christians try to make
their little ecclesiastical shows succeed by going easy on
the sins of society and using dubious promotional gimmicks,
the secular prophets are excoriating the meaninglessness and
absurdity of the world and berating the churches' loss of
nerve.  The great disloyalty of the local churches is to
forget that they are colonies of heaven whose mission is to
witness to, not to outcompete, the 'successful' rivals for
popular attention.

## IV

We must now look at the opposite side of the cultural
scene.  There are tendencies in modern culture which challenge the theses we have been developing.  There is the
tendency for basic institutions in urban society to become
relatively autonomous and hence to seek an existence of
their own, to write their own rules, to develop self-inter-
ested norms, to create their own language, and to elaborate
their own technostructure and secular priesthood.  Hence,
sub-cultures emerge.  They celebrate the differentiation and
specialization of civilization.  The autonomy so achieved is
like the Fall in Eden, disobedience and rebellion of the
parts against the meanings of the whole.  Cumulatively this
signals the alienation of the creation against the Creator.
Finite things are sought for their own sake and not in subordination to ultimate ends.  The false consensus of the sub-
cultures violates the needed consensus of cultural unity.

What do these tendencies entail for our whole endeavor?
First of all, we must acknowledge that in a complex society
fragmentation not only takes place as specialized institu-

tions grow, but fragmentation also develops in the accepted
standards of urban society. Examples of this are readily at
hand:

1.    There has been a three hundred year trend for economic life to be free of political, ethical, and ecclesiastical controls. This movement probably reached its peak, at
least in theories of business autonomy, in the nineteenth
century. Since then more accountability or responsibility
has been argued. The so-called 'welfare state' and socialism are expressions of this reintegration.

2.    Law has tended to be more positivistic. The merely
legal has become morally deprived of appeals to ultimate
principles and sanctions, but here again an appeal to universal human rights is reasserting itself.

3.    There is a tendency for government to become utilitarian and expedient, while it is also more inclusive in its
claims over the citizens.

4.    Art and music have separated themselves from the
sources of social meaning and from the popular life, creating a deep division between the 'great' artist and the
'vulgar' art. The arts are often technical, ingrown, or
esoteric projections of innovation.

5.    Education has largely lost its liberal spirit and
substance. Even the liberal arts have little enlivening or
common universe of discourse. The university is called a
diversity. Subservience to trade and utility has vocation-
alized them and specialized degree programs appear in hundreds of educational packages.

6.    Nations increasingly stress sovereignty and patrio-
tism as internal principles of cohesion and expend increasing proportions of national budgets on military security.
Internally they celebrate ethnic pluralism as if that were a
self-evident virtue.

7.   The churches are divided and self-absorbed and, despite growing doctrinal consensus, fail to practice visible organic unity.  Moreover, they are alienated from culture while being institutionally accommodated to nationalism, class structure, and even race and sex biases.

The above are only indicative of the data that must be considered when one is realistically pursuing the theme of Christ transforming culture.

V

What then becomes the task of the Church and the churches?   There is a fourfold responsibility:   (1) There must be a whole gospel for the whole person for the whole world.   A piecemeal gospel tied to individualistic ideas of people and the nature of society will only aid and abet the secularism and fragmentation already indicated above.   (2) Church leaders must learn to confront a culture simultaneously at all relevant points of social change.   Its decision-making must seek to set in motion through cumulative causation a constructive spiral where now a vicious circle is at work.   A small community of dedicated Christians can have a marked strategic effect.   Disciplined witness-bearing has always generated more spiritual power than large bodies of diffuse, uncommitted, and untrained church members who expect more nurturance from than sacrifice for Christ.   (3) The institutions of society must be redirected in terms of purposes and goals and hence the churches must formulate them and develop men and women who are motivated to achieve them.   In a period of rapid social change the purposes that canalize social energy generate great power.   Church leaders need understanding of the nature and control of revolutionary power.   (4) Since society is a web of decision-

making, the churches need sophistication in the strategy of
planning and persuasion, eliciting the participation of the
people whose welfare is affected by induced social change.

The church must renew itself with the same principles
and loyalties whereby it would change its cultural environment.  It must lead in self-criticism and self-reform, thus
being a model.  The church is, thus, not merely a theological institution, but its life has economic, political, educational, aesthetic, social, and communications dimensions.
The transformation of the culture must begin at the house of
the Lord.  How the church raises money, governs itself, edu-
cates its youth and adults, develops its art, conducts its
community, and relates its Gospel to the world must be coherent with the transformation it seeks in the corresponding
areas of its environment.  Meanwhile there is grave danger
that the churches will continue to sanction the secular
loyalties of the people to means and ends that resist rather
than enhance the realization of the Kingdom of God.

A few direct questions will point up the issues:  Does
the Church have a positivistic attitude toward law?  Does it
have a casuistry of legal loop-holes?  Is its canon law
progressive in method or is it used to inhibit change?  Does
it expect special privileges from the secular order for its
leaders?  How does it manage its real estate and profitable
investments?  What are its employment practices?  How does
it relate actual inequalities and spiritual equalities?

The problem has to do with both support and the appeals
used to get support.  Let one example stand for many others.
Why do so many church appeals for money feature the fact
that they are tax deductible?  The other day I received an
appeal to support a drive for better pensions for retired
ministers.  The whole appeal was constructed around the idea
of how much tax advantage there would be to a generous

donor. Missing was a New Testament type of appeal. For the
average tax payer there would be little advantage in such a
case, but the so-called 'leading' laypersons would have a
substantial incentive.  If response to God is the fundamental objective of church efforts, rather than fiscal returns, or the success of a pensions drive, then a nation's
tax policy might bear scrutiny more than its advantage to a
large giver.  The question of stewardship belongs to the
norms with which the church addresses the state's tax laws
and the church's budgets.

A useful concept in ethics may be helpful in clarifying
the moral dimensions of how Christ transforms cultures and
persons in them.  It is the distinction between 'spot'
values and the 'field' values which give them normative meaning.  The first are the specific values chosen at a particular time and place.  The latter are the ideals that should
govern them and which are invisible.  'Spot' values are such
experiences as this morning's breakfast, last night's movie,
a particular vacation experience, a business deal, a labor-
management contract, or a sports event.  'Field' values
include norms like love, justice, fairness, freedom, compassion, reconciliation, sportsmanship, honesty, responsibility.  When the spot values are chosen coherently with the
field value, the whole self assents to the self of the spe-
cious present; and the experience then has joy or happiness as the accompanying feeling.  When what is specifically
chosen violates its field value, negative emotions are
brought to the consciousness of the actor.  In an athletic
contest, for example, except for an occasional tie, one team
wins and one team loses.  Each has wished to succeed; neither wishes to fail.  But the loss is tolerable for the
loser and the sport retains its integrity if the rules of
the game and the principles of sportsmanship have been fol-

lowed and obeyed.   If not, the whole system of relationships between the teams begins to disintegrate.   The sport
has lost its inner meaning and coherence.   When success
(winning) regardless of means becomes the dominant value,
the field values, not merely the spot values, are negated.
The scandal of football 'fixes' is not simply the disvalue
experienced in a single game, but the threat to meaningful
rivalry becomes ominous for all.   Success at any cost is a
disintegrative force in modern life.

The same relationship applies to labor-management relations.   In collective bargaining the representatives of each
side seldom get just what they want, but if they have bar-
gained in good faith, and recognize this to have been so,
disappointments and compromise on certain issues are tolerable.   A field of common values sustains future specific
relationships.   But if either side believes strongly that
the rules of the game have been violated, or that either
side has taken unfair advantage (which means about the same
thing), there is bitterness and the result is conflictual,
even disastrous.

The Church may be said to have a special mission with
respect to the field values of society.   Its ministry
includes the coherence of the moral order.   It cannot and
should not draw up all the rules of all the games of soci-
etal interaction, but it should address itself constantly to
what Christ requires as to the spirit and the basic principles of social responsibility.   William Temple was wont to
say that ninety percent of the churches' work lies outside
the walls of local churches.   The churches should understand
the true field values of the basic institutions of culture
and nurture them.   While doing so it must address its own
success drives and its operating values as to whether its
daily 'spot' values are coherent with its Gospel 'field'

values.  The most inclusive field value is, of course, the
Kingdom of God.

Finally, what do all these considerations mean with
respect to the theme of Christ transforming culture?  First
we should recognize that all societies are in a state of
rapid social change, not just the less-developed ones.
Revolution is changing many of them rapidly.  The spot
values change more rapidly than the field values, but the
field values are also in a state of flux.  Science and technology, governments and corporations, are bringing new
values with them.  The churches should demand responsible
consideration of all induced social change, the whole ecological impact of all interventions in nature and society.
Purposefully to induce change entails a responsibility to
come to terms with the central values of nations and
peoples.  The churches' posture must be ecumenical and it
should seek middle axions such as that found in the idea of
a just, sustainable, and participatory society.

Secondly, the almost universal approbation by humankind
of the universal Declaration of Rights and Freedoms as formulated under the aegis of the United Nations shows that the
secular world wants and needs a coherent body of field
values, the articulation of a mythos that will provide peace
and unity.  Such goals can canalize the new energies of new
and old cultures alike.  The Church knows that this table of
rights and freedoms owes much to the ethos of the West and
that this, in turn, is deeply rooted in the Judaeo-Christian spiritual heritage.  But the field values do not con-
cretize themselves in spot values.  All participants co-
create in this process.  The churches must not turn over to
others the ultimate spiritual and moral concerns of the
people.  Though Christ has been at work in whatever good
world cultures have achieved in the past, he has called into

being a new community for a new age.  For this mission he
seeks a renewed community, 'new wineskins for the new wine.'
The relevant conception of the Church for this age is Christ
transforming culture.

## NOTES

[1] H. Richard Niebuhr, *Christ Transforming Culture* (New York:  Harper and Bros., 1951).

[2] Dores Sharpe, *Walter Rauschenbusch* (New York: Macmillan, 1942), pp. 82-83.

[3] David Bidney, *Theoretical Anthropology* (Columbia University Press, 1954).

[4] Margaret Mead, *Cultural Patterns and Technical Change* (Columbia University Press, 1953).

Social Problems and the Christian Hope
(1954)

In this essay we shall try to state what it means to relate Christian hope to social problems. We shall, therefore, not seek to show how any particular social problem is resolved or illuminated by Christian eschatology, but rather to clarify some of the issues which the main theme of the Evanston Assembly of the World Council of Churches (Jesus Christ the Hope of the World) raises in the social field. Theologically speaking the problem is that of showing the relevance of eschatology to the solution of social questions. In the minds of some people the term eschatology is associated with historical despair and pessimism rather than with an optimism that social problems can have an historically favorable issue. Is hope only "ultimate" and is pessimism realism for the present?

I
Can Social Problems
be Solved?

Dean Liston Pope in an address at Boston University School of Theology entitled "Can Social Problems Be Solved?"[1] separates the question of sin as a perennial human problem from social problems. "A social problem," he writes, "is not to be equated with the basic stuff of human nature or despaired of because man is a sinner. It may result from sin or be manifestation of sin, but it is recognizable as a *social* problem only when it emerges as social behavior and accumulates social form and content with all the relativities and impermanence of any social struc-

267

ture....Efforts to explain particular social problems in
terms of sin are generally fruitless, as it is a *tour de
force* to describe a transitory and sporadic form of social
behavior (for example, war) in terms of a presumably
continual and permanent human characteristic or perversity."
He goes on to argue that neither progress nor problems
should be accepted as absolute. "There is no support from
history or from scrutiny of human nature that *all* social
problems will ultimately be solved, in the sense that a
society without problems will emerge. But there are adequate grounds for the belief that particular social problems can be solved once and for all. Society is a fluid,
ever-changing realm; new problems generally resemble former
ones but they are never quite the same. To lose heart about
an immediate problem is defeatist; to suppose that it will
have no successor is fatuous."[2] Dean Pope here makes some
important distinctions that will help to dispel some current
confusions about Christian hope.

Christianity is a religion of redemption. It therefore
affirms that certain basic problems can be solved. Among
these are man's relationship to God, man's relationship to
himself, and man's fundamental relationships to his fellow-
men. Moreover, the Christian faith views all persons not
individualistically but as bound together inter-personally.
These relationships viewed in their broadest cosmic and ultimate contexts overarch and include the social problems which
Dean Pope discusses in the essay referred to above. It is
the relevance of these interpenetrating realms of ultimate,
historical and personal redemption which constitutes the
crux of our present enquiry.

## II
## What is a Valid Eschatology?

Christian hope is not so much a subjective state of mind as an adequate personal relationship to what God has done, is now doing, and will do until all things are brought to their final end. End here means both *finis* and consummated *goal*. Christian eschatology views social problems from the perspective of the self-disclosure of God as manifested in the prophets of the Old Testament and supremely in the life, teachings, death and resurrection of Jesus Christ. When social problems are considered eschatologically they are confronted and interpreted and acted on in the light of such events. That they are a source of deeper attitudes of hope (even psychologically considered) than most human beings today bring to social events rests on the faith that the mighty acts of God manifested in Christ embrace all people and all time.

Many persons, particularly Christians in American churches, tend to ignore the term "eschatology" because of (a) its apparent technical theological character, (b) its exploitation by Biblical literalists, and (c) its special association with sectarianism and apocalypticism. Nevertheless, Christian hope is always eschatological and the studied avoidance of the term by ministers is a serious mistake. There is grave danger that with the disuse of the term there will result a disuse of its essential ideas. In the jargon of the trade we might say that the surrender of eschatology leads to the existentialism of the immediate present. Christian hope which feeds on the present availability of ultimate resources is then surrendered to the private despair of a present moment of decision which lacks goal, ground or sustaining motive.

Christian eschatology (and there are other kinds, like the Communist view of history) sees all social problems not only in terms of their conclusion but of their relationship

to God's purposes.  The consummation of God's work in Christ
is the goal of history.  Social events are not isolated
islands submerged in a sea of meaningless infinitude.  The
social process has a fulfillment in God's consummation of
his creative and redemptive work.  The *ground* of this hope
is in the nature and character of God which has been conclu-
sively revealed in Jesus Christ.  Social problems find their
ultimate solution not in the immediate passing moment but in
Christ as *end* and *ground*, i.e. in the preserving, righteous
and loving activity of God.  The psychological basis of
Christian hoping, as we have already observed, arises from
the Christian's faith in this objective activity of God.
Faith, hope and love interpenetrate.  We love because He
first loved us.  What we hope for in society and beyond
history is empirically grounded in the love which has
already been made manifest and constantly manifests itself.
Love produces hope.  What we have faith in provides the
substance of what we hope for.  So faith and love are the
foundation of our hope for the future.

      (1)  It is evident from what we have said that a  valid
Christian hope is not an otherworldly substitute for social
action.      Indeed,  social  problems  are  more  seriously
confronted  because  they  have  an  eschatological  context.
Persons have eternal destinies; they give to economics,
family life, social work and politics a dimension of profound interpersonal concern.  Eschatology is not an alternative to social science, but saves men from disposing of man
on a superficial level or of considering him as simply the
product of social forces.  On the other hand, so-called
Christian hope which escapes into "spiritual" aloofness
above the world or to "positive thinking" of a
self-protective subjective character is morally
irresponsible and hence religiously unworthy.

(2)   Although the meaning of social events centers in
God who transcends history, the overarching purposes of God
are *not merely transcendent*.  Christians who leave everything to God or who depreciate the ability of persons to do
anything about their psychological or social conditions
deny, in effect, the creative activity of God.  Although
detailed social programs may not be deduced from Biblical
generalizations, the evidence is irrefutable that Biblical
revelations of God are concretely historical.  God calls to
men and women in the midst of historical situations.  One of
the most eschatological parables of Jesus, The Last Judgment, deals with the problem of persons and nations who were
or were not sufficiently perceptive and faithful to hear the
call of the Christlike God in terms of the social needs of
their fellow human beings.  A valid eschatology corrects
simple resignation, insensitiveness to others, lofty but
abstract idealism, mere contemplation of timeless truths,
and quietistic devotion to God "above" history.

(3)   A genuine Christian hope is not *apocalyptic*, as
that term has come to be used.  There are, to be sure,
apocalyptic elements in the Bible.  Jesus may have shared
some of them.  He and Paul may have been in error in the
timing of their "historical expectations."  But their hope
was not fundamentally apocalyptical.  Even when the apocalyptic passages have been "demythologized," we find an eschatological remainder which centers in the fact that God does
not go down in defeat in the Cross but triumphs over sin and
death.  The Kingdom of God overarches all social tragedies
and defeats and yet is in the midst of the community as ongoing norm as a power.  The most abysmal social evils do not
finally defeat God or exhaust the resources which he affords
all his anxious, frustrated and bewildered children.  Christ
does not come again *as* the apocalyptists  vainly hope, but He

does come again and again, for "nothing can separate us from
the love of God which is in Christ Jesus our Lord."

(4) Eschatology does not annul discriminate moral judgments and decisions in social situations. It does recognize
that all our judgments and actions are under the judgment
and mercy of Him who sent his Son to the Cross. The
majestic holiness and righteousness of God give more rather
than less significance to responsible compromises when
persons choose between the relatively better and the
relatively worse values presented in actual alternatives.
Therefore, not unspecified or merely general repentance mark
the experience of Christians, but obedience to the moral law
in terms that are specifically relevant to concrete historical occasions. God, being the most obligated of all persons, has an absolute stake in human discriminate decisions
marked by loyalty or disloyalty.


                                III
                    Christian Hope is Personal


What the Christian hope postulates is the radically personal character of existence. Social problems occur not in
a self-explanatory biological or sociological realm, but in
a realm which is metaphysically personal in all its ultimate
dimensions. The apparently impersonal is always a phase or
aspect of the personal which is concretely real. Nature and
society present, when studied for specialized purposes, certain impersonal analytical traits. These may yield important results for scientific study. Institutions and other
forms of group life may be behavioristically and statistical-
ly examined. Yet the human community is always more concretely real and complex than science can analyze and
describe. But the human community is but a part of ultimate cosmic society. The Christian hope accepts the reality

of the divine-human encounter as basic in this divinely created community. In the midst of the social collectivity man confronts the divine Person. Social hope is based in a recognition of interpersonal fellowship both horizontally and vertically.

The eschatology of Christian faith requires, as a consequence, that social problems be treated from the perspective of the whole person. People are not primarily subjects of the state, units of production and consumption, man-hour monads of labor, business prospects, items in a vital statistics schedule, social security numbers or variables in the barometric pressure of public opinion. Persons are not psychophysical mechanisms to be brain-washed and manipulated. They are members of a divine society, alienated, anxious, tempted, sinful, forgiven, repentant, justified or sanctified, and their relationship in this community of persons includes and transcends at every moment of time the events of human history.

The basis of Christian social ethics is not abstract ideals or impersonal laws. Love, the whole person acting in compassionate, responsible mutuality and good will, is the substance of the great commandment, for it is the outgoing power of God which holds men and women in community with Himself and underlies all genuine forms of community. Love is always concretely personal. In this enfolding love each is free. God does not coerce human will though He holds each responsible for his moral choices. We must recognize that freedom is essential to the religious relationship. Therefore, it is also part of social hope. All forms of freedom have their analogue in the respect which God accords his children.

IV

The Social Relevance

of Christian Hope

Christian faith gives to all scientific and philosophical quests in the solution of social questions a great
motivation. Without this motivation the special sciences
and technologies tend to arouse fragmentary, illusory and
false hopes. Their vocational goals are often not brought
to completion but are abstracted and isolated from their
true end. The full affirmation of the Hope gives perspective, unity and coherence to what otherwise becomes a partial, truncated and even sub-Christian substitute for the
social whole. Three such distorted forms of truth in
contemporary life are scientific humanism, democratic humanism and Communism. They all express natural human hopes,
but they all lead human beings astray when taken as substitutes for the genuine and coherent hope of the Christian
faith. Scientific humanism possesses much truth, but when
elevated to the place of one's sole philosophy of life it
tempts one to believe that the immanent level of social and
physical cause and effect is self-explanatory and autonomous. Christian eschatology frees people from imprisonment
within any one intellectual discipline.

Christian eschatology also frees a person from bondage
to the rival humanisms of Communism and democracy. On the
one hand, it exposes the atheistic contempt of the person
found in the demonic use of power which some Marxist
perversions of eschatology involve. At the same time the
Christian concern for social justice relates the basic human
needs of the exploited millions of humankind to a revolutionary program which will champion the lowliest person when
proletarian dictatorship will have surrendered to despair.
On the other hand, the Christian hope refuses to identify
capitalist democracy with Christianity. It thus frees men
and women from the complacent self-righteousness with which
the West tends to confront communist totalitarianism. It

exposes, for example, the pride and pretensions of all social classes, the dilemmas of majority rule, the idolatries of competitive self-display, the hypocrisies of the gospel of production, and the tyrannies of corporation domination. The Christian hope doe not repudiate the constructive realism and fruitful idealism of democratic life, but it calls all to the Lordship of Christ and the permanent revolution in all social relations under the power of the Cross.

Whether in persecution or social triumph, whether as successful leaders of stable governments or as martyrs, whether as social prophets or as humble followers the Christian hope holds before all persons the reality of eternal life in Christ, his Lordship over all life, his final triumph and the everlasting communion of saints.

## NOTES

[1]Subsequently published in John A. Hutchinson, ed.,
*Christian Faith and Social Action* (New York:   Charles
Scribner's Sons, 1953).

[2]*Ibid*., pp. 223-224.

# Christian Bases of Morality and Ethics for Today
## (Choosing Responsibly in a Revolutionary World)
### (1969)

Bishop Frank and esteemed members of the Council, it is
an honor and a privilege to present to you a paper on the
Christian Bases of Morality and Ethics for Today and to
relate that theme to some of the trends commonly called the
"new morality."

I

Permit me, at the outset, to define some terms and to
indicate the range of topics that I shall seek to cover in
this lecture. By *morality* I mean the personal and social
conduct of life. I mean the actual moral choices that persons and organizations make and the quality of their habits
of will and institutional decisions as measured by some
norm. Morality includes the degree of freedom from corruption on the part of public officials, for example, and the
tone of positive responsibility with which policies are
carried out. The conduct of the war in Vietnam and the conduct of Mayor Daly and the Chicago police are questions of
morality. On the other hand, *ethics* is the normative
science of choice. It deals with man's reflections on
morality and choice. *Ethics* is not the same as morality for
it deals with the bases of judgment and decision in matters
of morality.

It is confusing to entitle a book *Situation Ethics:
The New Morality*.[1] Ethics and morality cannot, of course,
be completely divorced from each other, but there is a

277

logical and a methodological difference between them, even
though there is no ultimate separation. Morality and ethics
are both involved in the words of T. S. Eliot that the greatest treason is "to do the right thing for the wrong reason."
Ethics deals critically with the question of the principles
(if there are any) which ought to be observed in making
moral choices. Whether there are any principles is one of
the crucial questions in the debate over situation or contextual ethics. It is important, I shall insist, not only
that we do the right things, but that we choose them and do
them for the right reason. If we recognize that there are
practical moral rules or guidelines, we must ask what is the
basis for such rules? Are all rules maxims or are there
rules which are universal, i.e. more than maxims, rules
which have the standing of laws or principles? We shall consider these issues in due course.

There has always been a "new morality" and an "old
morality." The new one gets old by-and-by. In one sense,
the "new morality" is a collective term for modes of behavior that threaten standards for which the church has stood.
But there are also new modes of behavior that express more
fully what the church proclaims than much of the "old morality." It is all very mixed up. The "old morality" includes
some attitudes that are as deep as loyalty to Jesus Christ
but some forms of "old morality" are quite alien to responsible society and the youth are often eager to point these
out. For its part, the "new morality" is a mixed bag of
idealism, freedom, protest, sexual hedonism, and emphasis on
the *now*. The "old morality" is a mixed bag of ideals,
freedoms, defenses, power structures, negative constraints,
and drives for future as well as present affluence. In one
sense the "new morality" is today's liberalism and the "old
morality" is yesterday's liberalism; the former is a radical

threat and the latter is a conservative defense. Neither is self-validating. Both are mixtures of "liberties" and "restraints" and the mixtures are partly determined by a distinctive vision of what a person ought to be and by a distinctive perspective on society.

The worst in the "old morality" has much in common with the worst in the "new morality" in so far as both are self-regarding, proud of parochial values, indulgent in pleasures of the body, willing to use other people for one's own ends, blind to the needs of the total community, insensitive to exploitation, and lacking in true humanism. Does it really make much difference if one is absorbed in a vulgar display of adult affluence or in a display of vulgar unkemptness and indulgence of bodily satisfactions by youth? Hypocritical conventions in the older generation can be matched by irresponsible conformism in youthful patterns of protest. Youth sometimes cries out: there is no comparison between the obscenity of four letter words for sex and anger and the enacted obscenity of war and racial injustice. The "new morality" may be an unaesthetic but idealistic alternative to a conventionally proper hypocrisy which uses law and order to mask violence. The "new morality" is often a self-righteous protest against a self-righteous complacency. And so, where there is much confusion, we need methods of clarity if we are to be responsible.

There is a need to recognize the reality of rapid social change but also the continuity between basic themes in changing situations. The same theme may be detected amid the variations on the theme. Many styles of clothes may be worn by the same person. There may be a conformism among today's protesters which robs their deviations of any radical significance. In other words, there may be a typology of student and/or adult morality which shows that it is not

very radical after all.  In an interdependent social system
all behavior is a symbol of interacting responses.

    Perhaps the main moral challenge which the American
society faces is this:  "responsible action in a revolutionary world."  This phrase is taken from Robert M. Bellah's
essay "Civil Religion in America" (*The Religious Situation:
1968*).[2]  Each of these terms is crucial:  (1) *Responsibility*
rather than freedom seems to be the majority's moral need;
(2) *Action* alone will convince those who are impatient with
hypocrisy and freedom deferred; (3) *Revolution* bespeaks the
multiphasic social change that upsets patterns of power; and
(4) *World* describes the scope of the theater and the drama
that is being enacted.  The moral confusion of American life
may be viewed as the many-sided many-levelled acceptance,
rejection, or evasion of a theme that history has handed us:
"responsible action in a revolutionary world."

    This paper has three parts:  I.  A continuation of this
introduction on the general moral situation of the nation;
II.  A long statement on method in Christian social ethics;
and III.  Some brief concluding observations.

    The present moral situation in the nation is not good
and in many respects it is deteriorating.  It is amazing how
relatively silent the local churches are on the innumerable
moral problems that confront persons, families, and economic
and political institutions.  The relative silence is probably due to two things:  (1) the local churches are too
confused to speak out and (2) their people are sufficiently
well-off within the status quo to be able to manage without
getting involved in radical protest or revolution.  For example, as Ralph Potter observes, bad as the abortion laws may
be and horrible as the choices are that confront the poorer
women, the typical middle-class church woman does not need a
change in the laws, since she has the resources of motiva-

tion, information, and money to solve her problem if she is
desperate enough. However, there is a new receptivity and
broad segments of Protestants are getting involved in the
abortion question. But the situation may be a paradigm for
many moral dilemmas ranging from birth control and the pill
to the draft and the war in Vietnam. People are too confused to be morally articulate and they do not go in for
reform if they can somehow get by personally. As the Kerner
report[3] says: the people lack the *will* to overcome their
racism—and so the nation bitterly drifts into two separate
but unequal societies. In one sense many people are developing the kind of sophistication in which they do not want
to impose their moral views on others; but in another sense
they do not see that their real interests are those of
responsible action for the whole community. They lack
*responsiveness* which is the precondition of *responsibility*. In any case, whether we deal with the sacredness of
life in the *fetus* or the mother, on the one hand, or the
sacredness of God's creation in the black poor—the church
is a mission and therefore the moral claims of the Gospel
must be publicly announced and efforts must be made to pene-
trate the moral texture of all social life. The church cannot settle for silence or merely private solutions.

To this Council a brief listing of some current moral
failure will suffice to show the scope and complexity of the
confusion and moral evasion: racism, poverty, militarism
and war, breakdown of the city's basic order and services,
enthronement of affluence, decline of standards in the mass
media, the stranglehold of big business and the dominance of
organization man, widespread sexual hedonism and the epidem-
ic growth of venereal disease, the decline of the family as
a moral force, the international irresponsibility of the
state, the growth of the industrial-military complex, the

collapse of the welfare system, urban violence, the escala-
tion of organized crime, and the extreme alienation of a
growing body of contemporary youth.

In each of these areas the rate of change is rapid and
each area has a tendency to influence several of the other
areas substantially.  All are part of a vast interrelated
social system.  Each is involved in a *causal nexus* that
defies easy analysis and resolution of dilemmas.  Each is a
direct threat to the gospel and each has some of its source
in the "old morality" of the Protestant churches, with the
possible exception of organized crime.  Each and all of
these are related to the overall challenge of *responsible
action in a revolutionary world*.  Though all of these forces
are an integral part of the American social system, there is
no single or overall power structure that controls them.
There is a plurality of power structures represented in
these moral areas.  The more dynamic of the power centers
develop ideologies which compete for the attention and energies of many people.  No simple moral strategy or private
gospel or moralism can greatly affect any of them because of
their deep rootage in society as a whole.


                                II


We turn now from these introductory and survey comments
to the more systematic discussion of ehtics as a method for
dealing with moral choice.

How shall we do ethics today?  Shall we be situationists or contextualists like Sittler, Fletcher, or Lehmann?
Shall we be defenders of a method like Catholic natural law
theory such as Pope Paul VI uses in his encyclical on birth
control?  Shall we appeal to rules after the method and
manner of Paul Ramsey?  Shall we refuse to choose radically

between contexts and principles as James Gustafson does?

In commenting on the "Situation Ethics" debate[4] E. L. Long, Jr. point out three features of it which are worth recalling. (1) The claim of the *person* who stands in the concrete situation, either as recipient or dispenser of neighbor love, is greater than the claim of any abstract conception of right. We may call this the personalistic demand or priority. (2) Situationsists and contextualists tend to regard the moral changes of our time as more to be welcomed and transformed than to be resisted or reversed. (3) The preoccupation of such ethics is with *method*. This makes the central ethical issue to be method, i.e. the ways in which moral decisions are approached and ethical judgments rendered.

I also believe that method is crucial particularly in a time of rapid social change, but method never takes place in a vacuum.

In the April 1, 1969 issue of *Engage* Howard L. Harrod of Vanderbilt deals with the foundations of social ethics today through a distinction between "Reflective and Involvement Ethics." He rejects the older distinction between personal and social ethics and also the older disjunction between love and justice which Reinhold Niebuhr employed. Says Harrod: "The disjunction at the heart of moral experience divides today along the crevasse between *thought* and *action* rather than any of the older divisions." The reflective ethicists he divides between those interested in more general, often long-term issues and those concerned with more specific, often short-term problems. As over against these two kinds of reflective ethicists he places the involvement ethicists. These are characterized primarily by their participation in the specific social movements that have shaped recent history. Here again there is

a distinction between those concerned with long-range issues
and those more closely involved in action. Harrod's own
call is to an ethics of integrity with a strong Christian
commitment. He wants *action* deeply rooted in the Christian heritage.

Whatever one may think of Harrod's classification, his
call to action requires some fresh thinking about method,
not least on how we relate the involvement and integrity to
the Christian heritage. How do we decide? What method
shall we use?

Situationists and contextualists appeal in some way to
*love* and to Jesus Christ. Paul Lehmann asks: "What am I as
a believer in Jesus Christ and a member of his church to
do?" Joseph Fletcher asks: "What does *agape* require in
this situation?" Both *posit* the Christian faith; they do
not seek to demonstrate its validity. They take their
stands there as their personal decisions. For them there
are no absolute rules to follow.

What response is made to this general ethical posture?
Serious scholars and critics point out that both terms, *love*
and *situation*, are quite ambiguous and particularly so in
the writings of J. Fletcher. Some also point out that the
thoughts of Lehmann and Fletcher deal inadequately with social *structures*. This weakness in dealing with structures
takes away much of their value for social ethics. Since
institutions and structural decision-making procedures are
deeply involved in the dilemmas of society, an adequate
method must be developed to deal with them.

Paul Ramsey has faulted both Fletcher and Lehmann by
insisting on the place of rules in moral judgments and decisions and showing that rules do not necessarily mean legalism in the pejorative sense of that term. Ramsey builds on
Frankena and goes beyond him. Frankena distinguished be-

tween *act-agapism* and *rule-agapism*. In *act-agapism* "we are
to tell what we should do in a particular situation simply
by getting clear about the facts of that situation and then
asking what is the loving or the most loving thing to do in
it." By contrast rule-agapism seeks "to determine what we
ought to do, not by asking which *act* is the most loving, but
by determining which *rules of action* are most love
embodying." Ramsey adds to rules of deeds the idea of soci-
etal rules, or *rules of practices*. What does love require
as a practice? There are rules of deeds and rules of practices. A rule of practice would be, for example, "Be loyal
to your spouse because marriage as a practice is the most
loving thing to do." Marriage is the most loving *practice*
and is not just a series of situations. It has to do with a
life-covenant taken as a whole. A practice is thus a structure, or a kind of institution. We ought to judge and
choose covenants, practices, and institutions, not just
deeds or acts. Marriage as a practice requires a rule of
love. Consequently, situation ethics is held by Ramsey to
be faulty because it tends to atomize and relativize unduly
some institutions and practices which as wholes are a responsible expression of love.

Fletcher himself cannot avoid an ethic of rules entirely, for in commenting on flexibility in relation to an abortion case he says: "No unwanted or unintended baby should
ever be born."

The above consideration by Ramsey is an important one
and carries our deliberations regarding morality and ethics
a considerable distance beyond Fletcher and Lehmann. Social
ethics must attend to structures, institutions, policies and
the like which are shaped by many persons and affect many
persons. In rejecting *legalism* we have still to deal with
the most *loving practices*, therefore with the rules of prac-

tices.

Yet, how do we validate a rule of practice like marriage, or, to take another example, the rights of inheritance?   I am not asking how do we get the United Methodist
General Conference to make a pronouncement or how do we get
a moral consensus of laymen and clergy, but how *ought* we to
*validate* an institution like marriage?   I am not asking how
do we get the rights of inheritance established into civil
law, but how *ought* we to validate private and family inheritance of property?   We are living in a time when social
changes are so widespread and rapid that we cannot be content with an appeal to present and past practices, customs,
and civil laws.   We are compelled by the social situation
and by the rationale of ethics to press the basic question:
Why ought there to be marriage vows?   Why ought there to be
rights of inheritance?   What are the universal principles of
moral decision-making?

Moral law, as I use the term, is not a specific commandment or enactment but is a principle, a universal, which the
person *ought* to obey in making up his conscience or in developing a moral rule or shaping an institution or practice.
The method of moral law goes one level deeper than Ramsey
and adds a whole dimension to the situationists and the contextualists, without denying the truth contributed by any of
them.   The method of the moral laws as you will note below
draws on the personalist tradition in moral philosophy particularly as developed by Brightman[5], but it updates him in
a communitarian way.

The method of doing social ethics which I have developed has some affinities with what has been analyzed above,
but its strength lies in a coherence which ties *three* disciplines together.   Christian social ethics requires a threefold interdisciplinary method.   It is open to the ethical

illumination and claims of theology (the Christian Faith);
it draws heavily from the analytical work of the behavioral
sciences; and it uses principles developed in philosophical
ethics.  Without an appeal and an openness to Jesus Christ
and the New Testament an ethic could not be Christian; without the empirical descriptions and analyses of the social
sciences it would lack concrete sophistication and social
realism; and without philosophical reflection on the principles or laws governing moral choice it would lack critical
integrity as a normative discipline.

Such a method which I shall now more fully describe has
the advantage of no absolute prescriptions of choice which
must be set aside as times change and in this sense the
ethic is relative; but it has the further advantage of seeking a coherent judgment and decision of choice that does not
compromise the disciplines it appeals to, but it leaves them
free to develop their own fitting autonomy.  Theologians,
philosophers, social scientists work with their own integrity even while collaborating on issues—and the Christian
social ethicist *internalizes* the three-way dialogue in order
to make the responsible decision which the situation calls
for.

*From theology* social ethics receives illumination or
revelation, motivation, perspective and an ultimate context.
In Jesus Christ we have an ultimate loyalty.  Theology makes
an ultimate claim and proclaims an ultimate disclosure, but
it does not provide a body of practical prescriptions valid
for all occasions.  We cannot deduce specific modern rules
from N. T. propositions.  The Kingdom of God is the New
Testament term for God's righteous rule, but it is not the
major premise of an ethical syllogism from which rules and
regulations can be clearly deduced.  In the twofold commandment—"Thou shalt love the Lord thy God with all thy heart,

soul, mind and strength" and "Thou shalt love thy neighbor
as thyself"—there is great scope and motivating power, but
there is no clear disposition of such questions as population control, national planning, or whether the parietal
rules of a university ought to be radically revised. Jesus
was himself more of a revealer than a reformer. And even
his reforms—like those dealing with the Sabbath—are
important more for their disclosures of ethical insights
than as precedents for Sunday observances. He set aside old
laws because of higher or deeper insights. But from what
Jesus said about the Sabbath we cannot deduce Sunday closing
laws.

   *From the behavioral sciences* we may expect an analytical description and partial interpretation of the social
situations in which individual and group decision take
place. American morality is heavily influenced by social
policy and social policy should depend greatly on the social
sciences. An adequate historical knowledge of a problem and
a thorough description of the forces at work are indispensable factors for sound ethical choice. More and more it
becomes evident that anthropology, sociology, psychology,
economics, and history are tools of sound social valuations.
The use of these tools tends to underscore the *relativity* of
morals, but they also show how dangerous it is to make value
choices apart from sophisticated empirical studies. Dennis
Munby has complained of the absence of technical competence
in much church decision making. He points out that many
church pronouncements on economic matters are painful reading to an economist.

   Take three current illustrations: hunger, population
control, and poverty. We cannot solve hunger's moral crises
by saying "Give ye them to eat" or "When saw we thee ahun-
gered?" Population control problems are not solved by

citing "Increase and multiply" or "Be not anxious about the
morrow." Poverty does not abate with recalling that "The
poor ye have always with you." It is a very sophisticated
and complicated world task to feed the hungry. What is hunger? Hunger is not just a problem of calories but also of
proteins. There are also institutional issues: What strategy of agricultural development is necessary? How does the
movement of vast amounts of wheat, for example, affect the
world market and the domestic market? In trying to feed the
hungry what sustained social policies are needed? The
ethics of population control is as dilemmatic as the ethics
of feeding the hungry. Shall one seek national across-the-
board policies? Is abortion a legitimate method of control?
How must social attitudes be changed toward family planning
and family size? What is the relation of population size
and family size to nation-building? Have hunger and population
control definite correlations with poverty? What is
poverty? What is the social composition of the statistical
class which may be described as poor? How is poverty related to the issues of education, race, sex, age, status-in-
life, geographical location, section of the country and the
like? I mention these only to press the question of finding
and using an adequate method.

The behavioral sciences help to discover the relevant
variables which must be considered in any serious social
decision. These sciences are themselves replete with value
judgments for the simple reason that they deal with people,
who are goal seeking and valuing creatures. Most social
science theories assume some doctrine of man. There is
always a dynamic interrelation between man and his environment, i.e. between person-and-community when an ethical judgment or moral decision is made. We may formulate this inter-
relationship as a question of *responsiveness*. The social

sciences    study    human    *responsiveness*;    and    personal
responsiveness as a social and psychological fact underlies
*responsibility* as  an  ethical  reality.    These  two  words
illuminate greatly the relation of social science to ethics:
*responsiveness* is the focus of behavioral science; *responsibility* is the focus of ethics.    Both responsiveness and
responsibility  are  functions  of  personality  taken  as  a
whole.

The  contributions  of  the  theologian  and  the  social
scientist need the assistance of the philosophical ethicist
to complete the task of doing Christian social ethics.  Theology  involves  ethics  and  so  does  social  science.  We need,
then, a model of ethical choice in order to make Christian
responsibility real and effective in the social order.

The  responsible  Christian  person  in  a  responsible  society  may  be  cited  as  the  model.    Through  the  idea  of  *person*
we  relate  the  disclosures  of  Jesus  Christ  as  person  to  contemporary persons.    Through the idea of *responsible society*
we  relate  the  theological  ideas  of  the  Kingdom  of  God  to
contemporary  social  systems.    Person-in-community  is  a
phrase which helps us to see and to say that man and society
cannot be adequately understood apart from each other.    The
person *ought* to be responsible and the structures *ought* to
be responsible.

In this philosophical approach we have a strong linkage
between  theological  insight  and  illumination,  on  the  one
hand,  and  social  science  and  social  systems  on  the  other
hand.    Moral  law  should  be  understood  as  the  principles
according to which the person ought to choose.    From this
perspective we may correct Fletcher and Lehmann and Barth
without  falling  into  the  limited  notion  of  rules  which
Ramsey adheres to.    Fletcher argues that values exist only
in response to persons.    Value is not an absolute, indepen-

dent existence but is always "value for a person." Sex, for
example, is not separable from personality. Some forms of
the "new morality" seek to do this. But the clinical
evidence is overwhelmingly against the view that sexuality
is separable in its effects from the persons related through
it. This idea Fletcher takes over from Brightman, but he
does not apply this principle coherently as Brightman did.
He approvingly quotes Brightman that "in personality is the
only true intrinsic value we know or conceive; all values
are but forms of personal experience." Love, says Fletcher,
is "goodwill at work in partnership with reason, seeking the
neighbor's good radically, non-preferentially." Love as
goodwill is a New Testament idea and so is neighbor-love.
It is in the idea of love *in partnership with reason* that we
must expound what I would call philosophical ethics—an
ethics of moral laws. Moral law is the structure of the
partnership with reason which informs responsible choice.

The body of moral laws which we may call the
Brightman—DeWolf—Muelder system has been elaborated into
about 15 principles (principles and laws are here used inter-
changeably) and can be grouped into four clusters. They are
normative principles of choice. I have elaborated them in
*Moral Laws in Christian Social Ethics.*[6]

One group are *formal* laws and command *consistency* and
*autonomy* in moral choices. We *ought* not to choose contradictions and the ideals we choose are imperative. Integrity and sincerity *ought* never be compromised.

The *second* group of laws go beyond these formal considerations. They are the laws of value. They command one
to choose values coherently, to elaborate and approve consequences, to choose the best possible, to choose the most
inclusive end, to choose the value *specifically* relevant to
the situation, and to develop a norm which will be an ideal

control over one's values.    In other words in the realm of
values there is a hierarchy of values which must be clarified and then chosen.

These laws of value point to a third group of laws, the
laws of personality.  Values are  of, by, and for persons.
We need laws of choice, therefore, that apply not just to
values but to the persons who experience and choose the
values.  Thus, there is a law of *individualism*, dealing with
the worth of the person choosing.   There is a law of
*altruism* commanding us to treat others as ends in themselves.   And there is the law of the *ideal of personality*
which commands us to formulate a conception of what a person
ought to be. ' That ideal ought to control our choices:  we
ought to formulate such an ideal.  For a Christian such an
ideal derives from the matchless person of Jesus Christ.

Persons,   however,  do not exist apart from society.
Hence a fourth group of laws is needed.  I call them communitarian,  for  they command us to choose as members of the
community.   The moral laws of community place the free and
responsible person in the context of a free and responsible
society.  The question is:  "In what social context shall we
choose?"   The communitarian laws respond:   "For the whole
community as requiring to be perfected."   There are three
principal moral laws of community: the law of co-operation,
the law of social devotion, and the law of the ideal of
community.   What do these mean?   The law of co-operation
states that "all persons ought as far as possible to co-operate with other persons in the production and enjoyment of
shared values."  The law of social devotion states that "all
persons ought to devote themselves to serving the best interests of the group and to subordinate personal gain to social
gain."   The final and climatic moral law states that "all
persons ought to form and choose all of their ideals and

values in loyalty to their ideals (in harmony with the other
Laws) of what the whole community ought to become; and to
participate responsibly in groups to help them similarly
choose and form all their ideals and choices." The moral
laws thus command social change and social reform. It is in
relation to the communitarian laws that Lehmann goes beyond
Fletcher  Lehmann asks:  "What am I as a believer in Jesus
Christ and as a member of his church to do?" The moral laws
embrace what Lehmann seeks here, but take in the wider context of many kinds of community and of world community.

Let us look at the characteristics of this system of
laws. It is a system. No one moral law stands by itself,
for the responsible life is a whole—and it is a whole
because personality is a whole and personality is an interpersonal reality in a community. One *ought* to perfect the
community in order to have a perfected person, and so on.

These laws are not *legalistic*. They do not prescribe
any predetermined moral content such as having or not having
an abortion, taking or not taking the pill, having or not
having parietal dormitory regulations, opposing or endorsing
a war, busing or not busing school children, and so on down
the line of the hundreds of moral situations with which persons today must deal. These moral laws are the normative
method of ethical reflection in that they command consideration of the whole range of the issues in every moral situation. In considering modification of abortion laws, e.g. it
does not suffice to think only of a woman's right to her own
body, but also of the sacredness of life, the consequences
of easy abortions, the relation of abortion to miscarriage
and murder, population control, welfare policies—in short
our doctrine of person and community. Self-determination is
not an absolute right. After the state's laws have been
modified, the person involved must still consider in her own

case whether to take advantage of the law or not. "What
does love require"needs the partnership of reason and the
community of reason.

It is my observation that most ethical method is one-
sided, vague, sentimental, or incomplete. We need to know
the paradigm of a wholistic moral decision. If the paradigm
is acknowledged and followed, we do not need to fear the
challenge of any alleged "new morality." My study of such
ethical choices as the making and dropping of the A-bomb
shows that crucial aspects of fully responsible choice were
neglected by one or more key persons in making the decision.

The moral laws, as we have seen, are not themselves
moral rules like——"Thou shalt not steal" or "Segregation is
discrimination." With respect to a question like steal-
ing the system of moral laws would have one wrestle with the
basic meaning and nature of property. What is property?
What kinds are there? What is the relation of property to
personal development? What are the consequences of acquir-
ing and consuming property in one way rather than in another? What are the short range and the long range consequences of my choices? What value is specifically relevant to
the present situation? How does this present situation and
my attitude toward it affect my life as a whole, my character as well as my external goods, my ideal of personality,
and my responsible participation in community life? At many
of these points in the paradigm of choosing my acts can be
illuminated by the Christian faith, on the one hand, and the
researches of the social sciences, on the other hand. We
have a heritage of answers on many questions and that heritage has many valuable ingredients, but the situation is new
and so we need a paradigm of moral laws to command us to
choose coherently. The moral laws are not a substitute for
Christian faith or scientific research. On the contrary,

*they command an empirical coherence of all the relevant*
*values and considerations.*

## III

There is an objection which many students raise at
first to such an ethical method as this. They say, "Who is
going to bother to learn 15 moral laws and apply them to
every moral situation?" The implied answer is: "Very few
people will do this." Most people like and want rules of
thumb to go by—something easy to apply. They want concrete guidelines. They are more comfortable when they
enshrine maxims with divine authority. My response is that
we need sound moral laws such as I have described in order
to construct and criticise concrete guidelines. Guidelines
are like middle axioms—less abstract than the highest ideal
values and less concrete than program decisions and
practices. Indeed, middle axioms can be trusted only if
they have been tested by more general and systematic ethical
reflection and commitments. Moral laws are not isolated
*ideals* of *value* like peace, equality, justice, and freedom. They are principles of the partnership of love and reason. They apply not only to personal situations but also to
structures and institutions. They link the motivations of
New Testament living to the concrete realities of rapidly
changing society. These linkages should not be short-circit-
ed by intuitions as to what ought to be done. Intuitions
are themselves subject to further critical examination.

Let us carry this methodological consideration a little
further. In the ecumenical movement we have operated with a
happily phrased middle axiom called the "idea of the responsible society." The "responsible society" is not a moral
law, but its validity as a guideline can be effectively test-

ed by the moral laws.  The moral laws do not require the
"idea of the responsible society" as the only fitting or
appropriate "middle axiom," but they are useful in sifting
all proposed "middle axioms."  They should be employed when
we re-write the Social Creed of the United Methodist Church.

   If we can help resolve the frontier issues of ethical
choice, we may win the respect of the professional leaders
of our society.  What are *some* of these issues?   Organ
transplants, the use of artificial organs, the moral and
operational definition of death, experimentation on human
beings, interference with the genetic code, the means of
population control, the methods of social change, the guar-
anteed annual income, the law of revolution, the goals and
limits of the welfare state, the participation of youth in
adult society, urban planning, the principles of regulation
of the mass media, and responsible decision-making in corporate technostructures.

   None of the above issues can be resolved by intuition
alone, by a direct appeal to Biblical revelation, and by the
sciences alone.  All involve subtle and precise definitions
of fact, complex matrixes of cause and effect, and adequate
notions of persons and community.  More and more of those
issues are being explored on an interdisciplinary basis.
Biologists and physicians are concerned over the power in
their hands, the human values for which they have a stewardship, and the question of *who* has the moral authority to
make *what* decision.  Law, said Chief Justice Warren, floats
on a sea of ethics.  The interdisciplinary conference on
Hunger and Development held in Beirut last April (1968), the
Washington Conference on Abortion as the Terrible Choice,
the Yale conference on transplants are all signs of a cooperative quest by theologians, philosophers, and scientists
for ethical answers.  Next December, for example, we shall

hold a top-level consultation in the areas of hunger and
population control, organ transplants and artificial organs,
and the control of behavior through genetic code manipulation. This will be done as part of the centennial celebra-
tion of Boston University and co-sponsored by the School of
Theology, the Department of Biology of the Graduate School,
and the America Association for the Advancement of Science.
The theme is the Identity and Dignity of the Person.

As Christian leaders we here should not be afraid of
the dimensions of relativity in our situation but we should
be faithful to the emergent coherence of truth in decision-
making. We can acknowledge with H. Richard Niebuhr that
Christin behavior is relative in at least four ways: it
depends on the partial, incomplete, fragmentary knowledge of
the individual; it is relative to the measure of the Christian's faith and his unbelief; it is relative to the historical position he occupies and to the duties of his station in
society; and it is relative to his ideas of the values of
things. These relativities can be expressed as the fourfold
crisis of *knowledge*, of *faith*, of *historical situation*, and
of *value*. The church should recognize that the bases of
Christian ethics and morality can be strengthened (1) by
reaffirming clearly its theological reference points, but
not using them to sanction morality in a legalistic way; (2)
by improving its mastery and criticism of the social sciences; (3) by examining afresh its hierarchy of moral values
and courageously applying them; and (4) by deepening its
self-understanding of the world historical situation and the
role of the church in it. In terms of the methodology of
Christian social ethics which I have presented, all four of
these responses are aspects of the theme "responsible action
for world revolution." They must be dealt with together
coherently and in an ecumenical spirit.

I have not said much about the "new morality" as a problem in sexuality.   There is no doubt about the excess of
sexual expression and its exploitation in business and the
arts, not to mention the new permissiveness among the young
and in more hidden ways among the adults.  Much of this "new
morality" is not to be credited to the *Playboy* philosophy of
sexual hedonism, though that has had its effect.   If you
want to brush up on the sexual lewdness with which Christianity has had at times to contend, you might get out your
dusty copies of Clement of Alexandria——and read what he says
about a civilization where the people seemed to wear their
bodies on the outside of their clothes, as he said.

The youthful sex permissiveness has been called a
pseudo-radicalism which turns to this side of life when its
protests against the obscenities of the Vietnam War and
racial injustice seem to make no dent on the national and
local establishments.   Eroticism, like alcohol and drugs,
has always served as escape and as pseudo-security for those
who were unloved, unregarded, exploited, coerced, and for
whom tomorrow was a prospect of terror and meaninglessness.
Take away the Vietnam War and many of the symptoms of youthful immorality will begin to disappear from the American
scene.   Take away the inhumanity of racism and the involuntary poverty of the ghetto, and a greater stabilization of
family relations will emerge.  Society is a social system
and this fact should impress itself on us when we consider
the Christian bases of morality and ethics in the United
States.  The great danger in eroticism as pseudo-radicalism
is that it leaves the basic immoralities unreconstructed.
It does great damage to the personality of youths, since it
short-circuits their physical and emotional energies.  Sex
is so deep a part of persons that when it is treated as
something in itself, personhood is violated.

The pseudo-radicalism of many young people takes other
forms than the attack on the old sex morality through
greater freedom and permissiveness. Their alienation like
the alienation of black persons roots in conspicuous failures and irrelevancies by powerful institutions. Idealism
in youth and in minority groups is mocked by the too slow
progress of the adult white world and the credibility gap of
its political and economic leaders. To be sure youth protests sometimes lack a cause, but this is not the case with
the revolution in race relations. To be sure the protests
and demands often show a lack of basic competence in the
areas where they wish shared decision-making. But who can
doubt the betrayal of youth by various Establishments? The
church has the resources to show appreciation for the protest against human alienation in today's world and it can
involve the "alienated" in a Christian revolution by involving the dissidents in an open strategy of social action
based on the methods of this essay. Their methods of "participatory democracy" do not work and will not work when
applied over a length of time. Sooner or later one has to
learn the hard lessons of institutional continuity as well
as the ephemeral joys of discontinuity. As Dag Hammerskjold
said, "In our time the road to holiness lies through the
world of social action" and for this reason I appreciate the
opportunity you have given me to open up the subject of
Christian social ethics.

**APPENDIX**

THE MORAL LAWS (W. G. Muelder, *Moral Law in Christian Social Ethics*, John Knox, 1966, pp. 51-53, 124).

A.  Formal laws:  "How ought we to choose?"

 1. Logical law:  All persons ought to will logically; i.e., each person ought to will to be free from self-contradiction and to be consistent in his intentions.

 2. Law of Autonomy:  All persons ought to recognize themselves as obligated to choose in accordance with the ideals which they acknowledge.  Or:  Self-imposed ideals are imperative.

B.  Axiological laws:  "What should we choose?"

 3. Axiological law:  All persons ought to choose values which are self-consistent, harmonious, and coherent, not values which are contradictory or incoherent with one another.

 4. Law of Consequences:  All persons ought to consider and, one the whole, approve the foreseeable consequences of each of their choices.

 5. Law of the Best Possible:  All persons ought to will the best possible values in every situation; hence, if possible, to improve every situation.

 6. Law of Specification:  All persons ought, in any given situation, to develop the value or values specifically relevant to that situation.

 7. The Law of the Most Inclusive End:  All persons ought to choose a coherent life in which the widest possible range of value is realized.

 8. Law of Ideal Control:  All persons ought to control their empirical values by ideal values.

C.  Personalistic laws:  "For whose sake should we choose?"

 9. Law of Individualism:  Each person ought to realize in his/her own experience the maximum value of which he/she is capable in harmony with moral law.

10. Law of Altruism:  Each person ought to respect all other persons as ends in themselves, and as far as possible, to cooperate with others in the production and enjoyment of shared values.

11. Law of the Ideal of Personality:  All persons ought to judge and guide all of their acts by their ideal conception (in harmony with the other Laws) of what the whole personality ought to become both individually and socially.

D. Communitarian laws:  "In what social context shall we choose?"

12. Law of Cooperation:  All persons ought as far as possible to cooperate with other persons in the production and enjoyment of shared values.

13. Law of Social Devotion:  All persons ought to devote themselves to serving the best interests of the group and to subordinate personal gain to social gain.

14. Law of the Ideal Community:  All persons ought to form and choose all of their ideals and values in loyalty to their ideals (in harmony with the other Laws) of what the whole community ought to become; and to participate responsibly in groups to help them similarly choose and form all their ideals and choices.

E. The Metaphysical law:  All persons ought to seek to know the source and significance of the harmony and universality of these moral laws, i.e., of the coherence of the moral order.

## NOTES

[1]Joseph Fletcher, *Situation Ethics:   The New Morality*
(Philadelphia:   Westminster Press, 1966).

[2]Donald R. Cutler, ed., *The Religious Situation:   1968*
(Boston:   Beacon Press, 1968).

[3]*Report of the National Advisory Commission on Civil
Disorders*, chairman:   Otto Kerner   (New York Times, 1968).

[4]Harvey Cox, ed., *The Situation Ethics Debate*
(Philadelphia:   Westminster Press, 1968), E. L. Long, Jr.,
"The History of the Literature of 'The New Morality'."

[5]E. S. Brightman, *Moral Laws* (New York:   The Abingdon
Press, 1934).   See W. G. Muelder, *Moral Law in Christian
Social Ethics* (Richmond, Va., John Knox Press, 1966).

[6]For a list of these laws see the appendix to this
essay.

# The Necessity of the Church
## (1956)


## Introduction

When one looks about him at all the denominations and
divisions in Christendom one may well ask: Are these denominations—are these churches necessary? Is there any church
which exists out of strict necessity? Strictly speaking the
Church is not a necessity, for the church is an historical
society and nothing historical exists in strict necessity.
Necessity is the logical relation of implication which
obtains between the premises and the conclusion of a syllogism. Immanuel Kant in seeking to refute the empiricism of
David Hume tried to show that necessity defines the category
of cause and effect in the field of knowing. It is a law of
the knowing subject. He tried to show that the field of
scientific knowledge of nature was characterized by strict
necessity, but he was agnostic about the realm of things-
in-themselves. Today we do not regard even casual relationships as necessary, but rather we find them intelligible in
terms of probability and recognize an element of indeterminacy in predicting the behavior of the elements of physical things.

There is, then, no necessity for the Church. Its reality must be found in another order of fact and interpretation. But why make so much of what may seem to be an
essentially semantic quibble about a word? Do we not mean
that the Church is indispensable in the purpose and providence of God? Nevertheless, it is useful to stay with the

303

category of necessity a bit longer, for doing so may assist
us in a proper humility regarding the Church.  It may help
us to be more specifically Christian.


I
The Non-Necessity of the Church


A topic such as the Necessity of the Church tempts one
to look at her from some vantage point outside the Church
from which one may view her grandeur and power, her relation
to society and civilization and from this standpoint to
pronounce on her indispensable contributions to culture and
humankind.  Has she not borne precious gifts to world history in every field?  Has she not been the mother of the
most precious values of the West and the Middle-East?  Has
she not penetrated darkest Africa with civilizing arts and
stirred the Asians' love of freedom and national independence?  But, even from a general cultural point of view, the
non-necessity of the Church is quite evident.

There are many cultures past and present which are not
built around the Church or its values.  Cultures may be
viable and integrated—quite stable in fact—without the
Church.  The Church is not a necessity in order to keep soul
and body together, or to carry on industry, or politics,
technology or science, or the arts.  World history can go on
quite oblivious of her.  She is not the presupposition of
even a religiously dominated culture.  Tibet and Burma,
India and Arabia have not found her a cultural necessity.

Not only culturally speaking but also theologically
speaking one must acknowledge the non-necessity of the
Church.  The Methodist heritage agrees with those who distin-
guish clearly between the Kingdom of God and the Church.
Here is one of the great issues of the ecumenical movement.
Some identify the Kingdom of God and the Church, but the New

Testament and church history both argue against such a view.
Jesus had much to say about the Kingdom; he had little to
say about the Church.    The Kingdom of God is a necessity,
for it belongs to the nature and character of God's righteous rule.    It has ontological being.    The Kingdom is the
standard by which the Church is judged.    Often God has acted
despite the Church.    He has overruled her.    The Kingdom of
God does not necessitate the Church.

Historically it is possible to have a people of God
without the Christian Church.    Some theologians give the
date of Pentecost as the birthday of the Church, but many
theologians (including some distinguished Methodist ones)
have always emphasized the continuity of the Christian
Church with the Israel of the Old Testament.    Such writers
are prone to treat the Church as the New Israel, or the true
Israel.    Clarence T. Craig has argued that because of the
continuity of the New Testament community with old Israel it
is better to say not that Jesus founded the Church but that
he redeemed the Church.

In any case it is quite clear that the Christian Church
is not a necessary precondition for ethical monotheism, or
the spirit for prophecy, or the proclamation that all should
"do justly, love mercy or walk humbly" with his God.    These
all antedate the Christian church.

Even in the Roman Catholic Church there is recognition
that the Church is non-necessary in a strictly logical
sense.    Charles Journet in *The Church of the Word Incarnate*
makes this fact the door to the great mystery of the hierarchy.    He writes:  "Doubtless God could have saved us without
becoming incarnate."    "Here certainly is a great mystery.
God could be the sole Actor if He wished.    He was under no
necessity to mingle human nature, always circumscribed,
almost always sinful, with the work of the sanctification of

the world.  He fully foresaw that in having recourse to the
ministry of men He would be only too often ill-served, and
would provide    some    with    arguments    against His goodness."[1]   The   New   Testament   stresses freedom rather than
necessity.   St. Paul with his exalted conception of Christ
contrasts the compulsive characteristics of the Law with the
free decision of God to take upon himself the likeness of
sinful man.   And St. John never speaks of the necessity of
the Logos to become flesh.   On the contrary, a totally
different category is appealed to:   "God so loved the world
that He gave His only begotten Son, that whosoever believeth
in him should not perish, but have everlasting life."   We do
not  come  to  the  Church  by  a  deduction  from  a  first
principle.

## II
## Non-Necessity *in* the Church

When we change our perspective from the question of the
necessity *of* the Church to necessity *in* the Church we find
also a great deal of relativity.   Even if the necessity *of*
the Church were granted it is difficult to prove the necessity of many elements *in* the Church.   Necessity is here used
in a derivative or secondary sense, as referring to what
fulfills the prerequisite conditions of an operation, process, relationship or institution.   Methodists, like most
Protestants, have posited the sufficiency of the Scriptures
for salvation and have measured the elements of the Church
against that as a standard.

1.   It is not necessary that any one form of Church
government be adopted.   Neither Christ nor the Apostles
prescribed any particular polity or order.   Several forms
may be consistent with the New Testament, but no one form is
required.

2.   It is expedient, Mr. Wesley taught (Sermon:   "A
Caution Against Bigotry," III, 7 (S, II, 119)), that whoever
preaches in Christ's name have an *outward* as well as an *inward* call, but it must be denied that it is absolutely necessary.

3.   It is not necessary that men be ordained in order
to preach.   Wesley in defending lay preaching said:   "Was
Mr. Calvin ordained?   Was he either Priest or Deacon?   And
were not most of those whom it pleased God to employ in promoting the Reformation abroad, laymen also?   Could that
great work have been promoted at all in many places, if
laymen had not preached?"  ("A Further Appeal to Men of Reason and Religion," III, 1C, 12 (VIII, 221-222)).

4.   This last point is closely related to the matter of
apostolic succession through bishops.   The Statement on "The
Nature of the Christian Church according to the Teaching of
the Methodists" approved by the British Methodist Conference
in 1937 said firmly and rightly:   "It is our conviction...
that the continuity of the Church does not depend on, and is
not necessarily secured by, an official succession of ministers, whether bishops or presbyters, from apostolic times,
but rather by fidelity to apostolic truth.   The office is
contingent on the Word, not the Word on the office.   Indeed,
the apparent discontinuity of office has sometimes been due
to a reassertion of the true and essential continuity of
experience, allegiance, message and mission."

5.   There is no necessity of having seven sacraments in
the Church.   Protestants generally agree that two suffice
because they are related in their institution to Jesus
Christ himself.   But even here there is no objective necessity in the sacraments.   Those who approach the sacrament of
holy communion, even though ordained by God himself, have no
grace conveyed to the soul, unless they trust in God alone.

Again, how profoundly right Wesley was:  "He that does truly
trust in Him cannot fall short of the grace of God, even
though he were cut off from every outward ordinance, though
he were shut up in the center of the earth..." ("The Means
of Grace," V, 4 (S, I, 259-60)).   "Beware you do not stick
in the *work* itself; if you do, it is all lost labour."

6.   Just as in the case of the communion service so
also in the case of baptism there is no necessity of grace
in the observance of the sacrament.  Baptism is not the new
birth and the new birth does not always accompany the observance of the ordinance.  There may be the outward sign where
there is no inward grace.

7.   It is not necessary that all members of the Church
agree in all matters to do with the creeds or with theology.
Indeed, it is not a necessity that any particular believer
have a consistent and completely worked out or clear theology in order to be saved.  In his sermon "On Living Without
God" Mr. Wesley refers to those well-meaning persons who
hold that "whatever change is wrought in men, whether in
their hearts or lives, yet if they have not clear views of
those capital doctrines, the fall of man, justification by
faith, and of the atonement made by the death of Christ, and
of his righteousness transferred to them, they can have no
benefit from his death.   I dare in nowise affirm this.
Indeed I do not believe it.   I believe the merciful God
regards the lives and tempers of men more than their
ideas....'Without holiness,' I won, 'no man shall see the
Lord'; but I dare not add, 'or clear ideas'" ("On Living
Without God, 14-15 (J, VII, 353-54)).


                              III
               The Church as Historical Community


     Let us return now to our starting point.   If there is

no logical necessity for the Church; if there is no theological determinism whereby the idea of Church is deduced from
the Kingdom of God; if, indeed, God's work in history precedes the organization of the Christian Church and continues
in the world affairs in realms and nations not effectively
touched by the Church; if also He must judge and often
overrule her work; if, moreover, some alleged marks of necessity in the Church do not really appear to have that strictness or rigidity which some aver—what shall we say? We may
say that the empirical Church is a fellowship in Christ in
history. The stuff of history marks her at every turn.
Like history she is personal, communitarian, human, waver-
ing, subject to contingency, buffeted from every side, accommodated and full of tension, institutionally anxious and
proud, full of good works and noble ideals, but also inter-
mittent in loyalty and often irresponsible or almost dead.

But as soon as we have introduced the historical nature
of the Church we must beware lest a subtle temptation will
drive us into a colossal error. The Church, it is argued,
is found where God touches men and women in history so that
they can be saved. It is consequently the earthly instrument of Christ in the days since his earthly incarnation
when he established personal contact with the apostles.
Thus in order that eternity might make contact with history
he has founded a visible hierarchy to serve as His instrument in contacting men. This is the essential argument of
Charles Journet in the Roman Catholic work I have already
mentioned: "The religion of the Gospel is not egalitarian
but apostolic; it is not a religion without intermediaries,
but hierarchic."[2] Thus out of the very historicity of the
Church the hierarchy is treated as *mysterious* and *miraculous* and not itself genuinely historical. The hierarchy, it
is argued further, must be divine; otherwise how could the

all too historical behavior of the church have prevented her
own self-destruction?  Protestants themselves sometimes talk
this way carelessly and enthusiastically.  "The hierarchy,"
we are told, "is *mysterious* and, as such, an object of
faith, in so far as it is a dispenser of the divine grace
and truth, and in so far as it is the instrumental cause of
the Body of Christ which is the Church."   But, Journet
argues, "it is also *miraculous*, and as such, observable;
inasmuch as in the turmoil and confusion of the world it
communicates a constancy, a persistence, to all that we can
see of the Church—a constancy of doctrine and of practice
which the laws that preside over the evolution of human
societies cannot sufficiently explain."[3]  When I read theologians who argue the divinely mysterious and miraculous
character of historical institutions by appealing to their
continuity throughout history as civilizations have come and
gone I wonder what a Buddhist Lama in Tibet might say or a
Taoist priest in China or a Vedantist in India.   Their
"miraculous" histories outdate the hierarchy of the Church.

     We must be very sober in the lessons we draw from his-
tory.   Yet the clue to the nature and mission—the vocation and responsibility—of the Church lies in a profound
grasp of the people of God as an historical community.  The
Church is indispensable to the work of God the Father, God
the Son, and God the Holy Spirit in history.  This means
that we must begin with the fact that the relation of God to
history is primordially and essentially personal and interpersonal.  God loves humanity.  Relationships are a matter
of ultimate concern to him.  Persons are the object of his
love and persons are the mediators through whom he expresses
his love.  He loves men and women directly, but he makes
visible his love to persons through persons in historical
situations.  In such situations we may speak of the Church

as indispensable only if we also recognize its relative and
derivative character and authority. This relationship is
illustrated in the Johannine passage, "You have not chosen
me but I have chosen you." The Church of Jesus Christ came
into existence as an historical event; its quality as event
is a persistent characteristic wherever its genuineness is
evident. It is an ongoing confrontation or meeting between
God and the corporate community gathered in the name of
Jesus Christ as Lord.

Karl Barth shocked many church persons in his preparatory essay for the Amersterdam Assembly by stressing the
Church as *event*. This led him to take a markedly congregational approach to the Church. In what he had to say about
this *event* quality he approached an almost eighteenth
century class meeting emphasis on experience of the Holy
Spirit. Barth's discussion of the Church is one of the most
evangelical aspects of his theology. By pointing to the
event in which by faith men and women meet their Lord and
are in communion with the Holy Spirit, Barth is noting the
historical nature of the Church's existence. He does not,
however, develop adequately the implications of this idea.
In his thought the *event* appears too much like a tangent
touching a circle, not an ongoing incarnation. We must go
beyond Barth to stress the permanent presence of the Holy
Spirit in the Church's historical life. We must emphasize
certain qualities of the personal relationship of God with
his people when they are gathered together such as (1) the
response of the people to God; (2) the transcendence of God;
(3) the immanence of God; (4) the comforting, strengthening,
and enlivening presence of God; (5) the love of God; (6) the
vocation of the Church in the purpose of God. The *event*
presupposes his Word and his real presence in the sacraments. In these relationships there is both continuity and

discontinuity.  God is the creative ground of the relationship, but he is also the redeeming seeker who judges because
he loves and who calls out a society of forgiven and forgiving community builders.  God and persons mutually transcend each other in freedom; yet the creature cannot express
free response were God not also immanently preserving him.
So we must say that together with transcendence and immanence there is enlivening personal presence in the Christian
fellowship of men and women.


                               IV
                  Not Association but Community


     On its human side the Church is a *response* in faith to
the love of God; it is a whole response, not of solitary
individuals but of a covenanted fellowship.  In other words
the historical event which constitutes the Church is always
a community.  Because God is love the event of personal
response generates a community of love.  Its common bond is
the gracious creative fellowship with Jesus Christ, the Son
of God.  This love takes the diversities of gifts and makes
them cohere in mutuality of service.  It brings every problem into the context of a responsible society of interrela-
tedness.  It sees every offender as a person to be reconciled internally, to God, and to the neighbor.  It views
every talent as an opportunity to enrich the fellowship
through sharing.  It calls the fellowship to be the sign of
a new history.  Thus we read in I Peter 2:9-10:  "Once you
were no people but now you are God's people; once you had
not received mercy, but now you have received mercy."
     This ethical and spiritual reality of being a *commun-
ity* under Jesus Christ stands in the sharpest contrast to
what is today called an *association*.  The Church is not an
association.  An association is a group of people who are

banded together to achieve some goal or who are organized to
promote some interest. One thinks of a taxpayer's association, or a medical society, a lawyers guild, or a civil
liberties union, a Parent Teachers Association, or a League
of Women voters. There are thousands upon thousands of
these associations. People are associated through them but
they do not meet as whole persons. Their central selves do
not communicate. They are not involved in each other with
an inclusive ultimate concern. In modern urban life these
associations jostle and bump against each other and compete
for support. They become interest groups which fragment personality and turn the whole ensemble into a bundle of discon-
nected roles and functions. Associations in our modern
societies are often powerful like the giant corporations, or
trade unions, or the Pentagon, the foreign office and the
State. These associations are in the business of self-pro-
motion and self-justification. To lead in these functions
the cleverest individuals are employed and their prestige is
exploited.

The Christian community is of a different order from
this. Paul writes in I Cor. 1:26-30: "For look at your own
calling as Christians, my brothers. You don't see among you
many of the wise (according to this world's judgment) nor
many of the ruling class, nor many from the noblest families. But God has chosen what the world calls foolish to
shame the strong. He has chosen things of little strength
and small repute, yes, and even things which have no real
existence to explode the pretensions of the things that
are—that no man may boast in the presence of God. Yet from
this same God you have received your standing in Jesus
Christ, and He has become for us the true Wisdom, a matter
in practice of being made righteous and holy, in fact, of
being redeemed."

When Christians ground their ethics not in an association to promote a cause but in a community focused in Jesus
Christ and sustained by the Holy Spirit, they appeal not
only to the goodness of Jesus' life but to the cosmic
Christ, i.e., to God in whom creative power and righteous
love are indivisibly one.  The fellowship is *in* Christ, in
and through the Spirit.  This ethical love sustains the
responsive community.  Yet, this cosmic ground of community
is historically active.  In Jesus Christ divine love is manifested in concrete historical form.  He is personal power
through the Church in human history.  The love of God in
Christ calls forth man's responding love.  "We love because
He first loved is."  This does not mean simply that the good
is worthy to be chosen.  Perfection motivates, of course.
But, beyond this, Jesus helped and continues to help men and
women to have faith that God does accept them.  This faith
is not dependent on any previous condition of moral excel-
lence or obedience.  Through faith in God as mercy persons
are reborn and their self-centered and anxious selves are
reconstituted.  Self-will is subordinated to love of God and
love of neighbor.  The self becomes grateful to God and
desires to do his will.  One becomes as a servant to human
need.  One serves one's neighbor like Christ.

The Church as a covenanted community is a community of
love and therefore in the purpose of God it does not exist
to serve itself.  It is God's people called to do his work.
It is an extension of Christ's incarnation; and Jesus'
commitment to the Kingdom of God constitutes the Church's
teleology.  God is in the community and always presses the
institutional church to build a barrierless community beyond
its institutional walls.  It is God's servant to the world
community.  It is a function of the churches to nurture and
discipline men and women in the Christian life to the end

that they may witness and serve in a visible unity.

The unity, witness and service of the Church as a teleological expression of redemption and the Kingdom of God
manifests the transformative power of Jesus Christ. The
Church is not the Kingdom of God, but stands under the judgment of the Kingdom in all of its actual earthly ministries.
Concretely, churches cannot serve, witness or be in unity
when they are segregated racially, or accommodated to economic class and privilege, or function as tools of colonialism and neo-colonialism, or are dominated by nationalism,
or become apologists for war and violence. When the
churches lack inner integrity, they cannot effectively
preach Christ. Worship, personal redemption, and social
reform constitute a single organic whole. By thus emphasizing community the Church takes the acceptable goals of competing associations and redirects their partial efficien-
cies into comprehensive task forces motivated by inclusive
ends.

This is what it means to have a community whose common
bond is Jesus Christ. The principle of this personal fellowship is qualitatively different from all associations, even
those organized for noble ideals. The love of God in Jesus
is not only a memory recorded in Scripture or a goal to
which one aspires but it is a present relationship in the
Holy Spirit which sustains and motivates. Consequently the
Church provides history with an ongoing concrete community
of love which various associations may emulate but which
only faith can produce. Associations provide humankind with
organizations devoted to ever-increased specialization of
purpose and differentiation of function; but what humankind
most basically needs is the coherence of real community.
The Church begets many associations, but it is only as they
find their fulfillment through service to the Kingdom of God

that they finally express their real vocation. The community they should serve is that same community which the church
serves as a redemptive society.

Now, the Church itself is constantly threatened by the
temptation and tendency to become one association among
others in modern society. Many view it as a special interest. This is the world's blindness and resistance. But the
greatest danger is from within the institutional life of the
Church itself: that it become a collection of concerns, of
causes, of functions, of agencies, of boards, of ministries,
and of callings. Youth work, children's work, women's work,
evangelism, education, missions, social work, social
action—and all the rest can finally so absorb the attention
and energy of the members that the *event*, the whole meeting
of God and his people does not take place. The event takes
place through worship and service. Hence corporate worship
and especially the communion service are indispensable for
the Church—and therefore for the salvation of the world.

V
Renewal of the Church

The Church is a fellowship which is meeting its Lord
and Savior, i.e., it is experiencing personal communion in
an integral responsiveness. But there is nothing automatic
about this experience. Actual churches can become less than
the Church. They can regress into a pre-Christian relation
to God. They act sometimes as if they were still looking
for the incarnation; as if they hoped a messiah would some-
day come; as if they did not know that He had come; that He
had concretely lived, died and been resurrected. This means
that they have lost the personal power of his presence, not
because of his willed absence, but because they have focused
mind, will and faith on something else.

Churches sometimes act as if they were external societies on the outside of an event, just spectators looking in.
They act like groups who are outside of something (a) that
either happened twenty centuries ago, or (b) that hopefully
might happen again, or (c) that might be going on somewhere
else now. This means that the empirical Church can become
disobedient; it can become indifferent; it can become un-
faithful; and it can die. There is no objective institutional machinery that can or will keep it alive. When its members have no corporate faith and when love has gone, there
is no outward order or structure that guarantees its existence. It can be renewed only through repentance and the
decision of faith freely made.

Yet the vocation of the Church is indispensable; for
her work and mission are done by no other group. Nowhere
else is to be found that community of memory and hope which
binds the whole history of humanity together and gives it a
center of meaning in personal and social salvation. Nowhere
else is to be found that community of thought and love of
truth that give both coherence and freedom to the mind.
Nowhere else is to be found the community of worship which
breaks down every social barrier whatsoever in the response
to the righteous and holy love of God. Nowhere else is to
be found that community of service which defines the neighbor as everyone. This indispensable Church is not a lofty
ideal, though it is defined in what has just been written in
a *normative* way. This Church is an objective reality
because her Lord is a living presence and the Holy Spirit is
in the midst of the congregation. The Church belongs to the
objective order of grace and redemption and therefore to the
order of continual renewal through God's initiative in the
Holy Spirit. The Church is renewed as it responds afresh to
the purpose of God. For the neighbor whom we learn to love

through the Church of Jesus Christ is that very person whom the powerful of the world treat as a means to ends which they are promoting.

## VI
## The Church as Indispensable Servant

The human element in the Church is a very large part of her life. We are not disembodied spirits. We are historically conditional men and women. We are of the earth earthy. But we also know that the earth is the Lord's and the fulness thereof. The Church has an indispensable service to all because of their very humanity and to history because its cultures are mediated by persons. Thus the Church as the humble servant of God is indispensable to express and witness to the perennial power of faith, not of perfect but of ordinary people. Its historical existence gives hope to the hopeless for this reason. The Church is not a community of idealists. Idealists can only form an association, or at best a sect. It is made up of the faith of persons as diverse as Peter, John, James and Paul. Moreover, the Church is indispensable not only because it carries the memory of the sinless Jesus Christ, but also because of persons like the apostle whose faith became the cornerstone of the Christian community—Peter, a quitter, a boaster, a coward. The New Testament is a story not of great women and men but of the work of the Holy Spirit on earth in our human history. It is this powerful fact, continually reenacted, that makes the Church indispensable to human nurture, to social welfare, to family life, to all responsible vocations, and to the community of nations. The Church is in every place called to be a voice for those who have no voice and a home for those who have no home. It should not pretend to be the Kingdom of God on earth but it is called to unceasing servanthood.[4]

NOTES

[1]Charles Journet, *The Church of the Word Incarnate*, pp. 10, 17.

[2]*Ibid.*, pp. 16-17.

[3]*Ibid.*, p. 21.

[4]A further development of the constructive themes of this address is found in my study book, *In Every Place a Voice* (Cincinnati, Ohio:  Woman's Division of Christian Service, The Methodist Church, 1957).

# The Togetherness of
# Men and Women
## (1958)

The right relation of men and women has become radically problematic in today's world. It is difficult to discuss the major issues because of fundamental disagreements on the meaning of terms, because of basic differences regarding the relevant facts, because of misgivings regarding the authority of these standards. These difficulties are pervasive in the realms of family life, work outside the home, community relations, the Church, and indeed culture as a whole. Only belatedly is the Church giving this critical situation serious attention. What attention has been given is fragmentary and mostly defensive—reactions naturally to be expected in an institution dominated in most important respects by the masculine half of the problem.

Until recently the Church has treated the relationship of men and women as fixed and settled. The new thinking in the Church is caused not so much by an imperative for truth, justice, freedom and love but by the radically new social situation of woman in the modern world. It is this new social situation that fundamentally affects her position in work, community, home, and Church. New roles successfully performed outside the family circle and the Church have threatened ancient patterns of culture and continue to demand radical reconsideration of points still withheld from the agenda of honest scrutiny.

What is masculine and what is feminine? What are the actual relations of men and women in the work-a-day world? Do these relationships truly reflect the polarities of men

321

and women or are they shot through with cultural prejudices,
fears, misunderstandings arising out of the past?  To what
extent are they overcompensations or based on erroneous
ideas of true personal freedom and equal dignity?  Should
the Bible be used as the standard to judge the situation?
What is the Biblical position or what are the Biblical
perspectives?  Do the Biblical perspectives have authority
or what authority do they have?  Shall the present social
developments be taken as good and hence as normative for
Christians and for Church life?

Some recent exegetical studies are giving me real concern.  There is a tendency in some circles to affirm both an
approval of the new roles of women in relation to men and to
hold to a strong authoritarian Biblical position.  But the
exegesis of many passages is today receiving a different
handling from that of several generations ago.  I am always
suspicious when this process takes place.  Of course, new
occasions teach new duties, but it is not always clear that
these new duties are also taught by Holy Writ.  It is also
clear that new occasions permit new truth to spring out from
the pages of Scripture, but it is doubtful that this new
truth is always the product of a careful exegesis of passages—whether in Genesis, Corinthians or Ephesians—in the
setting in which they were written.  We shall have occasion to note some illustrations below.

It is interesting to examine some of the recent interpretations of Biblical teaching on men-women relations in
general, in the family, in the Church, and with respect to
ordination.  In the interests of time I shall be selective,
referring mostly to papers written for the World Council of
Churches.

The Committee on Ecumenical Affairs of the Presbyterian
Church of Victoria (Australia) makes the following points:

"It is man as male-and-female and not as male alone who is
made in the image of God (Gen. 1:27)"—a central Biblical
concept brought out dramatically in the rarely quoted verse
of Gen. 5:1-2:   "In the day that God created man, in the
likeness of God made he him; male and female created he
them; and blessed them, and called their name Adam (i.e.
"man") in the day when they were created!   It is man as
male-and-female who is remade in the image of God in
Christ—this 'togetherness' is just as characteristic of the
'new man in Christ' as of the 'old man' in Adam.   'You have
put on Christ, there is neither...male nor female...ye are
all one in Christ Jesus.'" (Gal. 3:28).   Pastor Helmut
Pfeiffer (Berlin) says that Genesis 1 and 2 mean that the
man is nothing without the woman, and the woman is nothing
without the man.   They both discover themselves only through
the other.   Human marriage, however, is not the prototype
for man's relation to God; it is God's relation to man which
is the basis and prototype for all fellowship between men
and women.   "Every form of life lived in the image of God is
also a life in fellowship."   Pfeiffer appeals to recent
Biblical scholarship in asserting that Genesis 2 does not
advocate subordination, but partnership.   "The only question
it leaves open is, whether this partnership is exclusively
limited to marriage, or whether marriage is only the outstanding example of a partnership which should exist in
every sphere."   This partnership is distorted by the fall
and restored by the redeeming grace of Christ.

Andre Dumas has advanced most systematically the exegetical standpoint of mutual submission.   He acknowledges
that in the Old Testament period there is a hierarchy between the sexes which is taken as a self-evident and natural
fact.   The wife forms part of the property of the husband in
the Tenth Commandment (Ex. 20:17).   When making vows to the

Lord, a woman counts for just half the price of a man
(Leviticus 27:1-7). The minor status of women could be
related theologically to the disorder caused by sin but the
Old Testament, says Dumas, does not put forth such an expla-
nation. It describes the situation as an established fact.
The New Testament is also marked by this fact, but the
Apostle Paul did not aim at changing or evaluating social
conditions. Rather he admonished converts to remain in
their former status, but under the new grace of the Lord
Jesus Christ.

Floyd V. Filson points out that the plan of women is
generally marked by both honor and subordination. They were
not slaves, or chattel, or tools of men, as they were among
some ancient peoples. In both Testaments they are protected
from the capricious divorce of men, are given a place in worship gatherings, are recognized as important in home life,
and are assigned minor services in the religious community's
life. In Christ they are part of the one fellowship of
equally privileged believers (Gal. 3:28). At the same time
the place assigned is subordinate. In Gen. 3:16 the woman
is subjected to her husband and this pattern generally pre-
vails throughout the Bible.

In the New Testament there are many passages which
teach that the wife is to be subject to her husband (I Cor.
11:3; 14:34; Eph. 5:22, 24; Col. 3:18; I Tim. 2:11, 12;
Titus 2:5; and I Pet. 3:1). Filson points out that the
general practice of both Israel and the Apostolic Church
conformed to this teaching. In family life, in political
life, in social life generally, and in religious leadership
the dominant place of the man is clear.

On the family relations issue there are, however, some
significantly new emphases, especially in treating the New
Testament material. Pastor Pfeiffer skips over the passages

dealing with subordination in the family. Professor Conrad Bergendorff says that the concept of what is "natural" in God's creation is derived from the work and words of Christ and it is in the light of Christ's ministry that we should read the Epistles and the Old Testament. When this perspective is taken, it becomes clear that Paul is not interested in describing any natural superiority of man over woman, but thinks of them both "in Christ." On this basis Ephesians 5 is no anthropological study but an exhortation to Christian husbands and wives to see in their mutual relationships a symbol of Christ's love to the Church. "Since love is the principle that joins Christ and His Church, it must also be the principle that rules in the relations between man and wife." Any subjection of one to another, notes Dr. Bergendorff, is a voluntary condescension in love. Christ eliminates the grounds of the idea that either man or woman is superior.

Wendland takes special account of the so-called "house tablets" of the New Testament. These tablets show that no revolution has taken place in the sense of an overthrow of the historical form of society. The obedience, however, is overthrown; for the subordination becomes a free act of love, being defined by Christ. "Subordination" as defined by a secular legal order or a bourgeois code, and "subordination" as defined by the community of Christ are very different. "When the love of Christ penetrates human relationships, the 'subordination' becomes *mutual*, it applies to the man as well as to the woman (Eph. 5:21); it excludes the woman's bondage to the man, just as it excludes the man's treating the woman with brutality and unkindness (Eph. 5:25ff). ....Sex and Eros no longer have absolute control over men and women. The new order of love in the Body of Christ becomes apparent in the earthly order. Agape begins

to   purify   and   transform   Eros....(Yet)   there   is   no
'emancipation   of   women,'   as   if   they   were   now   freed   from
every   restraint  and  commandment  imposed  by  God  to  do  as  they
pleased,   or   only   to   fight   for   'rights'   in   the   Christian
community."[1]

The idea of mutual submission has been developed with
special thoroughness by Andre Dumas.  Dumas insists that as
the Apostles have put the Cross in the center of their dogmatic teaching, so have they placed submission at the heart
of their ethical teaching.   In I Peter 2:18-25 and in
Ephesians 5:25-33 the paradoxical relation of the ethic of
submission   and   the   dogma   of   the   Cross   is   explicitly
affirmed.  The first of these passages deals with slaves,
the second with wives.  Failure to read the Ephesian and
other submission passages apart from Christology provides
for an unrelenting conservatism, resulting in civic passiv-
ity, marital autocracy, and social paternalism.   On the
other hand, "the sterile controversy of the upholders of
hierarchy between the sexes versus the upholders of the
equality of the sexes could be by-passed, if the real context of the submission of the wives in the epistles were
more   closely   examined   and   clearly   comprehended."[2]   The
apostolic doctrine is *mutual submission*.   It expresses the
voluntary and spiritual interdependence, ordered by the
apostles to men and women.  This expression excludes the
overtly or covertly 'hierarchical' expressions, for the
latter are only intended as a circumstantial framework but
never as the doctrinal point of the passages in the Epistles
that refer to the sexes.  Here Dumas explicitly rejects Karl
Barth's ethic in the *Kirchliche Dogmatik* III/4, p. 189 where
he attempts to establish to either sex permanent, specific
qualities in the form of a divine institution of man as
"head"  and  woman  as  "follower."   "Reciprocity  no  longer

exists," says Dumas, "as soon as the interdependence of man
and woman becomes one-sided, as soon as you reserve for
women the functions of self-effacement, service, and silence
and to men the functions of responsibility, direction,
initiative."

When we turn to the passages that deal explicitly with
the Church or the Christian community we get an equally em-
phatic reconsideration of traditional interpretations. Pastor Pfeiffer holds that the New Testament position presents
men and women as equal before God and equal as members of
the Body of Christ. Though their differences in masculinity
and feminity are maintained they are "all *one* in Christ
Jesus." Every member of this Body has received special
gifts and is called upon to use them. He asks, "How can we
refuse to allow any member of Christ's Body to use the gifts
bestowed by the Holy Spirit?....Without mutual love, our
stewardship develops into a form of competition——instead of
using our gifts in God's service" (I Cor. 12-14). Much the
same point is made by Wendland but he adds a special
observation about the relation of the Church to the order of
Creation. "Paul does not regard the order of Creation as
something absolute and unalterable, which cannot be changed:
quite the reverse. In the Body of Christ a new reality
comes into being even amidst the society of the ancient
world and in every other society, which so works upon the
community that women have a new status, which in turn begins
to influence the social order."

Turning explicitly to the question of ordination it is
significant that several churches have recently opened the
full ministry to women because they did not find any valid
Scriptural reasons against it and because they came to
believe in removing all legalistic and unjustifiable barriers against people in general. Taking an historical inter-

pretation of the Scriptures they asserted that the Bible
neither prescribes nor prohibits a permanent and specific
social structure for the Church.

     Filson's recent study of the New Testament evidence on
leadership in the Apostolic Church is relevant at this
point.  He thinks a case can be made for the existence of
women deacons or more likely deaconesses, but that no historical case at all can be made for the existence of women as
"bishops" or elders.  Women were not regarded as entitled to
a place in the governing body of churches.  "The New Testament supports the view that before God men and women are
equal; neither sex is inferior to the other in access to
God's grace and gifts.  In the long run this can lead the
Church to conclude that women are eligible to all elected
positions of leadership in the Church.  But the New Testament writers never drew that inference."  Filson concludes
his study by saying that he does not think of the Bible as
prescribing permanent and detailed social or ecclesiastical
structures that bind all later life and thinking.  "It is my
conviction," says he, "that we must ask what organizational
and social pattern best expresses the Gospel message and
serves the Christian mission."

I
The Need for a
Wholistic Approach

     Scientific studies of culture have shown that signifi-
cant changes in one aspect of culture have effects in all
other aspects of culture.  No one aspect of culture is
always the cause of changes elsewhere.  Causation in a complex cultural whole is pluralistic and tends to be cumulative.  It is a nexus of partly dependent variables of differing intensities and power.  No one factor—be it religion

or economic life——is ever the independent variable which
determines the entire behavior of all the others. What is
the bearing of this observation on our theme?

Men and women bear significant relationships to each
other in all major segments of culture——economic life,
politics, education, the arts, family life, and religion.
If we are to deal significantly with their problems of
mutual subordination, co-operation, and partnership, or
conflict, competition, and isolation, we must pursue these
relationships throughout the whole range of cultural expression. The problems may be differently posed in different
social institutions. There are continuities and discontinuities. But in the last analysis the polarity of men-women
relationships must be understood in the community of the
whole. If Christianity and the Church have an answer to the
perplexing problems that pervade society they must deal both
with the segments and with total culture. The Church must
be aware of the extent to which its Scriptures, tradition,
and life reflect culture if it is to take creative initiative in transforming its own institutional life, the family,
the work world, and society as a whole.

General attitudes in Western civilization have been
colored by a number of philosophical and theological tendencies. Much Western philosophy has been dominated by types
of Greek thought which regarded the mind as the essential
reality in humanity and viewed sex as a merely animal feature. Despite the large role which sex plays in life, art,
and literature the interpretive work of philosophy has done
little with the duality-in-unity of men and women. Christian theology has often been written by men committed to
monastic or ascetic life or by persons who held such a
dominant clerical position that they took masculine values
for granted as the basically or decisively human ones. Even

in modern thought, both philosophical or scientific, the
concept of humanity which has assisted in the emancipation
of women has been one which was actually supra-sexual or
absolutely masculine in its norms. In such a context it was
inevitable that emancipated women themselves took masculine
values as the norms of freedom and equality. Now that we
have approached a period of radical reconception it is
amazing how little the centuries have to contribute to the
concrete analyses of masculinity and feminity and the
formulation of responsible relations of men and women to
each other.

The contemporary discussion of men-women relationships
still appeals to traits which are considered to be distinctively those of women. We have already alluded to Barth's
perspective, but others are also noteworthy. Pfeiffer says
that the special gifts of women seem to be: concentration,
a bent for practical matters, intuition, and reflective
thought. F. Buytendijk finds that the original "way of
being" for women is: that they instinctively want to protect things, and the world needs their care; that they value
everything for what it is as it is, and so they develop and
take care of things which already exist. These he places in
contrast to men, who regard the world as something to be
overcome, something to be transformed. Their sphere of life
is work, action, and the sense of creative responsibility.
A third writer, already noted, Professor Wendland, states
that the natural qualities of woman are her devotion, her
desire to be inconspicuous, and her need for protection. No
society, he adds, can disregard these qualities with impunity. Others suggest traits like tenderness and compassion as distinctively feminine.

To all such efforts it is well to respond in terms of
Erwin Nietzke's article on "Anthropology of the Sexes" in

*Theolojische Rundschau.*[3]  Most of these traits, he observes,
are typically human, not either only feminine or masculine.
Men and women, he stresses, are not side by side with one
another on this earth. They are, rather, face to face. The
individual always comes to know himself through his concrete
relation to the opposite sex. No one is an individual whose
traits are developed and accomplished in isolation. There
is, also, no neuter human being. Women blossom in the presence of men, and vice versa. This may be the key to a true
anthropology. There is a concrete polarity which cannot be
reduced to identity or simple unity and it cannot be "subli-
mated" into an individualistic structure. Interpersonal man-
woman response is a primaeval reality. The inter-relation-
ship is like a dialogue which sets up a process that is
handled rightly only in mutual responsibility. The responsibility is for one another and to one another.

Let us look next at some of the difficulties which
stand in the way of a maturer and juster relationship of men
and women in the church and in society. I shall list a
number of these recognizing that these difficulties exist in
varying degrees and in varying circumstances and that the
composite seldom reflects any concrete situation.

1.  Men are often not accustomed to co-operating with
women and regard them as competitors. Consequently women
frequently feel that men have no understanding for their
work. Men do not allow women adequate scope and do not regard the work they do with sufficient respect.

2.  Men find it difficult to recognize women as equals,
or even superiors in posts of responsibility.

3.  Men and women often deal with each other differently and on different interpersonal assumptions than they do
persons of their own sex. These contrasts are not adequately understood.

4.   Women often abandon their womanliness when they strive for co-operation on an equal basis. Sometimes they view men as their enemies, who never show them real consideration. Thus some career women view men with a chronic suspicion.

5.   Sometimes women struggle with men for power and deliberately use the special effect which they have on men for this end. The converse strategy is often the case also. Sexuality becomes an instrument of egoism and power over others.

6.   Some men unconsciously, or consciously, embrace a patriarchal view of life. This is often combined with a fixed conception of ecclesiastical or bureaucratic office. They identify the Gospel with a patriarchal prototype in institutional arrangements.

7.   Lack of healthy hetero-sexual adjustment in normal ways outside marriage often leads to a self-consciousness which disrupts equality of fellowship. This self-consciousness must not be confused with the form of mature reserve which takes place in true Christian love. The self-consciousness of immaturity is found in both the church, the professions, and ordinary work situations.

8.   Some difficulties arise out of the persistence of feminist patterns which are often only thinly disguised masculine protest. Some women cannot free themselves from the masculine ideal by which the world is patterned. The form of equal rights for which many struggle has a masculine rather than a human image informing it. Misunderstanding often arises in taking an abstract or isolated view of such doctrines as equal pay for equal work no matter how large a family unit is involved. On the other hand, the Church must understand at a deeper level that only equals can be partners.

9.   Mature relationships are often blocked and/or en-
dangered by the attitude of complete objectivity in sexual
relations.  The Kinsey Report may be criticized for reflecting and encouraging this attitude and for failing to relate
sex to human life as a whole.  Complete objectivity with
respect to sexual life may create as many problems as efforts to treat men and women as supra-sexual or neutral entities.  As Clemens Benda has clearly shown the erotic drives
in men and women must be handled within the context of agape-
love if the adjustment is to be personality fulfilling.  Personal and emotional factors can certainly not be ignored in
questions of sex.

## II
### Some Tasks for
### Study and Research

As a social institution the Church reflects within its
life many of the weaknesses and limitations of secular society.  Therefore in considering how the quality of Church
life and its leadership may be improved, indeed how the
Church's life can be renewed, it is essential to confront
these situations with frankness and honesty.  It is imperative that we draw upon the redemptive resources of our faith
in order to achieve the full benefit of the mutual responsibility and fellowship within the Church and at the same time
contribute to better interpersonal relationships in the family, the work situation, and society in general.  It belongs
to the vocation of the Church to ensure that men and women
have opportunity to use the fulness of their talents for the
benefit of society.

The Department on the Co-operation of Men and Women in
Church and Society in the World Council of Churches urges
the following program of study and service:

"(1)   The need to encourage and direct continuing study
of  the  roles  and  relationships  of  men  and  women  in  work
situations,   in   order   to   distinguish   the   basic   elements
inherent in relations of men and women from those induced by
our culture.

"(2)    The  need  to  evaluate  the  effect  upon  men  and
women  as  persons  and  upon  the  life  of  the  family  of  new
developments in women's employment.

"(3)   The need to consider the adequacy of the orientation and content of education in present-day society.

"(4)    The  need  for  the  Church  to  accept  responsibility
for  providing  sustaining  resources  of  fellowship  for  single
women outside their jobs.

"(5)    The  need  to  provide  within  the  service  of  the
Church counseling for men and women confronted with the conflicting values and demands of modern industrial life."

One  of  the  significant  characteristics  of  this  program
of  study  and  service  is  that  it  focuses  attention  on  the
inter-penetration  of  church  and  society.    The  Church  can
learn much from the new place taken by women in professional
and political life, the changing attitudes toward professional work of women, and what partnership in the secular world
has  to  teach  the  Church.    Unfortunately  in  most  of  the  work
situations  of  modern  industrial  society  real  mutuality  of
men  and  women  is  threatened  by  many  forces  which  cannot  be
ignored.    Despite  the  greatly  increased  gainful  employment
of  women,  they  do  not  enjoy  full  participation  in  many
occupations  and  tend  to  concentrate  in  a  comparatively
narrow range of work.  Opportunities for advancement and pro-
motion  are  frequently  restricted  because  traditional  attitudes  prejudice  conceptions  of  their  capacity  as  super-
visors.

Women  are  themselves  hampered  by  socially  inherited

images of their own relationships to the labor force and
conditioned by their concerns and responsibilities as wife,
mother, and home-maker.   Lack of clarity regarding the
occupational component of her role often gives a woman a
tentative attitude to work and a consequent unwillingness to
submit to the discipline of adequate education and vocational training.  Moreover, she is often too insecure emotionally to accept supervisory responsibility in work situations
that involve men.  It is significant that in the Church as
in other professions relatively few women have entered
leadership positions after these were opened.  The proportion of women in graduate professional schools is no greater
now than forty years ago.  With so many early marriages the
present fashion, there is little likelihood that women will
complete graduate degrees in any large number in the foreseeable future.  The social consequences of this for leadership
in American society is to continue the present pattern of
male domination in most supervisory roles all along the
line.  In almost every occupation a much larger proportion
of men than of women reach the high-level positions.  Between 1940 and 1956 the proportion of women along all professional and technical workers declined from 45 to 35 percent, though there was an increase in absolute figures.

     If time permitted I should like to relate these issues
to the dynamics of the roles of the marriage partners or
parents when both work extensively outside the home.  Preliminary studies undertaken in this area indicate a serious
disruption of familial relationships.  Since the Church has
a stake in the stability and soundness of the family unit as
the basic institution in culture, these problems should be
high on the agenda of concern and research in church related
institutions.

## NOTES

[1] D. Heinz-Dietrich Wendland, "What the Bible says about Man and Woman," in Elisabeth Hohn, ed., *Partnership* (World Council of Churches, 1954), pp. 96-99.

[2] Andre Dumas, "Mutual Subordination," a paper prepared for the Department on the Co-operation of Men and Women in Church and Society (World Council of Churches, Geneva, 1957).

[3] *Theologische Rundschau*, No. 3, 1954.

# Theological Aspects
## of Vocation
### (1960)

### I

God's work is creative and redemptive. This conception informs the Judaeo-Christian tradition concerning the divine activity. God is creator. He is the ground of being, the source of nature and of value. From all eternity he has been at work. "To be is to act and to act is to will," said Borden Parker Bowne.

God's being is not only energizing will but it is redemptive love. God's love radiates throughout creation. God's personal will is not only the ground of human society, but it takes the initiative in establishing and restoring right relationships among men. He seeks out man, for he loves man.

This conception of God as creative and redemptive stands in sharp contrast to other ideas of the nature and meaning of God and has important consequences for the doctrine of vocation. To think of God as the ground of truth, goodness, beauty, and love personally at work differentiates our thought of him from a being of impersonal truth, impersonal goodness, impersonal beauty, and impersonal love. Impersonal conceptions provide perhaps for the idea of God as ideals to be sought after, but not for the volitional empowering of God in terms of work and his identification with the worker in his weakness, sin, and resolution to trust.

### II

God's work is both transcendent and immanent in relation to nature and history.  God creates nature and is
immanent in nature but he also transcends nature.  As the
ground of physical things they are dependent for their existence on him but he is more than they.  The source of their
laws and principles is in him.  They are not self-created.
God's work transcends them not only in the sense that he
creates other realms of being than physical nature such as
persons and values but in the sense that nature is an instrument for the development and growth in meaning and value.
God expresses ultimate meaning through the transitory
manifestations of physical things.  In this way God transcends nature, but he is also immanent in nature.  In nature
man confronts the activities and purposes of God.  God's
purposes in nature set tasks and limits to man's work.  Nature is not ultimately impersonal or meaningless.  It is not
to be used carelessly.  The heavens and the earth declare
divine glory and show forth the divine handiwork.  The energies of nature which man seeks to control through work are
divine in origin and ultimate significance.

God's immanence and transcendence are found not only in
nature but also in history.  History in all its forms is
enclosed in the eternal purposes of God.  He rules and over-
rules history.  Through God the particular histories of all
peoples are made possible and through God the destinies of
cultures and civilizations are finally determined.  His purposes are at work in history.  His norms of righteousness
and love judge men and nations.  He guarantees the instability of all injustice and provides redemption for those who
turn to him in faith and humility.

God's self-disclosure of himself in history and supremely in the coming of Jesus Christ as sacrificial love expresses the ultimate meaning of work as religious vocation.

Jesus Christ is the center of meaning in history and as such
provides the criterion and the motivating power of man's
work.   Jesus disclosed not only the love of God which
transcends history, he expressed the power of God's love
within the vicissitudes and tragedies of history.  The meaning of Work cannot be finally appraised apart from what
Jesus symbolized and enacted.

Man is able, in part, to transcend history because he
is capable of self-transcendence. He can act not only within history; he can act on, for, and against history.   He
also transcends God in the sense that God has created him as
a being who can, within limits, defy God.  His own center of
being has been created with freedom to say "yes" or "no" to
any given content of experience.  This capacity of mutual
transcendence to God and of self-transcendence has, as we
shall see, important implications for vocation.


## III


God's work in nature and history provides the context
and the goals of man's work.  The manner in which God created man shows that he is interdependent.  He does not stand
alone.  He belongs.  He is not self-sufficient or independent.  Man's work is always cast in a pattern of social
interrelationships.  There are a number of acts which man
performs that are quite individual, but in his birth and
death, to mention only two aspects of his existence, he is
socially involved.  A firmament of inter-personal relationships surrounds his most private transactions.

In a universe where being is activity, action is the
natural and inevitable situation for man.  God works and man
must work.  Work is not a curse, but it is a condition of
man's historical existence.  It is, therefore, apparent that

man must be productive if he is to survive.  Individual persons must either work themselves or be served by others.
The necessity of work focuses attention both on the person
whose earthly survival is at stake and on the others who are
involved in his survival and productivity.  Because the person must act himself and/or be served by others in an interdependent destiny, work raises the basic questions of justice and freedom.  Men are tempted to think of work in self-
centered terms, but the realities of life require that they
consider their work in terms of its social involvements.  To
think of one's work in terms of self-interest is both foolish and irresponsible.

    Since God has created man interdependent, his work
should be organized so as to express and achieve community.
In the family and in small communities it is not difficult
to perceive that the roles of different members supplement
each other.  Though functions are different they should properly constitute a pattern of mutual service in behalf of
the common good.  In large and complex societies, with elaborate division of labor, it is often difficult to achieve a
sense of belonging.  Work seems anonymous, impersonal, and
competitive.  Piecework, mass production, and assembly lines
separate man from his work and the particular operation from
the whole of which it is a part.  The secularist and materi-
alist spirit tend to dominate life, for the created world is
isolated from the creator by man-made devices, and the material means of production and distribution tend to become ends
in themselves.  Despite these difficulties man has the assignment from God to create community.  Economic means must
be made subject to the spiritual goals of life in a society
where people know one another well and are concerned for  one
another's well-being.  No aspect of modern life is more difficult or challenging then transforming economic life into a

community building vocation.

Though man is interdependent and called to create community, God requires that this goal be achieved in freedom.
Freedom is a gift and imposes obligations. Work is a necessity, yet it involves freedom and therefore a decision regarding the motives which enter into economic life and the
goals for which it is carried out. Man is called to use his
freedom to create a responsible society. In the words of
the Amsterdam Assembly of the World Council of Churches, "A
responsible society is one in which freedom is the freedom
of those who acknowledge justice and public order, and where
those who exercise economic and political power are responsible to God and to the people whose welfare is affected by
it." Effective freedom is both a precondition and a consequence of responsible action. In fact, many persons are so
far under the power of economic and political forces wielded
by others that their work is still a kind of slavery. Their
condition becomes a challenge to those who are freer to come
to their rescue. Freedom enters into the theological understanding of vocation.

Since God's own work is creative love, all persons are
called to do his work in the name of creative love. Through
work creative love is to be expressed. In stressing this
point we must note, once again, the attitude of man toward
work, his motives in working, his need to arise above sheer
necessity, and his opportunity to share in God's own divine
activity on behalf of people. We must also note that in the
long historic struggle for food, clothing, and shelter human
material circumstances have often completely absorbed their
attention. The human family has still a long way to travel
before minimal material needs will be satisfied for the
majority of them. But even for the most abjectly poor it
must be asserted, as Jesus did, that "man does not live by

bread alone, but by every word that proceeds out of the
mouth of God." Man does not live by bread alone——and he
does not live by work alone when work consists of earning
his daily bread. Man's whole work is the inclusive expression of his total personality. In this larger sense work
serves man and man serves God. Work is not a curse; it is a
necessity; it is alienating when it lacks meaning; it gains
meaning when it signifies God's purposes in history.

IV

We are led to the conclusion that all work must be
judged by the the threefold principle of personality, community, and ultimate meaning. These norms of work determine
whether it properly fulfills the meaning of vocation.

As adequate conception of vocation will be personalistic. It will conceive of the producer in such a way as to
assign priority to the personal over the impersonal factors.
Human labor may be, in part, a commodity but the person
never. Personality which gives itself freely in love and
productivity will always transcend the necessary labor which
enters into the contractual responsibilities of any economy
or political society. Today many persons cannot truly express personal creativity in their jobs because these are
too routine or fragmentary, or for some other alienating reason. They may then have to achieve their larger vocations
outside economic life. This situation means for some that
they earn their livelihoods in uncreative ways but seek creative fulfillment outside their jobs. To set this situation
right is a fundamental challenge for religious groups.

An adequate doctrine of vocation will be not only personalistic but communitarian. There are different ranges of
gratification in the various jobs and professions of modern

society.  In work man may come to self-realization but such
realization is not the highest if it is self-centered.  Personal self-fulfillment or self-realization, properly understood, are not primarily fulfillment or realization of the
first person singular.  What is required is the realization
of certain tasks in society in the interest of the common
good.  The common good is, of course, the good of persons
but persons are interpersonal.  Through the universals which
bind them together they realize their personhood.  As a person gives himself to the tasks of service to other persons
and the common good he also fulfills himself.  Work is no
exception to the communitarian principle in personality.  It
is an indictment on personnel policy in modern industry that
so many persons are denied this opportunity by the way work
is organized and incentives are presented to both workers
and managers.

The third dimension of vocation is the principle of
ultimate meaning.  I am indebted to Victor E. Frankl for an
aphorism by Nietzsche:  "He who has a *why* to live for can
bear almost any *how*."  Man needs to find in work a satisfactory relation to the ultimate meaning of his life.  When
he learns to respond to God he can become truly responsible.
Man's freedom is meant to provide him the opportunity to
make a gift of his life to God.  Responsibility is the fulfillment of freedom.  As Frankl says, responsibility involves
a twofold reference to the world both *for* something and *to*
something.  In a true religious understanding of vocation
man acknowledges that he is responsible to someone—to God.

V

In the solidarity of the human family God has given men
and women a diversity of gifts.  St. Paul argued that the

Christian Community was a special fellowship under Christ in
which the diversity of gifts were to be united by the same
Spirit.  Different assets and capabilities were not to be
causes for absurd competitive claims and for rankings of
higher and lower, but all members in the church were to
recognize that they needed each other and were members of
the one body of Christ.  All were freely to share their
God-given talents for the upbuilding of the fellowship.
There is no finer parable of true vocation than this.  The
actual inequalities of personal gifts are transmuted through
the spirit of love into a responsible society of mutual
service under God.  This normative church is a paradigm of
vocation.

Though this normative church is a paradigm of vocation,
it is apparent that no actual church is a model for the
world of industry.  Nevertheless, God sets his children to
the task of transforming both church and society into a responsible society dedicated to justice and the increasing of
love to God and man in the world.  In the world of economic
life each person is called to develop a social environment
in which all persons can in fact be free.  Every worker is
called to play a part in this historic task.  Each person's
task is truly unique and yet each shares in a common
calling.

Within the church the common calling transcends the customary distinctions of roles as between clergy and laity.
All are ministers of God, for all are members of the body of
Christ.  The diversities of gifts do not comprise a hierarchy of callings.  At the present time, when the ministry of
the laity is receiving fresh theological attention, it is
important to relate it to the question of vocation.  The
laity do local church work, but their principal church work
is their ministry in the world wherever they toil, whether

in homes, hospitals, offices, trade unions, factories, or
parliaments.  Christ is the Lord of all of life.  The Kingdom of God is wherever a decision involving righteousness is
made.  For Christians all legitimate work is church work and
ought to be entered into in that awareness.  Where work is
impersonal, anti-social, or meaningless Christians and all
who acknowledge the righteousness of God have a special vocation to reform the social order in harmony with the creative
and redemptive activity of God.

## Diakonia: The
## Christian in Society
## (1968)

Everyman is person in society. Persons differ; societies differ; man's roles in society differ, but everyman is
essentially interpersonal and in society. Everyman is private and social. A person is a socius with a private center. The Christian man and woman, the Christian person, in
society is not distinguished from others in having a social
environment. The difference is to be found in his perception of his ultimate environment, of himself, and of others
in the social environment. This perception is related to
his faith, to his response to God, and to his responsibility
for and with his fellowmen. For the purposes of this exposition this self-understanding and awareness of others is formulated as *diakonia*. Although everyman shapes his life and
society in some degree and for some end, there is a distinctive vocation in that interaction of personal and social
formation when it is the calling of Christian *diakonia*.

Before outlining the theological foundations of
*diakonia* and some of its distinctive opportunities and
challenges in today's world, it will be useful to note more
fully man's general relation to his social surroundings, for
what is distinctively Christian is more clearly seen against
the background of what is the common human condition. This
approach is all the more valuable since the Christian's calling is with and for *men* and *women*; and all the basic human
relationships are problem areas for the Christian life.
Christians are called to go into *all* the world—and that
world is made up of a multiplicity of cultures, nations,

347

types of political and economic order, modes of social
existence, and the like.

In dealing with the person in society in a summary fashion the first thing to note is that all cultures have common
social themes and basic aspects of order.  All have family
life, political institutions (or government), economic
patterns and goals, institutions of communication and education, aesthetic modes of expression, and religious life or
at least institutions dealing with ultimate issues of life
and death.  The study of cultures shows that they are social
wholes, interacting systems.  Basic changes in any aspect of
culture are reflected in all the other parts of culture.
Cultures are created by man in his responsive interaction
with his environment. As he builds cultural institutions and
processes he changes himself in terms of the quality of his
experience, his ideas, his habits, and his attitudes.

Religion is related to culture in two fundamental ways:
(1) through the meanings and values that integrate its institutions toward unity and (2) in terms of the specific institutions of religion.  In the first of these ways religion is
related to the ultimate dimension of meaning and value in
all of the institutions of society such as family, market
place, government, school, mass communication, art forms and
the like.  In the second it is expressed in its own institutions such as cult, church, priesthood and church-related
organizations.  Accordingly, when the church asks the question of the place of the Christian in society it asks a two-
fold question:  (1) how can the Christian men and women
serve all the modes of social life so as to make them truly
human and meaningful?  (2) how can the church perform its
corporate service in society and prepare or train Christians
for their service in society?  Service to church is an offer-
ing to God in order that the love of God and persons may be

increased in the world.

As one looks at the total interdependent life of humankind today one notes at once that its cultures no longer
possess integrated unities of meaning and value. On the contrary, they are in a period of rapid social change—even of
revolution. Moreover, the church is also seeking to rede-
fine its witness and service in the world. Therefore, the
model of culture suggested in the paragraphs above can only
serve to outline more clearly the dimensions of the present
situation: the dimension of the unifying themes of man's
social existence and the corporate life of the church as a
community alongside other institutions seeking to serve them
and to redeem them and the persons whose existence they
shape. Christian faith and ethics speaks to the themes and
values of society as a whole, to the institutions, and to
the persons whose lives are lived out in the manifold processes of social activity. Depending on the situation in
which church and Christians find themselves, their service
must be directed now to persons, now to institutions, now to
basic ideas, now to concrete tasks, now to structures of power, and now to welfare ministrations.

Christians are dispersed throughout the world in the
most varied situations and circumstances. In some nations
of the West they enjoy a standard of living thirty-times
higher than that of people in some "have not" nations. The
gap of income and productivity continues to widen. In some
nations there is an acute overpopulation in relation to
available resources. In some nations there is imbalance in
numbers as between men and women. Again, in parts of the
world the percentage of older people is rising rapidly while
in others fifty percent of the population is now under
twenty years of age. Some nations have assigned to the
state almost all social welfare responsibility and have

deliberately restricted churches and private groups in educational and welfare activities. On the other hand, some nations encourage private and religious work in these spheres.
The panorama of church-state relations in the world covers
the most varied patterns. Likewise Christians are present
in the most diverse economies which were at contrasting
stages of development when measured in modern technological
terms. Therefore, no simple concrete answers can be given
to the question of *diakonia*: how ought I as a believer in
Jesus Christ and as a member of his church to serve my society, its institutions, and my fellow human beings?

Because no simple apriori answer can be concretely
given to the above question, it is all the more important to
note the reference points in the theological foundations of
*diakonia*.

The Christian stands in a relation of response and accountability to God in his work as creator, redeemer, and
Holy Spirit. These classical modes of speaking of God's
energizing are still fruitful as a context for the human
situation today. In relation to God as creator man is a
steward of the creation, a co-creator of society, with responsibilities to produce, and to care for the needs of
God's creatures.

The Bible presents man as having dominion over the creation, as one who is to care for God's garden. The tasks of
dominion and responsible stewardship are given to man as
man. These tasks are universal and precede man's role as a
Christian. Christian stewardship heightens these roles; it
does not excuse men and women from the secular order. Here
are found the work of persons as explorer, scientist, technologist, and administrator. God works and man works. Here
also are found the tasks of persons as co-creators but on
the subordinate level. There are orders of creation in

society and culture, but culture is a mixture of God's energizing and sustaining work and of man's creative response.
There is government and there are governors. What God intends and purposes in persons and government is shaped for
good or ill by their freedom and stewardship. As knowledge
and productive capacity grow one's obligation to serve the
neighbor through that productive capacity also grows. In a
world in which the productive capacity exists to wipe out
abject poverty it is immoral and sinful not to adapt production, distribution, and service to overcome poverty. In
an age when ignorance, disease, and famine can be alleviated
in a marked degree it is a default in *diakonia* to live in
static patterns of privilege. There is even an obligation
to revolution when justice deferred means that justice is
denied and when the order of legal justice is in fact an
order of injustice.

Man's call to serve is not only rooted in God's acts of
creation and man's stewardship, but in God's action in
Christ Jesus to redeem. God acts not only in creation but
in grace. Creation and grace are not conflicting divine
actions, for nature can be rightly viewed as God's first act
of grace. It is the Christ-like God who creates. God has
decisively acted in history to redeem man from his misuse of
the creation, of himself, and of his fellowmen.

Jesus began his preaching ministry by quoting an Isaiah
text which calls to service: "The spirit of the Lord is
upon me because he has annointed me to preach good news to
the poor, He has sent me to proclaim release to the captives
and recovering of sight to the blind, to set at liberty
those who are oppressed, and to proclaim the acceptable year
of the Lord." (Luke 4:18-19, RVS) In the parable of the
last judgment he says: "Come, O blessed of my Father,
inherit the kingdom prepared for you from the foundation of

the world; for I was hungry and you gave me food, I was
thirsty and you gave me drink, I was a stranger and you welcomed me, I was sick and you visited me, I was in prison and
you came to me....Truly, I say to you, as you did it to one
of the least of these my brethren, you did it to me."
(Matthew 25:34-36, 40). The contrasting words are stern:
"As you did it not to one of the least of these, you did it
not to me."

In Jesus Christ God discloses himself as redeeming
love. Each person's call is to respond in faith to God's
redemptive work made manifest in Jesus' life, teaching,
death, and resurrection. Deep calls to deep. Human love is
a response to God's love. "We love because He first loved
us." The worship of God and the thanksgiving that is offered to him for his gift of Jesus Christ, his forgiveness
of our sins, and our reconciliation to Him from whom we were
estranged creates a community of love. In this community of
love the people of God take upon themselves the ministry of
Jesus Christ *in* and *for* the world. To be baptized is to be
enrolled in the community of Jesus and his people. This
enrollment in its essential bonds is a commitment to the
church's corporate *diakonia* in the world and from this corporate *diakonia* there proceeds the individual Christian's
ministry of love. Love is the inclusive act of service in
which are embraced all the responsible acts of concrete duty
whether they be in the home, in the welfare agency, in political action, or in economic development anywhere in the
world.

When we speak of the Christian in society we say much
more than simply person-in-society, though these are not two
separate realms. We must emphasize Christ in the Christian
and Christ in the world and Christ in the church and the
church in the world. The boundaries of Christ's kingdom are

not found in the church as a social institution but wherever
servants of God are making responsible decisions in the
work-a-day world. The world is foe of the church when the
world is self-absorbed in the temporal sphere, but the
church is partner of the world when it is occupied with
temporal things and affairs as gifts of God.

Sometimes the church is so self-consciously focused
upon Jesus Christ and so exclusively Christological that it
loses sight of the full nature of the church and the kingdom
which it serves. It often forgets that Jesus Christ did not
come to be ministered unto, but to minister.

The church, therefore, has a major but not an exclusive
task to transform world society into a responsible society,
for God calls not only Christians but all men to be responsible stewards of creation and culture. The church has her
distinctive work, but she must also be ready to co-operate
with all forces of social justice, recognizing that God is
at work everywhere in contemporary history. The history of
God's work in the church and in the world is finally one.

*Diakonia* has its theological foundation not only in
God's energizing in creation, and not only in his loving
activity as revealed in Jesus Christ, but also in the work
of the Holy Spirit. Jesus appealed to the action of the
Spirit in his own ministry in the text cited above and he
promised his disciples that the Spirit would continue to
give them power after his death. The church was brought
into missionary existence with the outpouring of the Holy
Spirit at Pentecost and it was the power of love in service
in the primitive church that occasioned the first specific
reference to *diakonia* (more as verb than as noun). The
Spirit was to lead the church into deeper insights into
truth and love than the disciples had been aware of when
Jesus was with them. Hence Christians are called on always

to practice *openness* to fresh disclosures of love and truth
in the church and in the world. It is part of the
Christian's vocation to be open to the future and this means
an open responsiveness to God while old structures of culture and society are being torn down and new structures are
being created. In this openness to God's initiative the
Spirit must prove the "spirits" and this is accomplished by
responsible participation. The Christian is not called to
be a spectator but an actor in God's on-going creation and
lordship over history.

The service of the Christian in society, we may infer
from what has been outlined above, is in and through the
church and in and for the world. Service may be church
oriented and for the church primarily, church ordained and
for the world primarily, or Christian service in society
without special status or ordination in the church. The
development of the office of deacon and deaconess reflects
this.

The author of Acts does not use the noun "deacon" to
describe the men in Acts 6:1-6 but uses rather the verb form
to describe their function of "serving tables." The word
"deacon" is not found in Acts. In Phil. 1:1 Paul addresses
the "bishops and deacons" with the whole church in Philippi
and probably was referring to those ministers who were particularly responsible for collecting and sending the offer-
ing which he received for his needs. In later literature
the references to deacons are abundant and indicate precise
duties and ranks within the hierarchy of the church's ministry. The deacon ranked third, after bishops and elders, in
the ordained ministry. He was distinctly the bishop's assistant, being ordained by the bishop alone and serving him in
his liturgical and pastoral duties. We may note along with
assisting in the Eucharistic assembly and reading the gospel

that deacons sought out and visited the sick, the poor and
indigent—especially widows and orphans and prisoners,
informed the bishops of their needs, and carried the alms of
the church to them. Since they had many practical responsibilities and visited constantly among the people, there were
many temptations to one's self and one's family for gossip,
greed, slander, and intemperance. The inspiration for the
diaconate is Jesus' own example who "came not to be served
but to serve" and in a fundamental sense the diaconate is
the foundation of all the ministry of the church.

Space does not allow for more than a passing reference
to the role of deaconesses in the church, yet the service
and status of women in the church cannot be noted without at
least a brief notation. In the Eastern Church the deaconess
performed an important function and held an honored position. She cared especially for women and children of the
church, gave help to the poor and needy, and taught, particularly in the homes. Her position was symbolized by ordination at the hand of the bishop. She served at the altar in
administering the chalice at the Eucharist. In the pre-Ref-
ormation West the life and service of women in the church
found a greater place through abbeys and nunneries than in
parishes, though the prominence of persons like St.
Catherine of Siena in secular life must not be overlooked.

The idea of the deaconess in post-Reformation churches
resulted in three types of deaconesses. There is, first,
the German deaconess who belongs to a great deaconess mother
house stemming from the revival of deaconess work in the
early nineteenth century. Trained primarily as a nurse (or
as a teacher) along with Bible study, she works along both
these lines. These deaconess orders exist along-side the
church rather than within it. The second type, the
Anglican, is a recongized order of ministry within the

framework of church order.  The third type of deaconess is
found in Baptist, Methodist, and Presbyterian churches and
is analogous to the 'parish assistant' of the Reformed and
Lutheran churches and to the 'parish worker' of the Anglican
Church.  They work within a parish especially in the teaching of women and children under the direction of the minister or of a parish board.

In the Methodist Episcopal Church the deacons constituted an order in the ministry as in the Episcopal Church,
but without the *jure divine* theory of apostolic succession.
They were elected by the annual conferences and ordained by
the bishop.  Their duties were "(1) to administer baptism,
and to solemnize matrimony; (2) to assist the elder in
administering the Lord's Supper; (3) to do all the duties of
a traveling preacher."  Traveling deacons had to exercise
their office for two years before they were eligible to the
office of elder.  Local deacons were eligible to the office
of elder after preaching four years.

The deaconesses of the Methodists in the United States
were recognized as officials in the church by action of the
General Conference of 1888.  She took no vows:  "her duties
are to minister to the poor, visit the sick, pray with the
dying, care for the orphan, seek the wandering, comfort the
sorrowing, save the sinning, and, relinquishing wholly other
pursuits, to devote herself in a general way to such forms
of Christian labor as may be suited to her abilities."  Each
annual conference of the Methodist Episcopal Church through
a board, composed partly of women, exercized oversight over
the work and issued diaconal certificates to women properly
accredited.  In 1900 the bishops established a general deaconesses' board and  authorized  new deaconesses' homes.
Deaconesses were licensed and consecrated to their office
after two years of continuous probationary service and an

examination, being unmarried and 23 years of age.  Their
work became an integral part of the discipline of the Methodist Church.  The present definition of a deaconess in the
Methodist Church is as follows:  "A deaconess is a woman who
has been led by the Holy Spirit to devote herself to Christ-
like service under the direction of the Church, and who,
having met the requirements prescribed by Joint Committee on
Missionary Personnel of the Board of Missions, including a
period of not less than one year of probation, has been duly
licensed, consecrated, and commissioned by a bishop.  This
office entitles a woman to serve the Methodist Church
through any of its agencies in any capacity not requiring
full clergy rights."

Church-related services often require intensive
activity in the world.  And it is, therefore, to the large
concept of the worldly or social diaconate to which the
discussion must now return, closing any gap that is created
by the historic coming of the "people of God" into the wider
interdependent life of the "family of mankind."  One of the
most comprehensive forms of responsibility for the Christian
is participation in political order, for it is comprehensive
not only in the range of duties involved but also because it
embraces all persons within and without the church.

Citizenship is one of the principal aspects of the
Christian's service in society.  He must therefore reflect
on the right and wrong uses of religion in politics.  In the
contemporary world religion in many places enters actively
into the whole struggle for power and has been eagerly exploited by ruling and revolutionary powers for national,
imperial, or anti-colonial and liberationist ends.  The
Christian faith, being anchored in God's transcendent righteousness, may not be identified with any one political
order or party, and therefore regards all governments and

programs as provisional. Since it does not defend such
schemes as simple embodiments of the kingdom of God it
resists political ideology. Nevertheless, the Christian
must recognize that provisional decisions must be made and
that action must be taken in changing concrete situations.
Nationalist goals are today particularly troublesome for
Christians because the Christian faith makes universal
claims and hence transcends merely national objectives.

Political life is an arena of ethical ambiguity.
National regimes which are linked to atheistic ideologies in
some respects serve the common good. National regimes which
have a heritage in Christian culture may be idolatrous and
deny universal human values. But politics and religion to
some extent always concretely interpenetrate. The one is
never found without some relation to the other. Religion
plays a pervasive role in culture, including politics.
Government is a dimension of religious institutions. The
separation of church and state never eliminates completely
the co-operation of church and state and should, in any
case, not be identified with separation of Christian ethics
and political responsibility. In the political order the
Christian works in an ambiguous and provisional situation
and program of action.

This ambiguity should be constantly examined. Government is as pervasive a dimension of social life as is religion. That is, every social group presents some problems of
social control and has, therefore, a political dimension. A
family, an association of workers, a professional society,
or a church require government. It is ubiquitous. In this
sense the institution of the church is itself social and
political because it develops its own customs, regulations,
laws, forms of property, welfare administration, and the
like. For every nation the state performs the special

function of co-ordinating all the governmental aspects of
social institutions and of asserting its claim to a monopoly
on the use of ultimate coercive means in exercising social
control. By reserving ultimate coercion to itself it makes
for domestic concord among competing groups. Yet no organization of power is finally completely just and the Christian
man or woman must exercise political judgment and take
stands with respect to it. One is not morally free as a
Christian to abdicate responsibility or to default on participation in leadership or followership.

Christian ethics and political ethics thus have intimate relationships in the whole of society and may either
support and supplement each other or be in tension and conflict. The Christian should always remember that though the
state demands a monopoly of coercive power, the state does
not finally rest on physical force. Authority in political
government resides in rightful claims and hence is legitimated by spiritual appeals to justice, customs, consent,
tradition, humanitarian goals and the like. The idea that
government rests on force is a half-truth that begets total
error. Law rests on a sea of ethics and ethics roots in the
ethos of a people. Generally speaking, religion serves as
an integrative and conservative force underlying politics
and therefore religious and national loyalties tend to reinforce each other. The nation state is never above being
willing to exploit the Christian's national sentiments for
its own ends. For this reason the Christian's spiritual
formation must be ecumenical as well as national. As a
prophetic universal religion and faith Christianity has
goals that transcend national and parochial politics and
inevitably generates strain in modern sovereign states.

The political service of a Christian inevitably involves him in dilemmas. In order to serve his nation he

must to some extent accommodate his values to the going
values of the nation. On the other hand, if this accommodation is too primarily protective and conservative only, the
universal element in the Kingdom of God is betrayed.
Because of the hunger of mankind for a genuinely universal
community today all religious groups are called upon to find
ways in which they can create, on the one hand, a healthy
tension with their respective societies and, on the other
hand, develop those values which will truly bind humankind
together. The spiritual claims of universal love and justice are ultimate; the moral claims of particular governments are proximate and transient. A church that accommodates too fully to the political order either by domination
or being dominated by it must fail to perform its function
as bearer of the meaning of the unity of humankind under the
righteousness and love of God. For these reasons many Christians in widely different parts of the world have insisted
that the Christian should today support the secular or
neutral state as the best type of political government. One
of the implications of this position is that the churches
must be willing to forego activities which would make impar-
tiality and secular neutrality meaningless.

The universal demands of Christian ethics give the
churches the special responsibility of weaning people away
from the restricted values associated with ideas of national
sovereignty and to lead the people into the inclusive responsibilities which are symbolized by such organizations as the
United Nations and its many agencies. Effective political
influence by religion on politics requires a significant
degree of autonomy in ecclesiastical organization vis-a-vis
the socio-political order. To win and conserve a courageous
and prophetic autonomy is one of the major assignments for
the Christian citizen in the contemporary world and this

autonomy must be repeatedly recovered.

The witness of the Christian, we have noted, must be an ecumenical witness. In the bold language of the "Message" of the Amsterdam Assembly of the World Council of Churches we strike the key to service in the last third of the twentieth century:

> We have to remind ourselves and all men that God has put down the mighty from their seats and exalted the humble and meek. We have to learn afresh to speak boldly in Christ's name both to those in power and to the people, to oppose terror, cruelty, and race discrimination, to stand by the outcast, the prisoner, and the refugee. We have to make of the church in every place a voice for those who have no voice, and a home where everyman will be at home. We have to learn afresh together what is the duty of the Christian man or woman in industry, in agriculture, in politics, in the professions, and in the home. We have to ask God to teach us together to say 'No' and to say 'Yes' in truth.

In the spirit of this message we may elaborate the service of the layperson not only in terms of the meaning of vocation and work. It does not suffice for the *diakonia* to be restricted in laymen's and laywomen's organizations which raise money for church projects and organize time, talents, prayer, and programs in behalf of keeping agencies going. The present discussion must not be interpreted as belittling this necessary activity or devotion to it, but Christians are called upon to confront their duty in such secular spheres as industry, agriculture, the professions, and the home. If the world is to be made a responsible society, it will be so because laymen and laywomen together learn afresh how to make Christian decisions as a congregation dispersed in all the institutions of the community. When this is learned and practised the worshipping life of the congregation takes on new meaning and relevance. Evangelism and

education thereby become revitalized.  The service of corporate  communion  then  extends  its  sacramental  power  of
cleansing, forgiving and renewing love into areas of life
otherwise shut-off from it by narrow defining walls.

Vocation  as  work  involves  three  cardinal  principles:
(1) the principle of personality, (b) the principle of community, and (c) the principle of ultimate meaning.  Christians
in office, factory, farm, or mine must recognize that work
often fails to be put into the context of these questions:
(1) What does this work do to the people who engage in it?
(2) What does it do to significant interpersonal relations,
to brotherhood, and to structural relations in the whole community?  (3) What does it do to each person's sense of ultimate significance and to his concern for God's purpose in
his life?  These questions confront the Christian at several
levels depending on whether one is in a power position to
decide the shape or mode of work in an industry or factory
or whether one is an employee with relatively little power
in the economic sphere.  The temptation in either case to
evade the questions by referring them to impersonal processes or legal fictions for decisions must be resisted.
The Christian may have to organize associations in order to
exercise responsibility.

There are several factors which tend to frustrate the
sense of vocation.  One is the secularist spirit which
places emphasis on efficiency in production of goods rather
than on the development of persons.  Another factor is specialization of the various realms of work which isolate men
and women from each other.

Communication tends to become limited to skilled workers within a particular craft or profession.  A third factor
is separation of the person from his tools.  This phenomenon
which has been present since the introduction of the factory

system has become acute with automation and cybernation.
Men and women often feel hostile and powerless in the presence of productive forces completely outside their control
or interest. Fourthly, the substitution of mechanical processes for the powers of body and mind is supplemented by
the "organization revolution" in which individual thought is
stifled by the omnicompetence of bureaucratic instructions.
All these obscure the idea of providence in giving meaning
in one's daily work. A fifth factor is the mass character
of industrial society. A sixth is the mobility of modern
life. And a seventh factor is the fragmentation of men into
functions. A mass society where people are only functions
or roles to each other is one where respect is likely to
fade and people are tempted to manipulate others for their
own personal or group ends.

Despite all these factors and problems the Christian
faith dares to lift up the real meaning of vocation. Work
is a divine calling when persons under God match their
talents against the world's needs and thereby find their
field of service. But a job is not an end in itself and a
particular economic system is not self-validating. All
stand under the judgment of God and in this judgment the
Christian must look at the structure and goals of the economic order, not only at one's private station in it. Wherever
a person is at work, there is the frontier of the kingdom of
God; and in that place the coming of the kingdom is either
advanced or betrayed.

The shape of economic society presents special challenges to Christians when taken in the context of the rich
nations and the poor nations.

An International Theological Conference recently commented on this issue. The central fact of our world today
is total scientific, technological and economic interdepen-

dence.   Yet  this  unity  remains  a  brute  physical  unity,
lacking  the  moral  dimensions  of  human  solidarity  and  human
justice.   We  have  become  close  neighbors  in  space  and  time.
We  have  no  comparable  nearness  in  generosity  and  love.

Within  this  narrow  world  of  inescapable  physical  prox-
imity,  the  small  white,  Christian  and  Western  minority  are
rich  and  grow  richer.   They  make  up  not  more  than  20  per
cent  of  the  world's  peoples.   They  consume  some  75  per  cent
of  the  world's  income.   Moreover,  they  grow  richer  by  not
less  than  three  per  cent  a  year.   In  1965,  they  *added* to
their  existing  national  incomes  between  $60  and  $70,000
million——a  figure  which  is  considerably  larger  than  the
entire  national  income  of  all  Latin  America  and  twice  as
large  as  that  of  India  or  Africa.

These   facts   confront   the   Christian   and   humane
conscience  of  the  West  today  just  as  the  misery  of  Lazarus
once  cried  out  for  pity  at  the  gates  of  Dives.   Yet  the
peoples  of  the  West  can  hardly  be  said  to  recognize  the
issue  when,  year  by  year,  as  their  wealth  increases,  the
attention,  the  investment,  the  aid  they  give  to  the  poor
continents  actually  falls  away.   Each  year,  a  lower  proportion  of  a  rising  national  income  is  devoted  to  direct
assistance.   Each  year,  relatively  fewer  crumbs  fall  from
the  rich  man's  table.

This  burning  scandal——of  rising  means  and  shrinking
response,   of   increasing   affluence   and   deepening
misery——makes  a  mockery  of  all  pretensions  to  be  a  Christian
and  humane  society.   It  stands  as  a  total  obstacle  to  the
construction  of  a  neighborly  world.   It  threatens  with  resort  to  violence.   It  even  carries  within  itself  the  apocalyptic  risk  of  wider  war  and  ultimate  destruction.

After  recognizing  the  fact  of  the  various  forms  of
political,  economic,  and  church  life  in  modern  society,  it

is important to note finally, that the Christian family should be the healthy cell of the people of God and of the responsible society. To say what the family should be does not, however, make it so—and it does not describe even what the form of the Christian family must be. The phenomenon of rapid social change extends to all countries and affects family life in all of them differently. And although the family has been the tough and stable pivot of society in the past, it is today vulnerable at its center and pressed hard from many directions. We shall try to state some of the tasks which a Christian family should seek to fulfill, but at the same time we must recognize that the complementary roles of husband and wife, father and mother, are constantly changing along with all the relationships within the family and other units of society. In some places the woman is left alone as head of the family; in some the parents are migratory workers; in other situations men are taking more interest in the home and sharing responsibilities with their wives; and in yet others there is diminishing influence of parents on children who are caught up in the demands of competing social influences of all kinds.

It is not too much to say that all the primary sexual and familial relationships must be approached afresh in the new situations and no simplistic prescriptions may be given that would be convincing everywhere. Nevertheless, it is needful that Christian love and truth be spoken in a positive way and with realistic relevance to the most variant situations. The family and the church must be considered in each area in relation to a positive ministry making for responsible participation in the family and in the institutions that touch it dynamically. Respect for personality, for freedom in relation to order, for community development, and for educational growth and accountability are all essential.

In almost every place population control and sexual responsibility are relevant guidelines. Christian family
education must perceive its tasks not only horizontally in
terms of present pressures but also longitudinally, for men
and women are involved in life-long interpersonal solidarity
and hence responsibility must be based on mutual respect and
loyalty that spans decades and generations. While customs
change and institutions become mobile and while legal and
customary morality are put in flux, the Christian man and
woman must rediscover afresh in *agape* love the fundamental
requirements of marriage and family life. They will see
these most clearly if they also relate the basic Christian
faith to the problems and tasks which call for responsible
men and women in a responsible society of which the family
is the basic unit.

## NOTES

This essay is the original English text of "Diakonia:
*Der Christ in der Gesellschaft*."  In *Die Kirchen der Welt*,
Der Methodismus, vol. 6.  Edited by C. Ernst Sommer.
Stuttgart:  Evangelisches Verlag, 1968.

## Social Responsibility
## and the Local Church
## (1951)

A variety of social judgments about the Church and local churches have been made in recent years. Some relate to prophetic responsibility and irresponsibility. The Church is the Body of Christ. The Church is an accommodated institution. The Church is the Kingdom of God on earth. The Church is imprisoned in its culture. The Church is a world-wide fellowship. The Church is divided racially and nationally; it is a middle-class institution. The Church is the one institution which maintained a semblance of inclusive integrity during World War II. The Church is isolated from the intelligentsia and from the laboring masses. The Church is the community of the forgiven and the incarnation of Christ's spirit. The church is secularized and worldly. There is one conclusion which may be drawn from this variety of typical judgments; namely that the Church is a social problem.

The main concerns of this essay are the elements of social responsibility for the local church. How does it maintain its prophetic integrity? What are the criteria of prophetic integrity? What should be its strategy for social action? The local church in the community tends to reflect the social structure of that community. The church's structure may be broadly denominational in theory but it often tends to modify its functions and structure so as to satisfy the pressures immediately around it. How can it conserve its relationships to God and the people so as to carry out his purposes for the Church? Both nationally and locally

369

the context threatens institutional integrity.

I
## Criteria of Prophetic Integrity

The basic needs of people when related to the Kingdom
of God provide the context of the table of criteria for the
prophetic integrity of the local church.   Sensitivity to
human needs constitutes the most basic criterion and the
orientation to all the others, for it is persons in relation
to God and the creation of a just and loving community that
are the focal points of prophetic activity.   Jesus made
human need the point of relevance for an understanding of
God's love and will.

Basic human needs must be distinguished from mere wants
and interests.   Human needs relate to the aspects of life
that participate in self-fulfillment and actualization.   The
teleology of the Christian ethic is that men and women may
have life and have it abundantly.   Man has one great need
which is self-actualization; but self-actualization when
fully understood is not a self-centered idea.   For a person
is a communitarian being.   Men and women are interdependent.
Each comes to fulfillment only in community with others,
hence only in terms of truth, fellowship, love and justice.
A local church sensitive to human need must develop responsibility to the whole community.

Human needs are the biological and psychological bases
of human rights.   A right is a moral claim of the person
against the community with respect to the satisfaction of
some basic need involved in personal actualization.   In the
present crisis when human values tend to be sacrificed to
mass manipulation, the church's prophetic integrity will be
judged by its relationship to protecting human beings in
need.

A criterion which grows out of dedication to basic human needs is the inclusiveness of the church fellowship. The Gospel calls for a barrierless community of love, but many local churches and denominations are so obviously divided along racial, national or class lines as to constitute a continuing scandal. Equally scandalous is the absence of intercommunion among the churches. Can Christ be divided? The church's social ministry loses much of its effectiveness because it lacks faith in its Lord, especially in his including love. This ineffectiveness often exposes hypocrisy of the crassest sort.

There are many forces playing on the local church demanding conformity to the contextual status quo. Many expect the churches to pronounce as good what special interests regard as good and to denounce as evil what does not please established institutional culture patterns. On many ambiguous issues the churches are expected to be silent lest the spirit of conflict and possible contention be aroused. But the Church of Christ must express independent social judgment. Its prophetic integrity is measured in part by the issues on which it is articulate and the issues on which it is silent. Local churches often purchase peace with cowardly silence. On all issues the churches must speak with a relevant objectivity and through concerned critical participation. Social hysteria often knows no middle ground between extreme positions on crucial issues; Christianity should illuminate the middle ground from a vertical perspective of prophetic transcendence.

A fourth criterion of prophetic integrity is genuine community. The local church is often just a congregation associated for worship. But the church should be a genuine caring community and its members should engage responsibly in various community-wide expressions of their Christian

vocation. To express Christian responsibility the local
church must grow in spiritual depth beyond being a Sunday
morning audience to being a valid group of convenanted participating Christians. Worship should create a community of
love and service. But these virtues are nurtured in relatively small groups characterized by critical, creative and
responsible participation. One of the most effective
antidotes to the poison of mass hysteria is the purgative
power of free critical discussion. Mass-mindedness is not
Christian-mindedness. A mass mind is not the mind of free
persons, informed by the spirit of love disciplined by reason and justice, but a psychological condition wherein the
masses are manipulated by those who control mass communication. There can be no independent social judgment, no inclusive fellowship, and no sensitivity to basic human needs
where people do not participate freely and responsibly in
small groups. The church can be a great bulwark against
totalitarian trends by developing Christian cells of fear-
less thinking and conscientious  acting on social questions.

To implement the qualities of group life which we have
noted, it is required that the local church nurture a wide
base of democratic leadership. Out of the practicing community of praying, thinking, studying, planning, and service
there should emerge many new leaders among the lay people.
The Church should study its own effective talent and its
potential talent in order to rear a generation of men and
women who are both Christian and democratic. Too many
churches simply take over from the culture around them "leading" secular lay persons as their "churchmen." The net result is that the work and the standards of the church tend
over the years to conform to the approved secular standards
of these "leaders." No greater need exists in the church
than the development of its own leaders who arise from its

own type and quality of community experience. Social classes not well-represented now could undoubtedly be noted among the new group. The leadership would represent all segments of social life and develop Christian communication among persons now alienated along class and national and racial lines.

The criteria thus far mentioned deal with the function and structure of the church as community. We now turn to one which is specially relevant in the present crisis. The prophetic quality of a church is now being tested by its loyalty to the principle of and its active defense of conscientious persons denied personal freedom in the social order. This means all those persons in the church and out who are willing to exercise their responsible freedom in a critical way and are seeking a better social life for all. Pressures demanding political orthodoxy and intellectual conformity threaten the foundations of American life and quench the hopes of a united world. But many churches are silent in their defense of civil liberties and civil rights, because they lack faith and therefore courage. If the churches do not defend the conscientious independent and critical minds in the present crisis, the churches are disloyal to the spirit of truth and of human dignity. For Christians religious freedom is at stake in all the freedoms, for where human dignity is oppressed God's vocation in people is denied.

The church's prophetic ministry is judged not only by its defense of the souls of free men and women, but by the pioneering it is willing to do in their thought and action. The sickness of the churches is often evident in its unwillingness to challenge the present distribution of political and economic power. It is not the duty of the churches as such to build institutions for the manipulation of power in

national or international politics or to take over the operation of the economic order.  But the effectiveness of the
churches' social ministry is largely circumscribed by the
structures and processes of the status quo.  We need church
pioneering in social doctrine, social work and social action
because social power must be brought into harmony with Christian vocation and God's righteous rule among men and
nations.

     The final criterion is self-criticism.  A church which
has learned to fulfill the foregoing norms will be able to
receive the ongoing judgment of God on itself as rebukes
which work for salvation and perfection.  Self-criticism is
a form of humility and meekness.  It makes a community
strong in faith, clear in purpose, and courageous in a
crisis, for it relates itself to the will of God and thus is
freed from the shackles of institutional self-interest and
self-will.  Today there is a growing self-criticism, but
complacency still predominates at all levels of churchman-
ship.

## II
### The Strategy of
### Social Responsibility

     Social responsibility expresses itself primarily in the
form of social doctrine, social work and social action.  Social doctrine means the development of sound theology made
relevant through Christian ethics to the major problems of
society.  Unless the mind of the church is well-informed
with clear thinking about the theological basis of Christian
action, the message will be obscure.  Theology should not be
made a fetish; experience is prior to doctrine; the springs
of action are not derived from syllogisms or propositions.
But theology is a constituent aspect of coherent prophetic

evangelism. Sound theology must be thoroughly informed with
relevant social data and the findings of the social sciences.

Sound social doctrine is not obvious. There are rival
social creeds and ideologies in the church. For example,
there is an otherworldliness which discusses piously and
sentimentally the whole range of Christian subjects but
denies action in history in favor of a transcendent life to
come. There are forms of eschatology which are apocalyptic
and therefore separate Christian doctrine from social
science and social work. There are forms of eschatology
which repudiate apocalyptic interpretations but which put
the hope of mankind so remotely in the future, when God will
consummate the age, that no specific present duty emerges to
view. Indeed, the temptation of all excessive stress on
eschatology is to emphasize God's role in history to the
exclusion of significant human initiative and decision.
Again, there are social doctrines which are relevant to present needs, for example in the economic order, but which so
subordinate the social order to ecclesiastical control as to
promise only ultimate church domination. Such are some of
the social encyclicals of the Roman Catholic popes issued
since Leo XIII. There is much wisdom in these encyclicals,
but the over-all effect is (a) to undermine democratic
institutions like the public school, (b) to encourage authoritarianism in politics, (c) to confirm class domination in
the West, and (d) to invite a holy war with the U.S.S.R.
Individual distinguished Roman Catholic thinkers have been
more creative than official encyclical pronouncements.

Sound social doctrine will relate freedom and other
creatively. It will show how the legitimate hopes and needs
of people are related to the ultimate hope of Christianity.
It will have a universal perspective on the conservation of

natural resources everywhere in the world with a program of
conservation, such as soil and water conservation, in the
local parish in rural areas.    The leading idea which
includes all others is expressed in theology as the Kingdom
of God, and in Christian social ethics as the "responsible
society."

The religious conception of an economically responsible
society is one in which men and woman freely acknowledge
responsibility to inclusive justice and public order; one in
which economic goals are not divorced from the welfare of
society they ought to serve; one in which political authority and economic power are responsible both to God and the
people; one in which economic activities are understood as
means to larger ends, but in which the person can nevertheless actualize himself; one in which the people have freedom
to control, to criticize and to reform their political and
economic institutions; one in which power is widely distributed throughout the whole community and one in which justice
and equality of opportunity are established for all.    The
religious conception is an integral conception in which the
church is both a conserver, a critic and an inspirer of creative approaches to the meeting of human needs.    It is a conception in which economic life finds its rightful place in a
doctrine of redemption both in history and beyond.

The second form of social ministry is social work.
This includes both case work and group work.    Social work is
the most developed form of the church's social ministry.
The natural responses of sympathy and mutual aid, fortified
by the example of the loving Lord, have undergirded the
works of charity from the earliest days of the Christian community.    Certain parables, like the good Samaritan, direct
teaching, like the Sermon on the Mount, and fellowship among
the disciples have made social work effective with a minimum

of doctrinal theology. There is always something one can do
in a situation of distress, without waiting for the fulfillment of history or a structural change in the social order.
When all external aid or resources fail, one can always
share distress with understanding, fellowship and love.

Social work needs however, to be done better than it
has been in the past. In the Christian churches it needs
development in three directions. First, it needs to be
grounded more deeply in Christian doctrine and therefore in
the knowledge of the deeper needs which people have. Food,
clothing and shelter are indispensable aspects of social
work; but man does not live by bread alone, nor by raiments
or good housing alone. Secondly, social work in the
churches needs to be less superficial and sentimental in its
methods. Case work and group work should be integrated in a
community, so that all the agencies of community can work
together cooperatively. Poor social work, even when sincere-
ly done, may cause people to deteriorate in character.
Thirdly, social work needs to be coherently related to
social action, so that it does not become a substitute for
the love which is expressed in social justice. The poor
need "not charity but a chance." Oftentimes church philanthropy and social work prevent intelligent social action.
Thus the givers of philanthropy have sometimes short-circuited God's will in society because immediate symptoms of distress were ministered to rather than constitutional causes
of evil in the economic and political order. Church social
work, therefore, needs to be theologically deeper, technically better, and profoundly integrated in community reconstruction.

Social responsibility expresses itself, in the third
place, in sound social action. Social action differs from
social work as first aid differs from preventive medicine or

as limited preventive medicine differs from regional sanita-
tion engineering. Social work concentrates on focusing present resources to meet human need. Social action focuses on
community reconstruction. The two belong together in a
continuum of social process.

Social action in the local church requires that it be
well-informed and well led. High ideals do not guarantee
successful social policy. The minister must know how to
lead the democratic process through the pitfalls of prejudice, complacency, rash action, and unnecessary community
conflict. It is often said that the Gospel is dynamite; so
it is, but often it just explodes in the pulpit and blows
the church down. Dynamite should be entrusted only to the
informed engineer. So the minister must know how to handle
controversial issues. The minister must know how to maintain the unity of the fellowship in the bond of peace. Such
peace is not the absence of conflicting interests, but is
rather the common faith and mutual respect which persons of
differing interests and convictions have in each other and
in God. The minister must not isolate himself from the
people nor segments of the people from each other. The
power of the gospel must be harnessed to manageable units of
group action. Ortho*doxy* needs ortho*praxis*.

The minister should not say "I" when he can say "we."
He should never egocentrically separate himself from the
inclusive frame-of-reference of the Christian fellowship.
He should not dogmatize with conclusions when the people
have not been led to consider the premises carefully and to
appropriate them. If the minister is well-grounded in social doctrine and has served his people well in forms of
social work, he will not easily sever the common bond of congregational unity. There is much to draw on in the Scriptures, in Christian history, in the official social legisla-

tion of the churches to provide the basis for discussing
controversial problems in the spirit of "our" tradition,
"our goals," "our Lord," "our common hope."

The minister will know the techniques of the forum, the
study committee, the class, the debate, the hearing, the
unofficial work-shop and the like in initiating change in
social attitudes. He will know how to balance a program
with varying points of view. He will not place the absolute
sanction of Christianity on any specific program. He will
know that real advance is not to be measured in a church
community by parliamentary manipulation, not by the official
change of voting for resolution B instead of resolution A.
He will know that the real criterion of growth is what happens to the people as they move from position A to position
B. Prophetic integrity is not belligerence but the spirit
of God achieving his purposes in group relations. His
purposes are redemptive rather than judgmental. Christ came
not to condemn the world but that the world through Him
might be saved. The last word is not victory of a cause, or
defeat of opponents, but reconciliation.

Social action can be improved through action-research.
Action-research has been popularized and developed, for
example, through the work of Kurt Lewin and the experiments
carried out in the field of group dynamics. Of special significance is the process whereby the attitudes and action
patterns are changed through self-education and group decision and concrete projects. Instead of study being done *for*
a group or community *by* outside experts, action research is
self-instituted and unites action *through* participation in
decision making with survey and research. The truly remarkable social discoveries made within this field-theory frame
work should lead the pastor to realize that the most effi-
cient path of conversion is not from sermon to social

change, but in terms of small-groups approaching manageable
units of action with freedom and democracy. Old prejudices
never die; they just fade away with the dawn of action-in-
sights. The answer to many sterotypes is not ideological
refutation but experimentation in action-research. Action-
research has demonstrated the superiority of democratically
conducted groups over autocratic ones, thus providing empirical confirmation of the faith in democracy in the very area
of discipline in which autocratic method has claimed superiority. Christian love and democratic processes tend to confirm each other in small groups.

The strategy of social responsibility must recognize
the sharp distinction which obtains between community and
the interest associations. The Churches must keep the principle of association subordinate to that of community. Interest associations are for the most part competitive with
one another. They exist for the gaining of limited and
limiting objectives. They seek control over scarce values
and stimulate the drive for power and success. There are,
for example, over sixteen hundred trade associations in the
U.S.A. Corporations are themselves interest-limited associations. About fifteen million workers are organized in great
labor associations. More than half the farmers belong to
agricultural associations. Physicians and other professional men are likewise organized in interest groups. These
associations do not collectively make up community, though
they tend to dominate both urban and rural society. A true
community is no more a collection of associations than a person is a bundle of interests or wants. Community requires
many common value-impregnated beliefs, mutuality of concern,
and cooperation. Community development must succeed in sub-
ordinating the associations to itself or it will be torn
assunder by them.

Baker Brownell defines a community as follows: "(1)  A
Community is a group of neighbors who know one another face
to face.  (2)  It is a diversified group as to age, sex,
skill, function, and mutual service to each other.  (3)  It
is a cooperative group in which many of the main activities
of life are carried on together.  (4)  It is a group having
a sense of 'belonging,' or group identity and solidarity.
(5)  It is a rather small group, such as the family, village, or small town, in which each person can know a number
of others as whole persons, not as functional fragments."[1]
Some scientists will challenge this definition.  R. M.
MacIver defines community as "the common life of beings who
are guided essentially from within..., relating themselves
to one another, weaving for themselves the complex web of
social unity."[2]  What is of special importance in these
definitions for the churches is that of deep interpersonal
relationship.  The churches should help build community,
whereas they are often competing and divisive associations
which disrupt community growth.  Questions of size and geog-
raphy, while significant, are not so important in the social
ministry of the church as common values that are conjunc-
tive.  As Arthur E. Morgan says, "The existence of a community is determined, not by the amount of organization and
social machinery, but by the extent to which common needs
and interests are worked out by unified planning and action,
in a spirit of mutual interest.  In such a community there
is common acquaintance, and common purposes and standards
are defined and maintained."[3]

The laity of the churches serve the work-a-day world in
many associations.  Here their Christian vocation is put to
the test, for Christian vocation calls them to relate what
is partial to the whole, to surrender fragmentary self-will
and desire to God's will, and personal interests to the

common good.   It belongs to the social strategy of the
churches today to revive a sense of organic Christian
vocation and to put it to work in community integration.
The failure of society to achieve mutuality and integrity at
the grass roots where the associations exercise their pressure, invites the state (the most powerful of associations)
to superimpose order from above in coercive ways.   For people rendered anonymous and impotent in the functional fragmentation of urban technology, the church has much to offer
as a genuine community of personal wholeness.   Since persons
are created for brotherhood, Christian vocation is fulfilled
only in community building.

    The answer to the problem of the competing multitude of
voluntary associations is not, therefore, coordination by a
superior power, or their destruction.   Indeed, the voluntary
association is a foundation stone of western freedom.   The
church must protect the right of voluntary association or it
will itself be threatened.   But the answer to fragmentation
is solidarity in social life in which whole persons respond
to one another as whole persons.   In the church and in the
cooperative life of community, persons can be led to interact deeply and realistically.   Workers associate for good
causes such as the right to have unions of their own choosing.   But the church must develop a tactic of bringing the
organized groups in American and world economic life together to face and consider their common responsibilities as we
have outlined them above.

    In dealing with the power of associations the churches
must conserve a constructive view of the role of government.
Today the church is tempted to join in the popular and
reactionary abuse heaped on government in the name of stat-
ism.   It is, to be sure, essential to maintain the separation of church and state, but it is equally important to see

in the state a useful servant of the community whose offices
may be used for the conservation and development of freedom.
The church must be under no illusions of the power tendencies of the state, yet it must distinguish between the
repressive tyranny of totalitarianism and the unity of order
with freedom which responsible government involves. In
other words the church must appropriate the practical wisdom of R. Niebuhr's remark: "Man's capacity for justice
makes democracy possible; but man's inclination to injustice
makes democracy necessary." It is part of the Christian
faith that the protection of justice which makes democracy
necessary is grounded in the ultimate triumph in man of the
sonship under God over the inclination to injustice. Just
as the Church is not only a possibility but a real fellowship of the forgiven, so democracy in the social order is
not only a possibility, but has in part been already realized. That which has been thus far realized gives substance
to the social order that is hoped for.

## NOTES

[1]Baker Brownell, *The Human Community* (New York:  Harper and Bros., 1950), p. 198.

[2]R. M. MacIver, *Community* (London:  Macmillan and Co., 1924), p. 34.

[3]Arthur E. Morgan, *The Small Community* (New York: Harper and Bros., 1942), p. 234.

The Christian Faith and the
Renewal of World Mission
(1963)


I
One Human Destiny

Contemporary world events have caused the Church to
enter a period of self-examination. Whether the Church in
its God-given vocation of unity and mission will be truly
renewed depends on how radical its reform will be. In a
period of radical self-examination we tend to look to performance and to practical demonstrable results, but we need
equally, or more basically to look at faith in the Church.
When one is in a questioning mood there is no limit to what
questions may be asked. Doubts, fears, guilt, anxieties,
feelings of impotence, perplexities, and confusion inevitably result. I shall address myself to the Christian faith
as both what is believed in and the trust, commitment, decision, and believing that are involved in the renewal of
faith. Men and women are dimly aware of *one human destiny*
today. They are convulsed in political, economic and cultural revolutions. They are universally bent on creating an
industrial, technological, and scientific civilization.
They are participating in a world market which cuts across
ideological frontiers and national sovereignties as well as
cultures whose ancient religions are more radically challenged by events than is the Christian Church. How ultimately adequate their faiths are is one of the primal issues
of our age.

In an address before the Central Committee of the World

Council of Churches in Paris in August, 1962, Principal John
Marsh spoke on the theme:  "The Finality of Jesus Christ in
the Age of Universal History."  He made four points which
provide the setting of *my own confessional convictions*.
*First*, "human history has become recognized as one, in a
sense that was unknown and indeed impossible, in previous
ages."  *Second*, "whether we have known it or not, history
has all the time been universal."  *Third*, the resurgence of
other world religions, "their strenuous attempts to
modernize themselves and their doctrines, may be seen in
depth as an attempt to claim a part in the universal history which, we are all coming to feel, we all share."
*Fourth*, not only the world religions, but the great
politico-economic power blocs have come to see the inescapable unity of the history of humanity.

II
The Ultimate Assertions
of Christian Faith

It is not possible for modern Christians to make more
ultimate assertions about Jesus Christ than have already
been made, indeed were made in the early Church.  Explorations into outer-space, on the one hand, and the quest for
global unity, on the other hand have not changed the universality or the absoluteness of the claims of faith about God
and man.  St. Paul's and St. John's claims are hard to
exceed.  To be sure, the early Christian had a cosmology
which modern man cannot effectively use and they lacked
knowledge of many cultures and other religions.  Their faith
was not, however, finally dependent on their knowledge of
cosmology or anthropology because it emerged from a revelation that had come in the "fullness of time."  In one respect the question is not whether their faith was big

enough, but whether it was too ambitious.

"When all things began," says John, "the Word already was. The Word dwelt with God, and what God was, the Word was. The Word, then, was with God at the beginning, and through him all things came to be; no single thing was created without him."[1]  Paul makes equally exalted claims: "For in him the complete being of God, by God's own choice, came to dwell. Through him God chose to reconcile the whole universe to himself, making peace through the shedding of his blood upon the cross—to reconcile all things, whether on earth or in heaven, through him alone."[2]  "You are now the people of God, who once were not his people; outside his mercy once, you have now  received his mercy,"[3] says Peter.

The point is that the vision and revelation received by the early church is profound and capacious enough to take in all modern knowledge and historical events. The question is whether we are profound and capacious enough to renew their faith-act in ourselves and in the Church. Within this faith-act both Christians and non-Christians, all cultures and nations new and old, are related to the one central story of all history at once cosmic and human. It is the story of God's creation of the world and of its redemption by the same Word, creative, incarnate, crucified, risen, ascended, triumphant. God's action in Jesus Christ is not simply something done *for* historical man, it is an event *in* human history. God is not only *for* us, he is *with* us and he seeks to work out his purposes *in* us and *through* us. Jesus Christ discloses the justice and compassion of God, but he discloses God by an historical act. To be sure, the claim that Jesus disclosed God is a very human claim. It is an act of faith.

This act of faith invites the consent of the whole mind and involves the free decision of the will. It relates us at once to the cosmic ground of all being, to our fellow creatures, and to all history.   All religions are involved in this event and Christian faith is involved in all religions.   All history is involved in this event and this event involves all history.   The event is, therefore, not isolated; and all interpretations of humanity and ultimate decisions by men and women *must* refer to it.   But since it is not isolated and therefore is genuinely historical, Christians must understand that God is involved in all history and not only in the history of Christian communities and the Christian Church.   Whenever Christians go in this world or in outer-space it is one world and one universe.   The God who was in Christ, whom Jesus Christ disclosed and who loves the world through Christ, is already there.

Christian faith in the cosmic and historical action of God does not entitle us to make absolute claims for our expressions about that faith.   These are very human products. Our propositions about Jesus Christ are themselves historical.   They refer to events and acts which are other than our creeds.   Our acts of faith are conditioned by our beliefs, but he for whom the universe was made and who perfected the pioneer of our salvation through suffering, and who calls us to unity and mission, is not conditioned by those beliefs. We believe not in our beliefs, but in God; we adore not ideals but reality; we belong not to a mythical character but to the historical Jesus; we cling not to admonitions but to the cross; we live not by hearsay but by first person experience, as deep responds to deep.   Moreover, we do not proclaim that we are the light of the world, or that the Church is the light of the world, or that our creedal formulations are the light of the world.   When we say that Jesus Christ is the light of the world and the hope of the world, we do not say that we own him or define him or control him

or circumscribe him. Death could not contain him; certainly
Christian groups cannot. It is not only in our darkness
that the light of the world shines. Christ shines everywhere, but many men and women have not appropriated him in
acts of faith.

Renewing the faith of Christians and the Christian
church is not primarily an act of repetition but a rebirth
of prayer and worship and the re-establishment of a coherent
view of humanity in its primary relationships. Bernard of
Clairvoux, the great mystical reformer of the Twelfth century who has been called the conscience of his age once affirmed: "I will light my fire at the flame of meditation."
The "Beyond" must be found "within." In the subjective
depths the objective reality must be affirmed. Through
objective worship the renewing act of faith grafts the
depths of private and public life into the mysterious depths
of divine Spirit. There it finds unity and power.

In his denunciation of despair, Emmanuel Mounier, the
great French personalist, writes: "In the strictest sense
of the word, Christianity was to graft human history into
the very heart of divine life, through the mediation of
Christ Incarnate. Thus the three theological unities are
inseparably welded together: the unity of God, the unity of
history, the unity of the human race. In the solidarity of
these three unities we have the framework of the idea of the
collective progress of humanity."[4] But being grafted into
the divine life does not make the course of history a linear
success. The movement of history is dialectical, not
linear, and so Christians must constantly face disaster and
defeat and they must fight for the renewal of their faith in
all periods of history. Man is in dialogue with himself,
his world, his fellow-men, and with God. Especially his
worship is dialogue.

The integrity of the individual worshiper even when
deeply involved in communion with God has never been more
profoundly stated than by one of the Brethren of the Common
Life in the Fourteenth century, John Ruysbrock: "That mea-
sureless Love which is God Himself, dwells in the pure deeps
of our spirit, like a burning brazier of coal. And it
throws forth brilliant and firey sparks which stir and/or
kindle heart and sense, will and desire, and all the powers
of the soul, with a fire of love....As air is penetrated by
the brightness and the heat of the sun, and iron is penetrated by fire; that it works through fire the works of
fire, since it burns and shines like fire....Yet each keeps
its own nature—the fire does not become iron, and the iron
does not become fire, for the iron is within the fire and
the fire within the iron, so likewise God is in the being of
the soul. The creature never becomes God as God never
becomes creature....The union takes place in God through
grace and our home-turning love."

Our Christian faith to be renewed must not only be
aflame with the fire of prayer but it must be morally
grounded in the righteousness of God. Our hope is in God,
but hope in action means mission. Christian optimism is not
only radically mystical; it is radically social because the
hope of a world to come awakens the desire to organize the
world around us. Communion with God creates community among
men. As Mounier says, "The hereafter is here and now
amongst you, through you, or it will not be for you." The
universal God creates the universal church and the universal
human community through us. This means a radical reorientation of those Christians who resist being the instruments of
God's coming kingdom. Such a radical reorientation requires
that men think through what the idea of our common human
destiny really entails. Men must conceive their destiny as

idea before they can translate it into action.  The threefold unity of God, of human history, and of the human race
is the enemy of all parochialism, for it discloses that our
mission is one and its frontiers are everywhere.  It defines
a radical ministry for clergy and laity alike freed from the
leading strings of sex, class, race, and nation.

The ministry of the laity is often described as responsible action within the jobs they have in the present social
order, but this idea must be enlarged and deepened to be
understood as eschatological ministry.  All laypersons stand
at one time and place, but there is a new community to come
into being.  Old orders change giving place to new.  God's
kingdom is breaking in at the frontiers of today's world,
but those frontiers are everywhere.  Therefore, the ministry
of the laity is a revolutionary one which transcends all
present human frontiers of market place, job description,
political alignment, or constitutional sovereignty.

### III
### Christian Faith and
### Christian Ethics

The Christian faith is lock-stitched into Christian
ethic.  This ethic is supra-national and therefore calls
upon every member of the Christian church to assume a universal and inclusive political, economic, and social responsibility.  All Christians must expect tension and conflict
between the ecumenical Christian community of which they are
organic parts and members and the national communities in
which they hold citizenship.  Their political responsibilities are ecumenical and are not finally defined by transient
national histories.  What can a Christian learn from a
Buddhist like U Thant?  Here is a man who approaches mankind
from an inclusive perspective.  He is dedicated to creating

conditions whereby the big power blocs can come to a greater
understanding of each other's point of view.  Once the "free
world" and the Communist bloc come to trust one another, U
Thant believes the arms race can be reduced.  He has repeatedly decried expenditures by the big nations on missiles,
rockets, and space projects.  He contends that the money can
be better put to use in underdeveloped nations, for mankind's greatest enemy is poverty.  In this connection U
Thant does not hesitate to take a stand for immediate cessa-
tion of testing of nuclear weapons by everyone everywhere.
He said recently, "The division of the world into the rich
and poor is much more real and much more serious, and ultimately much more explosive, than the division of the world
on ideological grounds."  He believes in what he calls the
"universality" of the United Nations, which means that he
favors membership for Communist China.

   What can Christians learn from this?  Does this mean
that such are the leadings of the Buddhist ministry of the
laity?  Does it mean that sober men of good will are led to
common judgments?  Does it mean that the "peaceful co-existence" of the living world religions postulates a common
faith in the "peaceful co-existence" of states?

   U Thant's various policy ideas correspond to strong rec-
ommendations taken by various denominations, by the National
Council of Churches of Christ in the U.S.A., and by the
World Council of Churches.  Unfortunately, they are not the
working faith of enough American Christians and such lack of
practical faith is a stumbling block for many non-Christians
who judge the churches by the touchstone of effective
witness for peace.

   To some, such policies as the ban on nuclear testing,
and the admission of Communist China into the United Nations
have little to do with Christian ethics and faith.  But

ortho*praxis* is as central as ortho*doxy*.

The world requires of adherents of Christian faith responsibility for leadership towards world coherence. Christian faith should free people from enslaving habits of mind and action, from crippling and restricting institutions and from ancient good which now is uncouth. Can a renewed Church lift the hearts of men as much say as "the common market" in Europe? The Committee on the Christian Responsibility for European Co-operation writes: "the new perspective of European co-operation has raised expectations in the hearts of many people in politics and society, and has come as a surprise after the breakdown of the old European order following decennia of war, gloom, and political crisis." The recent report then adds: "This sense of discovery of a new area of constructive effort and of hope for the political future is often stronger in the minds of those who are actively engaged in the life of secular society than among leaders of the Christian churches in Europe."[5] The Committee lauds the principle of the European Economic Community which makes it an *open one*, working for the economic progress of Europe and the world. However, one is still deeply disappointed in a Christian Committee which is finally oriented in the sterility of anti-communism. After lauding the responsibility of the rich nations towards the developing and the poor nations, and after observing that the Western world needs to put its monetary house in order, the crucial orientation of this committee comes to the fore. The report says: "However, hopes for the future could also be lost if the West were to lower its nuclear shield....It is therefore urgent that the new-found strength of Europe be reflected in a new balance within the N.A.T.O. alliance rather than in any third force tendencies." In the perspective of Christian faith for world mission one must protest

against the parochial defensiveness of policies limited by
N.A.T.O. loyalties.   It was this same lack of Christian
creativity which marred and crippled the resolutions on
international relations at the New Delhi Assembly.[6]   It is
this same tendency still to think in European and Western
terms which damns as hypocritical Christian expressions of
concrete international order.

When Christians retreat from the concrete existential
judgments of the present into the generalized abstractions
of the faith, they often betray a clericalized, and what is
worse, a professional theological retreat from ethical and
policy decisions.   The ministry of the laity of which we
hear so much today must express its faith concretely.  To be
sure no political or economic order may be equated with the
kingdom of God and all organizations of power are at best
ambiguous.   Nevertheless, there are today tens of thousands
of lay Christians in overseas service; and their witness
will be telling in the future developments of the Christian
community.  The fact that they are in constant communication
with the leaders of new nations in Africa, Asia, and South
America only underscores the crucial character of their witness.   If the older missionary effort by ordained missionaries was compromised by their naive and unwitting entangle-
ments in Western imperialism, whether economic, political or
cultural, what must we think of the compromise of the widely
acclaimed ministry of the laity in the persons of overseas
Americans, to mention only one group?

For good or ill the new missionaries are proclaiming
whatever gospel they profess.   As Abraham K. Thampy notes:
"Foreigners coming to India are not involved in a purely
economic activity, a mere business enterprise....When engineers or technicians come from the West, they have to bear
in mind that our younger generation is learning more than

technique. It is watching you very closely. This is the
time to 'gossip' the Gospel. In India the Christian influence is negligible because the Christian population is so
small. Yet I do not think that the old form of missionary
activities is possible any more—nor necessary or desir-
able. Therefore, when I look at this big issue of foreign
collaboration I look at the technicians coming out from the
West as technician-missionaries of the new age, as new missionaries—especially because we are already in living touch
with similar missionaries from the communist world and in my
contacts with some of them I found that they are not only
experts in engineering, but experts in something more than
this. It is here that the Church in the West can be a sort
of reference group to these technicians going out to the
economically underdeveloped countries like India." But what
kind of reference group is the Christian Church in the midst
of revolutionary change? Mr. Thampy says, "As an active
member of the Church I feel that the Church in India has
failed to take sufficient note of this change....The leadership of the Church is very middle class in its outlook, it
cannot understand or appreciate the problems of sections of
people below the so-called middle class....Hence it is my
conviction that Western industrialists can use their power
not only to help the changing Indian industry, but also to
'gossip' the Gospel to the changing Asian society."[7]

In using this illustration from India my principal
point is to show that the Christian faith has a doctrine of
the church and of ministry which needs renewal. The idea of
the people of God here employed belonged also to the early
church which held such bold and cosmic claims of Jesus
Christ mentioned earlier in this address. The doctrine of
the Church and its mission is integral to our faith and
ethics. An age of universal history with its recognized

interdependence of human destiny finds its meaning in acts
of faith which show forth compassion and obedience to God's
revelation.

IV
### Christian Faith and
### Scientific Viewpoints

The realm of science and technology has become a source
of grave ethical complexity and spiritual perplexity. This
comes about in three ways: (1) Every nation today links
its destiny to the rapid development of science and technology. To this end it organizes its natural resources and its
education of youth. (2) The scientific outlook becomes a
competitor of the religious outlook on life, so that scientism becomes a rival faith to Christian faith. Not only in
the Communist world but in the whole world many have come to
doubt that a Christian world view is compatible with the
scientific method and outlook. (3) Because man's destiny
seems to be subjected to impersonal technology and the awful
consequences of thermo-nuclear war, a despair has overwhelm-
ed both scientists and cultural leaders. The end-point of
the scientific age seems to many to be militarism and automation—and the two are not significantly different triumphs of the mechanization of man.

What does Christian faith reply to such perplexity and
despair? First of all, it is not Christian faith to pronounce nuclear doom on the human race. Though we live face
to face with the possibility of nuclear suicide, Christian
living is not a kind of catastrophism. As Mounier says, that
would be only a mean-minded interpretation of history. On
the other hand we must exercise enough faith to stop building bombs and to build and rebuild the world's social
economy.

In the second place, men have known for a long time
that science will not save them. They have followed it
because it will serve them. Long before World War II many
saw that the military misuse of science would desolate the
world. With the coming of the atom bomb and continued testing, almost everyone has a sense of disillusionment about
science and technology. Yet almost everyone knows that
science will be a dominating factor in the future and youth
will be intensively disciplined by scientific education.
This scientific and technological training will become universal in society both East and West and in the non-aligned
nations. It will be a constant factor in the emerging world
civilization. Science by itself is no savior, but science
has already become the order of the day. Men despair of science, but like the Sorcerer's apprentice they cannot stop
it. The despair leads some of them to nihilism. This philosophy is not only rowdy. Today it is armed. Yet Christian faith must lift science into a coherent philosophy of
nature, man, and history, thus saving men from both despair
and nihilism. How can Christian faith accomplish this?

The Christian faith must take a more serious and sober
view of science than it has done. It must respect and use
science as a liberating method and as a mechanical servant
of freedom and welfare. In taking a serious and sober view
of science theology will exercise a proper stewardship over
it as one of God's precious gifts to the mind of man. In a
coherent philosophy fact can never displace value, mechanisms cannot displace purpose, science can never displace
God. Christian faith has the resources of a personal view
of ultimate reality and a purposive philosophy of history in
which God has a personal stake.

The great metaphysical issues in the debate about God
and science have long been threshed out. Alternatives like

naturalism, idealism, materialism, realism, existentialism,
and personalism have been thoroughly explored.  In relation
to any and all of these Christian faith has had an effective
dialogue.  At the moment the great crisis is not a scientific threat to theology on theoretical grounds.  The great
failure of Christianity can be said to have been a pastoral
one.  The Church has turned over to others the intellectual
and spiritual care of man.  She has forsaken the common man.
She can regain the leadership in pastoral care which she
ought to assume whenever she will again take upon herself
the role of saving-servant.  The resources of the Christian
faith in Scripture, tradition, and reason are hers to use in
her servanthood.  Men and women need a newly formulated expression of Christian coherence, a unified view of human
existence whereby the scattered pieces and movements of life
can be referred to a meaningful whole.  Such a unified view
will  inevitably  contain  much  critical  dialogue  of  the
church's own pastoral derelections to modern culture.

As Christian faith continues its dialogue with modern
science it will favor an open society.  Philosophically the
Christian faith inevitably expresses itself in personal categories, but theology along with all other doctrines within
living  history  is  subject  to  constant modification.    It
unites fidelity to absolute human values, despite guilt and
sinfulness, with progressive historical experiences.

The university of today provides a kind of parable for
the Church and for modern Christianity with respect to the
open society and the open dialogue.  Formerly many regarded
a university as a place where tested knowledge was transmit-
ted to the young.  Research was an essential but minor
adjunct to the great body of common knowledge -some of it
classical, some of it contemporary.  Today a university is
tomorrow's society living in anticipation.  It is research

in process.  The student steps into a moving stream wherein
knowledge is in the process of being made.  Knowledge and
the student are both in the making.  So too with the expressions of Christianity.  Faith in Christ means a church in
action, a church being made by divine-human action which
shapes the world which it serves.

NOTES

[1]John 1:1-3 (New English Bible).

[2]Colossians 1:19-20.

[3]I Peter 2:10.

[4]Emmanuel Mounier, *Be Not Afraid: A Denunciation of Despair*. Studies in Personalist Sociology (New York: Harper and Bros.), pp. xiii-xiv.

[5]*European Issues*. No. 17, October 29, 1962.

[6]Third Assembly of the World Council of Churches, 1961.

[7]Abraham K. Thampy, *Laity*. November, 1962, pp. 27-28.

# Christian Responsibility
## With Respect to Revolution
### (1962, 1967)


I


The Church has a positive responsibility with respect to the social order. Its involvement is direct since salvation is an integral whole of persons-in-community. Social action is not a peripheral by-product of the church pursuing other goals. In itself social action is not the gospel, but the gospel to be whole includes political along with other concerns. To speak of social action "in itself" is an abstraction with little meaning. This essay differs, frankly, from the position taken by Gustave Weigal, a leading Roman Catholic who says: "Religion can contribute to welfare of the general community; it can help society. My only worry is whether it should. It certainly cannot be the prime purpose of religion to make secular enterprise more satisfactory. That can indeed be the consequent of religion. But consequents are not the goals of deliberation; they are casual accretions to the proper goals of a planned effort."[1] Human salvation and social salvation are interpenetrating processes. The one cannot be complete without the other.

The notion that Christian responsibility is only indirect has defenders among Protestants as well as among Roman Catholics. Waldo Beach argues for an "indirect" relationship as follows: "The Church does not exist in order to produce racial justice, or to achieve racial inclusiveness in its own life. The Church (sic) exists to honor its Lord and Head, through a corporate life of worship and service. Its racial inclusiveness within, and its witnesses for racial justice without, are the inevitable by-products, not the intention, of this corporate life in Christ."[2]  Such a division of mission and unity would seem to violate the nature of the church.  Where racial inclusiveness is violated, worship is not truly corporate; and where racial injustice without is condoned, Christ is dishonored.  Racial inclusiveness is a precondition of *Christian* fellowship.

Christian responsibility to be political must also be prepolitical, for the state rests on a firmament of law which has deep social foundations.  The present essay will emphasize the inclusive context of political change and revolution and in this it follows the position developed at the Oxford Conference in 1937.  "Whatever limitations there may be on the action of the church as an organized society, Christians must give expression to their faith not only in what one may call the pre-political sphere of the aims, standards and values that determine political action, but also in the field of concrete political decision and political struggle.  To doubt this would be to deny the sovereignty of God over the whole of life and to surrender large areas of life to the unfettered control of the forces of evil."[3]

The life of worship and the call to radical social action must not be divorced.  Harry F. Ward once quipped that "mysticism is the refuge of the tired radical."  Edgar S. Brightman has replied, "If you are going to be a mystic you must pay attention to God, and if you pay attention to God you must be radical."  The axe of God is at the root of all institutions.

In a remarkable essay prepared for the Amsterdam Assembly (1948) Jacques Ellul deals with the failure of the

Church in the context of the situation in Europe. The
failure of the Church he noted in three areas: (1) "The
Church has left the care and protection of man to others."
(2) "The Church has left to others the responsibility for
revolution." And (3) "The Church has left to others the
responsibility for the spiritual life of the peoples."[4] Of
these three the second thesis bears directly on the present
essay. Professor Ellul writes as follows:

> The Church exists in order to insist on constant
> change in society and civilization, in order to
> bring them more in conformity with the order of
> God. This is a mission of "permanent revolu-
> tion." But the Church has completely lost sight
> of the fact that an order of God exists and it
> has accepted the established order of things.
> Hence instead of representing values of trans-
> formation and judgment (justice, freedom, etc.)
> founded on Jesus Christ, the Church has merely
> stood for conservative values and has left the
> revolutionary functions in the hands of politi-
> cal parties.[5]

There is a certain Trotskyist flavor to the term "permanent revolution" but as employed by Jacques Ellul it presents an image which discloses the heart of the Christian social ethic. It involves such concepts as judgment, crisis,
mission, conversion, fundamental change, and transformation.
There is in it an eschatological element of hope for men
and society. Hope involves the prospect of release from
captivity. Mission is hope in action. A permanent revolution in Christ is an ongoing eschatological event in which
God guarantees the instability of every order of injustice,
since it mocks the creation; Christ effects redemption for
those who accept God's new order in faith; and the Holy
Spirit creates a new community in Christ. This on-going
revolution takes place concretely in history, therefore in
earthen vessels, and therefore it involves the constant
reformation and renewal of the church as well as of society,

for Christ is the meaning of man, society, and history.

The doctrine of "permanent revolution" is not universally acknowledged in the Church. Some parts of the Church
lack a sense of the political responsibility of the Church
entirely. Some parts of the Church wrongly translate the
idea of political responsibility into church political parties. In no part of the Church do we find an unambiguous
awareness of the relation of political revolution to the
mission of the Church. Where the responsibility of the
Church for revolution is unacknowledged, the mission of the
Church is not fully accepted. Since mission is hope in
action, the Church has a permanent vocation to take steps to
release all people from whatever bondage holds them. Political revolution derives its meaning from the nature and destiny of man.

From what we have just said we must place political responsibility within the context of a view, well described by
H. Richard Niebuhr, of Christ as the transformer of culture.
One of the great names in this tradition of Christian social
ethics is Augustine. Niebuhr says of Augustine: "Christ is
the transformer of culture for Augustine in the sense that
he redirects, reinvigorates, and regenerates that life of
man, expressed in all human works, which in present actuality is the perverted and corrupted exercise of a fundamentally good nature; which, moreover, in its depravity lies under
the curse of transiency and death, not because an external
punishment has been visited upon it, but because it is intrinsically self-contradictory."[6] Augustine could see
clearly as a Christian that it was not Christianity that was
causing the decline and collapse of Rome but the self-contra-
dictions of its total culture. The false will and the false
loves were the root sources of the decay. But within the
womb of the old society, as Marx would put it, a new order

was in the making.  The source of that new order was not
where Marx would have looked for it.   In the womb of the
Roman Empire a new love and a new will had been conceived.
This new love was creating a Church which would one day
shape a new civilization.

Along with Augustine, Wesley belongs in the tradition
of Christ's transformation of culture.  In Wesley this motif
is part of his idea of perfection.  He shares with Paul,
John, Augustine, Luther and Calvin the insight that Christ
"is no new lawgiver who separates a new people from the old
by giving them the constitution for a new kind of culture."
"Christ," says Niebuhr, "is for Wesley the transformer of
life; he justifies men by giving them faith; he deals with
the sources of human action; he makes no distinction between the moral and immoral citizens of human commonwealth,
in convicting all of self-love and in opening to all the
life of freedom in response to God's forgiving love.  But
Wesley insists on the possibility—again as God's possibility, not man's—of a present fulfillment of that promise of freedom.  By the power of Christ believers may be
cleansed from all sin, may be like their Master, may be delivered 'in this world.'"[7]

S. Paul Schilling develops the Wesleyan theology of
salvation into a completer theology of society.  He says:
"...a conception of Christian social responsibility which
centers in the gospel of redemption has a built-in point of
contact with Wesleyan thought.  It may also provide a perfect medium for working out the social implications which
were clearly present in Wesley's teachings but which Wesley
himself never fully developed.  There are thus three good
reasons for believing that in the concept of redemption we
have found the key principle for a sound theology of society.  (1) A social theology centering in salvation broadly

interpreted will be true to the deepest meaning of the Christian gospel, which calls on men to respond in trust to God's
redemptive work for mankind.  (2)  It will provide an integrating center for the ecumenical doctrines which Methodists
and other Protestants have actually regarded as socially
significant.  (3)  Finally, it will build on and develop the
major emphasis of the Wesleyan tradition itself."[8]  Thus the
doctrines of justification by faith and of sanctification
become relevant to the ambiguities of social and historical
reality.

      Put in terms of the controlling middle axiom of ecumeni-
cal social ethics the idea of "permanent revolution" is expressed as the "responsible society."  Although this idea is
broader than that of political responsibility, no adequate
treatment of this latter is possible without the context of
the former.  Formulated just after the close of World War II
its language has the vitality of world-wide rapid social
change.  "Man is created and called to be a free being, responsible to God and his neighbor.  Any tendencies in State
and society depriving man of the possibility of acting responsibly are a denial of God's intention for man and his
work of salvation.  A responsible society is one where freedom is the freedom of men who acknowledge responsibility to
justice and public order, and where those who hold political
authority or economic power are responsible for its exercise
to God and the people whose welfare is affected by it."  To
this definition the following commentary was added by the
Amsterdam Assembly:  "Man must never be made a mere means
for political or economic ends.  Man is not made for the
State but the State for man.  Man is not made for production, but production for man.  For a society to be responsible under modern conditions it is required that the people
have freedom to control, to criticize and to change their

governments, that power be made responsible by law and tradition, and be distributed as widely as possible through the
whole community.  It is required that economic justice and
provision of equality of opportunity be established for all
members of society."[9]

     The political sector of culture plays an enormous role
in the responsible society.  Therefore the state must be
truly responsible if the society is to achieve a responsible
character.  In its relation to society and the state the
church must be free to witness to its Lord and His design
for the world.  The Church must combat any denial to human
beings of an opportunity to participate in the shaping of
society.  The Church must condemn any attempt to prevent men
and women from learning and spreading the truth.  In no
society is responsibility permanently won.  In all societies
responsibility must be constantly renewed.


                              II


     Political responsibility is lock-stitched into more
inclusive duties.  But political activity is the key to so
much else that happens in society and culture because the
state lays down the rules of the game for economics, communications, education, and much else.  To the state is given a
monopoly over ultimate social coercion.  Though Christ cannot be made captive to the state, political governments can
quite effectively limit the actual social expression of the
Church.  State, culture, and economic order are generally
quite interdependent and mutually interpenetrate.  Reform or
revolution in one area is hardly effective without corresponding changes in the other parts of culture.  Political
revolution is so significant because political responsibility is so comprehensive.

In the emerging new nations of Africa and Asia the agenda of political revolution never stands alone. For example, in an Indonesian conference sponsored in 1957 by the National Council of Churches of Indonesia and the World Council of Churches, the findings dealt with "The Social Goals of New Asia" and included resolutions on (1) ethical foundations of government and the political responsibility of Christians; (2) the social goals of economic development; and (3) problems of independence and interdependence and the impact of the West. It also dealt with the role and responsibility of mission boards in the West. In a revolutionary situation political concern has many facets because government is a dimension of all organized social groups.

The situation in newly independent countries is quite different from those situations in the West where, historically, segments of the society have effectively resisted the excessive growth and power of the state and where even the idea of a welfare state is continually under attack. Asian Christians "desire to share more fully in the life of their nation and to contribute their best to it in the light of God's revelation in Christ." This desire is often canalized in terms of an expressive nationalism that permeates the whole social order and places the Christian in an ambiguous position. There is the temptation to limit the universal demands of the Christian social ethic to the political units which themselves stand under judgment.

## III

Today the Christian cause is not the major source of social change in the revolutions of Asia, Africa, and South America. Many factors are at work. In some countries revolutionary leaders have no interest in the Christian Church.

In others the Church is not politically significant.   In
some the Church has neither the theological understanding,
the leadership, nor the social "know how" to move with significant effectiveness.   Historical circumstances and theological insight vary greatly from one continent and nation
to another.

Wherever major and rapid social change is taking place
the following factors are generally involved:  (a) new ideas
of social justice with rising hopes among the people for a
better day; (b) widespread technological revolution; and (c)
the upsurge of nationalism.   Nationalism is often but not
always associated with the idea of national unity based on
democratic principles, the rule of law, and supported by the
idea of a universally literate and informed citizenry.   The
prime movers, as Egbert DeVries calls them, are new economic
forces, technological instruments and know-how, released
spiritual forces, social and cultural factors, and political
power.[10]  These prime movers may have little historical or
contemporary connection with the Christian cause or the
Christian Church.

In these areas of rapid social change Paul Abrecht sees
Christians involved in four major ways:  As citizens they
must help define the goals of new political and social life.
They must also participate in thinking about the patterns
and structure of the new institutions which must be shaped
and developed to fulfill these goals.   They must elaborate
the conception of man and society needed for these institutions and presupposed in the goals.   And Christians must,
finally, perform a ministry of love and service amid the new
social circumstances.[11]

In assessing the ways in which Christians will relate
themselves to the major revolutionary movements we may introduce at this point a recognition of what DeVries calls the

carriers of social leadership, the catalytic forces, and the
inhibiting factors.  The conveyors are in part carried along
by the prime movers but they are also agents with interests
and  agents  in  situations  affected  by  the  catalytic  forces
and  the  inhibiting  factors.   Stated  conversely,  the  carriers
include:    (1)  the  newly  emerging  educated  classes  and  the
whole  educational  program  of  the  nation;  (2)  the  women  in
their new roles in work and family and in their women's movements;  (3)  the  teachers  who  in  the  new  situation  play  a
decisive  role  in  forming  ideals,  defining  goals,  and  focusing  emotional  power  through  ideas;  (4)  the  new  industrialists  who  have  such  a  large  stake  in  the  economic  developments;  and  (5)  the  prophets  of  new  order  who  are  able  to
appeal  to  the  hungers,  needs,  enthusiasms,  resentments  and
aspirations  of  the  people.

These  carriers  operate  in  the  context  of  catalytic
forces  and  inhibiting  factors.   DeVries  would  include  among
catalytic  agents  "status  seeking"  and  the  "profit  motive"
and  a  general  abuse  of  rewards  for  efforts  to  change  the  old
order.   They  include  also  the  desire  among  the  younger  generation  to  be  different  from  the  older  generation.   In  other
words,  there  is  tension  among  the  generations.   Hence,  there
is  a  tendency  of  the  young  to  denounce  old  institutions  and
customs.   Psychologically  this  means  oftentimes  that  the
white  man  is  treated  like  the  old  man  and  missionaries  may
be  denounced  as  "colonial"  or  old-fashioned.

Other  catalytic  forces  are  the  cumulative  social
protest,  the  moral  indignation,  and  the  prophetic  fervor
which  revolts  against  the  old.   These  may  blend  into  yet
other  forces  like  the  emotion-laden  mass  movements  with  ever
accelerating  datelines  for  independence  and  freedom.   Such
mass  movements  may  reject  reason  and  even  be  harmful  from  an
economic  and  political  point  of  view,  but  they  affect  the

whole of social life. They may cause a constructive social
force to over-reach itself and become demonic.

Turning now to the inhibitors of rapid social change we
may note the fear of taking risks including the lack of
experience with handling social change. We may note also
that in traditional society there is marked perpetuity from
generation to generation. Family life, property rights and
vested interests in present social status illustrate three
forms of such perpetuity. Moreover, the existing order has
always a sacral character. Economic life, as well as family
and government, have in Asia and Africa this sacral dimension. There is fear of upsetting the magical or sacral
order of social arrangements. If, then, agriculture and
medicine are to be improved, there must come about a certain
secularization of culture. Christians need to know how to
develop a proper Christian secularization along with new
Christian vocation.

Another factor inhibiting social change is the traditional rejection of individual deviation in social behavior.
Where collective life is highly organic in its tribal heritage the deviant person is thought often to be crazy. Part
of the present revolutionary situation is the need for widespread acceptance of social innovation. The rejection of
individual deviation, however, plays into the hands of blind
revolution when the carriers of change become highly emotional mass movements, for the deviant behavior has here no
more status than in the traditional culture patterns.

Finally, we must cite the official protectors of the
old order. They work often behind the scenes in the family,
in government, and in the religious sphere. The general
conservative role of religion, including the church, must
not be overlooked. We can hardly overestimate the religious
tendency to associate "eternal" values with the status quo

in the basic institutions of society.  We need only to
remember Russia before 1917; Germany before 1914; Franco
Spain; the traditional Church in South America; the general
tenor of pre-conciliar papal encyclicals on social questions; and the role of certain Protestant churches in South
Africa and the southern states of the U.S.A.  Whenever an
older society has been deeply integrated and pervaded by
religious values and sanctions, political revolution will be
accompanied by a major conservative reaction in the religious sphere.


                               IV


     In trying to relate the Christian Church to contempo-
rary political responsibility we cannot overlook the
paradoxical character of Christian leadership and institutions in the area of rapid social change.  Besides repre-
senting only a tiny minority in many countries the churches
have not created the "role expectation" of leadership in
political revolution.  They were socialized by many forces
which made them accommodate both consciously and unconsciously to colonial and imperial powers.  This is not to
deny the inherent radical character of the Gospel, but the
missionary movement did not anticipate the age in which a
totally new situation has emerged.
     The churches have to find a new set of relationships in
their respective national environments.  M. M. Thomas said
at The New Delhi Assembly:  "The Church's identification
with Western culture and power on the one hand and the
Church's pietism and fear of organized group action to
change political and social structures on the other hand,
have been hindrances to the development of a positive
responsible relation to the people's struggle for a new

life."[12]  It is in politics, he adds, that the fear of the
world is most marked, inhibiting Asian and African
Christians from proper participation.

In the 1930's and 40's Western churches and missions
were still providing the main leadership for Christian thinking on social problems in Africa and Asia, and few national
church members were expressing themselves on these questions.  This situation has been changing as the conferences
of the past decade and a half in Asia and Africa show.  But
there are inhibiting factors which need correction.  There
is, first of all, a theological conservatism which does not
provide the theological basis for an ethical analysis and
criticism of social problems.  Abrecht says, "This drag of a
theological tradition which is under-developed in relation
to the life of man in society is clearly one of the major
obstacles to the ethical creativity of the younger churches
today."[13]  Secondly the old theological formulas do not help
sufficiently in social criticism.  Many of the applications
were developed by Westerners before the present surge of
rapid social change, so that new native leaders have to
rethink theology in relation to a new social situation.  The
problem is all the more radical and urgent because the
church leaders have to work in a context not only of a fresh
theological-ethical formulation but also of scientific
studies of social institutions and movements.  In very few
places are people trained to think at once in theological-
ethical and social scientific terms.  Meanwhile the classical and basic doctrinal issues persist and must be understood and mastered.

The problem is not only one of theological formulation
but also of adequate ethical leadership.  The 1959 International Study Conference on Christian Action in Rapid Social
Change reported the critical need "for better training of

pastors in Christian social ethics related to the real problems of social change, and they for their part have a responsibility to train the laity for their evangelistic and pastoral work in society."[14]

Another way of stating the problem is that theological
education itself does not know how to confront the revolutionary reality and is tempted to substitute simply more
intensive Biblical thinking for knowledge about and acquaintance with the real world. There can be no effective leadership of the Church in relation to political responsibility
in a revolutionary age when men and women lack the intellectual tools for analyzing their fast moving society. Political intuition based on Biblical theology alone may be highly
irresponsible.


                                    V


Political responsibility has, then, a close relationship to a revolution in education. This is one of the most
serious problems which humankind must face, for educational
traditions may resist and reject the principle of "permanent
revolution" which we proposed at the beginning of this discussion. A brief excursion into the traditions and motivations of education will bring these issues into sharper
focus.

A variety of traditions strongly influence the social
purposes of contemporary world education. Historically some
started to build the pyramid of education from the top.
Spain built universities in Peru and Guatemala in the early
sixteenth century and in Manila in 1611, but left the
countryside illiterate. In the Belgian Congo the pyramid of
education was built from the bottom upwards. Other areas
begin in the middle, but in every case there is a relation

between educational policy and the basic philosophy of society. Many parts of the world are today paying a heavy price for traditions of education that commit the gifts of youth to serve a class or an elite and not responsible interdependence of classes and peoples.

On the other hand, where people see that nations must be lifted from the bottom, countries have known how to combine education and training in fruitful ways. In some European countries primary education has been linked in adolescence with adaptation to techniques in agriculture, home economics, hygiene, cooperatives and the like. Formal and informal education were seen as a whole.

Of great importance in this connection has been that educational tradition in the agricultural regions of the U.S.A. which united public education, both elementary and secondary, with the university, as in Iowa State University and Michigan State University. They have their shortcomings but they have shown how farmers and engineers could enter the great educational line of splendor without any sense of inferiority as workers on land, in the mines, and in the forests. Theirs is a marriage of dirt and dignity which two-thirds of humankind desperately needs. Is it any wonder that Michigan State University at East Lansing has a larger number of its faculty with service outside the U.S.A. than almost any other University in the whole U.S.A.?

One of the important emphases in Communist countries is the recognition of the need for training local cadres of leadership in government, industry, and society. Let us suppose that in Asia, Africa, and South America at least one local leader is needed for every one hundred families. Here are some 400 to 500 million families. This means a minimum of 4 to 5 million local leaders are needed to fulfill a great variety of functions. And how important are strong,

clean, healthy local institutions!  In a time of rapid social change the dearth of well-equipped local institutions
is a serious threat to society.

It is one of the hardest problems of the present time
to turn the talents of the gifted to the lifting of the
local village level of leadership.  For many, rural life is
the symbol of poverty and the past and the city is the
bright light that gathers country moths around its dangerous
and deadly flame.  Even theological education has often been
a transmission belt of escape from rural existence rather
than a matrix of motivation to serve and save it.

One of the great contributions which some Americans are
making to the social and economic revolution in India is the
witness of our college trained agronomists working side by
side with less well-trained Indians in the clearing of jun-
gles, the ploughing of virgin soil, the planting of fields
and orchards, and the general exhibition of the dignity of
dirty overalls dedicated to human uplift.

Sociologists have long recognized that in the U.S.A.
one of the great functions of education has been vertical
mobility.  By means of education people improve their relative social status.  It is a way of climbing up the social
ladder.  By it class and caste lines are overcome as one
moves from lower to middle to upper class standing.  Of all
the means that men and women have tried to improve their
lot, in the U.S.A. education has been the generally most important—up to now.  But whom shall the educated serve?

There is no necessary correlation between the over-all
wealth of a country and its educational level.  In Latin
America, for example, generally about 40 percent of the
population above the age of fifteen are illiterate.  Moreover in countries like Mexico, Guatemala, Ecuador, Peru and
Bolivia large groups of the original Indian population have

lived through conquest, colonial periods, and the years of
independence without ever becoming completely assimilated in
the national life. *The UNESCO Courier*[15] points out that
Costa Rica, a small agricultural country which boasts that
its school teachers constitute its only army, has a proportion of illiterates as low as in most advanced countries on
the continent. On the other hand, Venezuela, with the
highest per capita income in Latin America (thanks to its
huge oil reserves) has a comparatively high percentage of
illiteracy. "Education in Latin America is the privilege of
a small minority which has access to the various levels of
the educational system while the great majority of the population is neither equipped to make an effective contribution
to economic development nor able to take a full share in
democratic life."[16]

It must be added, in all fairness, that major projects
in primary or elementary education are being undertaken in
many of the countries and that local and rural education are
major objectives. Yet the question remains—after illiteracy has been abolished—"what are the substantive national
goals after the double negatives represented by 'abolishing'
and 'illiteracy' have been removed?" At this point the
fundamental educational philosophy becomes crucial. Political revolution apart from sound social education is indeed
superficial and very dangerous.

In his study of areas of rapid social change DeVries
found that there is an urgent need to expand and at the same
time to reorganize university education. He found that in
the Philippines and in India there is a huge number of unem-
ployed people with a B.A. or even M.A. degree.

Much of the restlessness of Korean youth is traceable
to this type of social situation. The root trouble, however, is not only the kind of education which they received

but the motivation for education which they possessed. They
do not seem to know *who* they are or *whom* they should serve.
In the competition for jobs thousands find their way to
American universities and colleges in the hope that with an
additional degree from the U.S.A. their competitive position for the few available openings would be enhanced. Meanwhile, whole areas of rural life and local leadership at the
base of the social pyramid go begging. Today[17] the military government of Korea has put the whole educational system into something of a strait jacket. All high school graduates take governmental exams, are sorted as to what kind of
higher education they may take, are assigned to specific
colleges and universities (thus closing many which are sub-
standard), and take a government exam before colleges and
universities may grant degrees. In the process the civilian
point of view is often overlooked. The relationship of political revolutions to education is quite apparent, however.

From this evidence of acute areas of rapid social
change some observations may be drawn. (1) There is need
for a massive strategy of service to the base of the social
pyramid. (2) Because of its past heritage of association
with rulers, upper classes, non-agricultural and non-manual
labor, most young people in Asia, Africa, and South America
tend to link education with privilege and status at the top
rather than with commitment to the whole community and responsibility to those at the base of the social pyramid of
class and status. (3) The benefits of education in vertical mobility are so great that the gap widens between the
top and the bottom of the pyramid. "To him who has shall be
given." From him who has not shall be taken many things he
now has. The benefits of science and industry are cumulative. Consequently the gap between the illiterate and the
educated becomes wider; so also the gap between the rural

and the urban areas; finally also, the gap between the un-
skilled and the professionals. Unless the educational
system has balanced goals the present values of revolutions
in the new nations will be sacrificed to new exploiting
classes and power groups.

VI

Does the Church have the power or the motivation to
accept Christian responsibility for permanent political revolution? If we examine the Church in the United States we
must give a very cautious and sober answer to this question.
America is not in the mood to prosecute much by way of revolution either at home or abroad—and there is a tendency
toward consistency between the values of religious institutions and those of the cultural institutions which provide
their context, their membership, and their support. In
other words, the integrative function of religion tends to
make it accommodate heavily with the society in which it is
embedded. Integration and conservatism have much in common.

As we compare American life and the integrative role of
religion in areas of rapid social change, it may be useful
to examine more closely three levels of consensus required
for the social integrative function of religion. (1) At
the lowest level are the accepted ways of doing things, the
norms or prescriptions for daily action. We have already
noted that these ways take on a certain sacral character.
(2) At an intermediate level are the ideal-values which the
norms and prescribed behavior embody or further. These are
the ideal ends which make the lowest level of norms seem
worthwhile and good. (3) At the highest level are beliefs
concerning the nature of persons and the world, that is, the
ultimate view of reality that makes the ideal-values both

viable and rational. If there is unity and coherence among
these three levels and harmony with the surrounding culture
there will be little tension or conflict between religion
and society and the force of religion will be essentially
protective and conservative as in many traditional societies.   A nation tends to socialize its religious institutions in this general integrative direction.

     In the United States there is both integration and con-
flict.   At the lowest level of prescriptions American life
is full of conflict.   For example, there are the Protestant-
Catholic conflicts over marriage, family, and education;
there is the scandalous controversy over racial segregation
and desegregation; there is widespread crime and corruption;
and there is doubt as to what norms in daily life are right.

     When the prescribed ways of behavior are in conflict,
to what are the people committed? Are they committed to the
local norms (e.g., segregation and parochial schools), to
ideal-values which free them from captivity to worn out standards, or to ultimate beliefs that release them to recon-
sider their ideal-values?   For example, is segregation or
the democratic dream their commitment?   What is finally
sacred to the people, that is, for what will they finally
sacrifice?   Where prescriptions of action (daily norms) have
become ultimate (like the American way of life), beliefs are
their servants and are exploited to support them.   On the
other hand, unless the beliefs are clearly spelled out, so
that people know what conduct they mean, opposing values
which are concrete tend to win out.   A split develops
between    abstract    beliefs    and    specific    behavior.
Ideal-values and ultimate beliefs may be short-circuited and
mask the betrayal of these values by practices which
actually belie them.   In time a social deception settles
upon people who sense no conflict between Christ and

culture.

Whether and how the Church will serve as a conservative integrator of society or as an innovator depends not only on the level on which commitment is made, but also on the structure of authority in the community. Authority in this context means the ways in which power and decision are legitimated. In government one naturally thinks of legal authority and its sanctions. But there are at least three other important types of authority. These include the social pressures and sanctions of private groups, the transcendent or supra-social referents (God, Christ, the kingdom of God), and personal integrity or individual conscience. The church has responsibilities to this whole firmament of authority. If the church is tied too closely to race, class, clique, or political pattern, it can quickly lose its moral authority to champion change when these secular norms and customs are challenged. When the Oxford Conference in 1937 said, "Let the Church be the Church!" it affirmed imperatively the church's need to regain authentic authority. From this perspective the churches seem to have lost much of their authority to effect social change. They cannot, however, regain their social authority for change simply by more social action, but they have to be renewed in commitment and mission from within. Revolution roots in radical worship.

It would be an error to suppose that the institutionalized churches of the U.S.A. are today the most important and powerful integrators of American society. Other value centers may in fact be more "sacred" to most Americans—including the missions in the churches. Today churches may be providing a declining moral consensus in the nation even while their memberships are growing. The nation's normative local structure shows signs of disintegration. It is conceivable that the church is absorbing more into its institu-

tional life and local behavior from secular society than it
is giving to that society by way of standards, motivations,
and guidance.   Present-day revolutionary movements in the
world are not drawing heavily from the *transcendent* beliefs
of American or Western Christianity.   They are constructing
their own secular ideologies which have an appeal like that
of transcendent religious belief.   Yet the predominant
appeal  of   the   church   is   harmony—and   this   emphasis
encourages the infiltration of the church by alien elements.
Harmony is not the gospel.

One reason that the church is not more of an innovator
in American or in world society is that it does not make
*explicit* how men ought to behave, for what ends they should
live, and for what reasons.   The church lacks effective control and criticism of local practices by middle axioms, and
of middle axioms by transcendent beliefs.   It often operates
at such a level of vague abstraction that other social
forces fill in the middle axioms and the practical prescriptions.   To exercise the ministry of permanent revolution the
church must induce specific conflict on issues.   Christian
reconciliation cannot by-pass Christian judgment.

If the church is to be effective in social action there
must be unity and not conflict of judgment within the church
on what goals are more important or urgent than others.
There must be agreement on the action requirements of achieving a goal, once it is chosen.   Thirdly, there must be agreement over which office or institution assumes responsibility.   For example, the 1960 General Conference of The Methodist Church debate over its jurisdictional polity system
illustrates these three dimensions of social action predicaments.   There was conflict between the explicit goal of
achieving racial justice by eliminating the segregated Central Jurisdiction and the often unstated goal of preventing

a split into a Northern and a Southern Church.  The second
dimension focused on the method, in decisive action by the
General  Conference  *or* voluntary  and  permissive  action,
church by church, annual conference by annual conference.
The  third  dimension  related  to  the  role  of  leadership
assumed by the church in relation to society.  In what may
be a descriptive paradigm for some other basic issues, The
Methodist Church acted as follows:  "The General Conference,
with frank facing of the conflicts, kept open the dilemma,
although it chose temporarily unity over desegregation, permissive over decisive action, and a supportive rather than
prophetic role for the church in relation to action by
public institutions."[18]

VII

We may bring these several strands of argument into a
summary conclusion by suggesting, once again, the dilemma of
church leadership in rapid social change and certain guidelines for action.
    1.  The Western Christian's experience with political
revolution has shown a varied pattern of reaction, conservatism, acceptance, and positive concurrence.
    2.  Whatever Western Christian political experience may
have taught the church cannot be applied simply to Africa,
Asia, and Latin America.  In part it is misunderstood because of past linkages to colonialism and imperialism, however close or remote; in part it is misunderstood because
leadership must now come from the lands themselves; and in
part because new occasions teach new duties.
    3.  A major need in areas of rapid social change is
thorough-going education in theological social ethics.  Theology, ethics, and social sciences need coherent integration

in terms of the varying social situation.  Sound Christian
social ethics is interdisciplinary.

    4.   The Church must recognize that its mission is not
to avoid revolutions of our time, but to seek out the action
of God in them, and to witness to Christ's kingdom with a
gospel of inclusive salvation, inclusively expressed.

    5.   No one pattern of social, economic, or political
order may be identified with the gospel of Christ.  Since
Christ transcends revolution as well as all cultures and
social orders, the churches in the new nations must be
particularly aware of the universal elements in the gospel.
If this dimension is not heeded, they will fall into the
same nationalistic limitations which have inhibited the
manifestation of the responsible society in Western nations
where Christianity is much older.

    6.   Participation with non-Christians in nation-build-
ing is both required and it has grave risks, especially when
the Christian community is small.  This danger is particularly present where Christians have recently lost their privileged status and place as leaders of social service and welfare.   Yet participation is of the essence of political
responsibility.   He who voluntarily does not participate
forfeits the right to criticize political action.  The principal rights for which the Christian will contend are those
which relate to the fundamental rights of all.

    7.   It is particularly dangerous for Christians to
organize into a Christian political party of their own.  The
reasons are that the gospel does not provide such a political position and a Christian political party makes for special concern for narrow communal or churchly interests.  The
Christian community must strive for freedom, justice and
human dignity for all.

    8.   Christians will support the idea of a constructive

neutral or secular state.

9. The making of new states into political unities in behalf of traditional national religions inhibits the "permanent revolution." Traditional religions tied to traditional politics make for the repudiation of both in an age of revolution and reconstruction. Christians must discriminate between reactionary and constructive appeals to religion.

10. A modern state will have to assume comprehensive social responsibilities. The social substructure of the political order is of major concern to the Christian, who will attend to the responsible family, responsible education, and responsible agricultural and industrial relations, as well as to the political general welfare.

11. Western parliamentary forms of democracy are not viable unless a suitable social foundation has been provided for them. Democracy is not a mechanism primarily; it is a responsible ethical reality with appropriate structures and procedures.

12. Christians have a special responsibility to bear witness to the political needs of the whole of humankind. While new nations are being built, the world political order must also be reconstructed.

13. No greater need in the social witness and service of the churches for Christ exists than that of a renewal of the Church, whereby men and women are motivated to lift the social pyramids of their various societies from the bottom.

14. The "permanent revolution" is addressed to every nation.

## NOTES

[1]John Cogley, ed., "The Present Embarrassment of the
Church," in *Religion in America* (New York:   Meridian Books,
1958), p. 224.

[2]Waldo Beach, "Ecclesiology and Race," *Union Seminary
quarterly Review*.   XIV, No. 2 (Jan., 1959), pp. 22-23.

[3]W. A. Visser t'Hooft and J. H. Oldham, *The Church and
Its Function in Society* (Willett, Clark and Co., 1937), pp.
199-200.

[4]Jacques Ellul, *"The Situation in Europe,"* in
preparatory volume of Amsterdam Assembly, World Council of
Churches, *Man's Disorder and God's Design*, 1948.   Vol. III,
pp.59-60.

[5]*Ibid.*

[6]H. Richard Niebuhr, *Christ and Culture*   (New York:
Harper and Brothers, 1951), p. 209.

[7]*Ibid.*, pp. 218-219.

[8]S. Paul Schilling, *Methodism and Society in
Theological Perspective* (New York:   Abingdon Press, 1960),
pp. 209-210.

[9]Amsterdam Assembly of the World Council of Churches,
*The Church and the Disorder of Society*, 1948, p. 192.

[10]Egbert DeVries, *Man in Rapid Social Change* (New York:
Doubleday, 1961).

[11]Paul Abrecht, *The Churches in Rapid Social Change*
(New York:   Doubleday, 1961).

[12]M. M. Thomas, "Comments at the Third Assembly of the
World Council of Churches,"   (New Delhi, 1961).

[13]Paul Abrecht, *op. cit.*, p. 49.

[14]*Ibid.*, p. 52.

[15]*The UNESCO Courier*, June, 1961.

[16]*Ibid.*, p. 34.

[17]1962-1963.

[18]Herbert E. Stotts and Paul K. Deats, *Methodism and Society: Guidelines for Strategy* (New York:  Abingdon Press, 1962), p. 33f.

## TORONTO STUDIES IN THEOLOGY